Menhennet,
Truro.
2nd September 1974.

A CORNISHMAN AT OXFORD

The Education of a Cornishman

A CORNISHMAN
AT OXFORD

A. L. ROWSE

Fellow of All Souls College
Oxford

JONATHAN CAPE

THIRTY BEDFORD SQUARE LONDON

FIRST PUBLISHED 1965
© 1965 BY A. L. ROWSE

REISSUED IN THIS FORMAT 1974
JONATHAN CAPE LTD, 30 BEDFORD SQUARE, LONDON WCI

ISBN 0 224 60924 6

PRINTED IN GREAT BRITAIN BY
LOWE AND BRYDONE (PRINTERS) LTD, THETFORD, NORFOLK
ON PAPER MADE BY JOHN DICKINSON AND CO. LTD
BOUND BY JAMES BURN AND CO. LTD, ESHER, SURREY

CONTENTS

To
JACK SIMMONS,
fellow House-man,
most constant of friends

'*C'est l'œuvre d'un soi bien plus extérieur, non pas du moi profond qu'on ne retrouve qu'en faisant abstraction des autres et du moi qui connaît les autres, le moi qui a attendu pendant qu'on était avec les autres, qu'on sent bien le seul réel, et pour lequel seuls les artistes finissent par vivre.*'

Proust, *Contre Sainte-Beuve*

PREFACE

MANY people have asked me to write a sequel to *A Cornish Childhood* and I have always intended to do so. But more than twenty years have elapsed since then, a much longer interval than I had expected, filled with so many other things and so much work to be done.

The tribute that I value most to that earlier volume – among hundreds of letters from all over the world, while the book must have been taken to the heart of the public, for it long ago passed a hundred thousand in circulation – was reported to me by an Oxford friend, an eminent historian. Two doctors were discussing the book in the train from Paddington; one said, 'There are many books written *about* childhood; this one gives the sense of what it is really like to be a child.'

I had expected that the main interest of this volume – perhaps of some use to the medical profession – might lie in its exposure of the psychology of illness, the psychological accompaniments of pain, of which I had more than my share in these and subsequent years. But it has worked out rather differently – as is apt to happen with a live work of art. Mainly because of the detail of the early diaries upon which the book is based, I observe that its main theme is to reveal the whole process of education of a scholarship boy from the working class in the nineteen twenties. As such, even if it has no other interest, I hope it may be read as a contribution to the social history of the time.

All education, it has been said, if somewhat superfluously, is self-education. Here is an account of the process, more concrete and detailed than any that I know. But the detail is the whole point of the book: how otherwise, how more convincingly, can one expose the development of a mind, in all its intimacy, all its crevices, the ups and downs of temperament, the encouragement one received, the discouragements and set-backs, the excitements and ardours day by day, the stress and strain, the loneliness of it all?

I cannot be too glad now that I kept all those diaries and docu-

ments – perhaps with the instinct of the embryo historian – for
without them I should never have been able to recover the facts, let
alone the atmosphere, the voices, of the time. It is curious what a
creative, shaping instrument the memory is: some things were quite
different from the way I had remembered them – but there are the
diaries for a control. Mark Pattison in his *Memoirs* quotes a remark
from Mozley's *Reminiscences*, celebrated in their day: 'People may
perhaps remember what they saw and heard forty years ago, but
they cannot so easily remember what they were themselves.' Here
I have the diaries to tell me: there is no belying them.

I foresee that the book may add fuel to the Welfare State's demands
for more and more and more expenditure on education. Well,
I cannot help that, and anyway I am all in favour of the education of
the educable.

A. L. ROWSE

Trenarren House
St Austell
Summer vacation, 1963

Prologue: Spring in Cornwall

COMING back from my second winter in California I have run into a cold and sulky spring in Cornwall. Yet never have I seen the garden here at Trenarren look more beautiful. Colours: bright gold of the swathes of daffodils on the bank opposite the upper study where I write, from which I can see the cherry-red of one rhododendron, the crimson, pale pink, magenta, waxy cream, a rosy white of others. There are the butter-yellows and lavender-pink of primroses, white of narcissi, saffron of those trumpeting or ox-eyed daffodils, a myriad greens, the deep sea-blue of grape-hyacinths. The sea itself through the retarded, reluctant trees (after a long winter of ice and snow) is of a rare, pale blue – last evening under a rain-cloud there were different bands of thunder-purple-blue and a clear cerulean; now this moment, the morning relenting, the bay glistens summery under the sun.

When I was a schoolboy, living up nearer the china-clay country on the slopes of Tregonissey, I used to come down to this pilgrimage spot on the headland, and climb up on the granite hedge to pry into its seclusion. There was the enchanted garden – rhododendrons, camellias, japonica, mimosa flowering away to no one at all; for the family never lived here after the first war. No smoke rose from the chimneys; it seemed a deserted place, with a Sleeping Princess atmosphere. It became my *princesse lointaine*: 'if only I lived there', I used to breathe, ensconced by the eucalyptus, now vanished, leaving a hole in the sky as trees do when they go. My father, not long before he died – so my mother told me – came to look round the gate, and said, knowing my fixation, 'Well, he may come to live here one day, but I shan't live to see it.'

I suppose it showed a touching confidence on one side, and a proper respect for a 'gentleman's place', an old manor-house of the gentry, on the other. He belonged to a generation that had not lost the faculty of respect; and, simple clay-worker that he was, he was in return well worthy of respect himself, as I realise more and more as

I grow older and think of the difficulties in life he had to contend
with. (He had far more than respect from me: fondness, love, and
as he grew older, and I more and more ill, care and protection
nevertheless – more than he got from those more indubitably his
own: a theme I well recognised when I came upon it years later in
Gide's *Les Faux-Monnayeurs*.)

Even now when I am based on Trenarren and the enchanted
garden is at my disposal, it is its fate still to be deserted, for I am half
the year in America – longer there than anywhere else, here or at
Oxford. But, then, I have been so rooted in both of those, never
having been out of Cornwall until, at seventeen, I went to Oxford to
try for a scholarship and, since then, having spent half of every year,
often more, at Oxford. Nowadays, I feel rather like Dr Johnson who
one day said to Boswell how odd it was that until middle age he
never went anywhere, hardly ever left London, and then in later life
he was for ever gallivanting about the world. In his case his poverty
accounted for it; in mine, illness.

If I were in California now, Easter past by mid-April, the camellias in the garden of the Huntington Library – there are twelve
hundred varieties of them! – would be going over. Each time on
leaving I have gone round the ravine and the slopes above the
Japanese garden, where we have such good walks and talks in the
lunch-hour, all by myself to say goodbye to them. The cactus
garden will be ablaze with the red-hot pokers of the aloes, the full-
grown chorisia with magnolia-like flowers white against the blue
Californian sky now over. So too with the sweet-smelling osmanthus
or tea-olive, scattering its fragrance over the porch where we take a
mid-morning break, the lemony scent of South African cyrtanthus
coming up from below. But the fleshy-leaved crinum with its
Annunciation-lily flowers will be coming on as they will be here for
summer, along with the deep sea-blue of agapanthus – both serving
as a link between Cornwall and California. Though here there are
no mountains, like the San Gabriel range I have in view from my
window there, ochre-coloured and shadow-blue, pale lavender this
winter dusted with white at the top, and the farthest peak of Old
Baldy a serrated cone under snow.

There are so many links and comparabilities between Cornwall and California, not only the flora or the climate – the climate of Cornwall is much that of northern California, mild and damp, not that of southern California, where I pass the delicious winters – but among the people and the memories. Cornish miners have left their marks everywhere where there are minerals. Up in the high sierra behind Sacramento there are still two communities largely Cornish – Grass Valley and Nevada City, with their graveyards full of familiar names. In San Diego for Christmas – with the peninsula of Point Loma dominating the inlet much as Pendennis does Falmouth harbour – I was surprised by the number of Tre-, Pol-, Pen- names in the telephone directory. I need not have been, for there must be more Cornish folk in the United States than there are in Cornwall. Like William Saroyan with his three hundred thousand Armenians – perhaps I am a kind of Saroyan, an inadequate one, of the Cornish folk scattered about the world.

Many of them read things I write, send me messages, or write me letters. Once, when lecturing at the Clements Library at Ann Arbor, Michigan, the two front rows were filled with folk who had come in from Detroit. There are St Austell people in the suburbs of Los Angeles, where my sister lived in the years after the first war. On my first visit to California, twelve years ago, I met – believe it or not – someone who could be described as almost an original 'forty-niner'. This spry old gentleman had been taken out as a baby in arms in those years at the very beginning, actually in 1851 – he was now in his hundredth year. He was a Nicholls of St Austell, and had been 'home' to St Austell once, if not twice, in the intervening century.

Numbers of people have asked me when I am going to give them the sequel to *A Cornish Childhood*, and urged me to go on with it. Before leaving California this time, I promised my friends there that I would. Little do they, or anyone else, know what difficulties there will be in writing it – or I should not have allowed twenty years to pass before tackling it. *A Cornish Childhood* stopped short with my leaving home for Oxford at eighteen, and I have been able to make the excuse, which was true enough, that it was after then that things began to be complicated. But there are other, and worse, difficulties.

One of them is hardly serious, and one with which I am professionally familiar. Getting down to my task this sullen, inclement

Easter, I am taken aback by the sheer bulk of the materials I have accumulated. Not only are there the volumes of diary that I have kept going ever since I was a schoolboy – so that my exiguous publications are but the top one-eighth of the iceberg – but there are note-books, scrap-books, exercise books full of lecture-notes, abstracts of reading, commonplace books, engagement-books, besides essays, papers, stories, poems and innumerable notes for poems, pocket-books in which the thoughts, observations, sentences, inscriptions, descriptions, phrases of the day have been pinned down like so many thousands of butterflies by a mad entomologist. (But my mad entomology has been the pursuit of life on the wing, yet at a remove: *spectateur de la vie*.) In addition to all this there are hundreds of letters, cards, post-cards, papers, not only from other people but my own. For, obsessed with the idea that I should die before my time – not unreasonably, considering that I came near to it three or four times and how closely I lived with it all those long duodenal years – I got into the way of asking family and friends to keep my letters.

The result is that here at Trenarren, as at Oxford, there is a Rowse *Archiv*. Perhaps it was an appropriate inspiration for a budding historian, or at any rate some evidence of a bent for becoming one, when for years there was no other. At any rate, getting down to preparing the ground, I was appalled by the mounting heaps of manuscript poured forth from emptied drawers, upon desk, tables, chairs, floor of my upstairs study. As I was sorting the stuff into some chronological order, I heard myself say: 'This is as bad as historical research.' But I reflected that historical research is my profession, and that at least I should not suffer the nightmare of the researcher – absence of material.

The real difficulties in the way of writing this book are psychological, and acutely personal. Indeed, all my grown life I have had great difficulty in facing them. The facts of our family life were not as they seemed, or at least as they were represented, to ourselves and the outside world. One or two friends have been good enough to say that a prime quality of *A Cornish Childhood* was its honesty. I should not like its successor to fall short in that respect, though the difficulty in this is much greater, primarily with myself. A perceptive reader of T. E. Lawrence's *Home Letters* will see the point at which Lawrence learned the true facts of their strange family life, and the trauma the boy suffered in consequence. Perhaps thereby came the genius – but Lawrence could never face the fact honestly: his friend Namier told me that even in the last year of his life he denied it to him. I suppose honesty must be a prime requisite for an historian, however difficult when it affects first of all himself.

When gathering together my materials to begin, this rainy morning of daffodils and blue sea at Trenarren, I came across something that upset me strangely. It was just the marriage-certificate of my mother and father all those years ago, 21 February 1893, at Charlestown church. There it was, all in order: 'Richard Rowse, age 28, bachelor, son of William Rowse, miner.' (The miner had long been dead.) 'Annie Vanson, age 24, spinster, daughter of Edward Vanson, farm labourer.' The only witnesses were her parents, Edward and Fanny Vanson; duly made out and signed by parson Ferris. I wept to come upon this unexpectedly this morning – the simplicity of it and of their condition, the story behind it, the piece of paper that remains in evidence of the event from which our family story flowed. Now seventy years ago, a complete life-time after, and they lie in their grave together in St Austell cemetery, not far from William Rowse, miner, of the document.

Kept together with it in a little book was his last letter to her, written in pencil from the Infirmary at Truro. In it he says, 'I not hade any letter from Les.' I was ill again in Oxford. They told me that he kept asking for me in those last days. I am glad to think that I was good to him, as he had been good to me.

I

Christ Church: Initiation

A Cornish Childhood ends with the lights of Oxford – as they might be reflected in Mercury, the fountain-pool in Tom Quad, on the evening of my arrival, 11 October 1922. Every season has its particular beauty at Oxford, but I think of autumn as most characteristic of the place – the rich, ruddy colour of the creeper that covered Meadow Buildings, the plum-skin bloom of mist in the Meadows and about the quadrangles. Everywhere was the sound of bells: the deep reverberation of Great Tom that became so familiar, the hundred and one strokes at five past nine at night to call home the original number of students, the near-by sighing chime of the Cathedral bells from the squat Victorian tower, against the building of which Lewis Carroll levelled his pamphlet about the 'meat-safe', with his portrait of the design – a perfect parallelogram. Across the Meadows to me in my room were blown the sound of innumerable other bells: the clack of solitary tintinnabulations of colleges calling their undergraduates to chapel or hall, the chimes of a city church, or, loveliest of all, the full peal from Magdalen tower on May morning, that years later came to have a more affecting and personal connotation for me. If I had read Hopkins then, as I had not as yet, I might have had these among the many others in my head to express what I felt:

> Towery city and branchy between towers;
> Cuckoo-echoing, bell-swarmèd, lark-charmèd,
>   rook-racked, river-rounded ...

There was all the thrill of coming in at Tom gate into the grandest quadrangle in Oxford, those echoing stony spaces that gave one a lift of the heart, the parapeted mass of Wolsey's Hall on the right, the arched opening to the Cathedral straight ahead, and between them the splendid Hall staircase – on which there was singing by the Cathedral choir in summer – and the lugubrious dark passages and stone steps that led to Meadow Buildings, where the Scholars were kept. When I met the famous journalist, and former member of the House, Henry Nevinson, he put forward the view that the authorities tucked the Scholars away in Meadows so that they might catch pneumonia and die of it. True, the walls and staircases streamed with damp all winter. When Daudet on his visit to Oxford looked out over the marshy Meadows from a window in the Ruskin-inspired Buildings, he summed up: 'C'est le rhumatisme vert.'

Meadow Buildings meant nothing of this to me: I was in Elysium there that first term, indeed all those nine terms I spent there as a Scholar in college, for the first time in my life with a room of my own. Indeed a set of rooms – sitting-room in front looking to the south out over the Meadows, large, somewhat gaunt bedroom at the back, and a little pantry-scullery-cum-coal-hutch, more used by my scout, old ruddy-faced Frost, than by me. 'My rooms are beyond my wildest expectations,' my Diary records. I crept up the stairs in the twilight, after my long journey from Cornwall, peering at the name above every door, somewhat daunted, until I arrived in front of my own. 'Walking into the enormous sitting-room, I felt quite lost. I could not believe that this was the room for me. Why, it is twice as big as our front room at home.' I was much impressed by the large square of patterned red carpet, and the thick rug in front of the fireplace, in which a coal fire leaped up to welcome me.

Here I was much at home for the next three years: Meadows VI. 6, high up on the second floor at the end of the building, an attic storey above me, and with an outlook on the elms of the Broad Walk (planted at the Restoration and now coming to their end), the cow-pastures of the Meadows and the line of trees that marked the Isis, my horizon. I owe much to those rooms: they gave me shelter in those most impressionable and formative years in which I grew from schoolboy to graduate. They were the scene of the formation of friendships, of much more company than I had remembered, of endless discussion and argument (from which one learned more than from all the dons), of intense application and reading, a great deal of writing – essays, notes from books, Diary, poems – companionship and solitude, much enjoyment of life, some ecstasy and, familiar creatures, some pain and heartache.

Overjoyed as I was at my good fortune, beside myself with excitement, I at once began to worry. 'There is one thing that worries me above all others: have I been put into expensive rooms? ... I cannot afford to get head and ears into debt, without ever knowing what I have to pay out. So this morning (my first) I intend to call upon the Steward or the Senior Censor.' A few weeks later, 'one of the delights of being in Oxford is to have letters from father. The last I had was worrying: he with twenty others had been paid off from work at Carclaze. God, what are things coming to? I'm wondering now what mother and father are doing at home.' Though I wanted to work hard for History Previous in the vacation, I felt I couldn't 'go home to live on father, and he out of work'.

These were the years of the 'Geddes axe', miserable economies in education that had the year before nearly ruined my chance of getting to the university at all, and held up others of my schoolfriends, years of increasing unemployment and no Keynesian ideas, or any ideas at all, how to deal with it. Is it any wonder that from the first I was a Labour man? In any case, it was quite clear in my own mind that to be a Conservative just because I was moving up in the world and going to Oxford was beneath me. Pride forbade any such piece of vulgarity – and pride, inherited from my mother, was a keystone of my character. So I was a Labour man, inevitably and – with my temperament – keenly, aggressively, loyally, though not without some scepticism.

On the private side – and there was then, as there has always remained with me since, a strong distinction between public and private in my life – one other thing was no less evident. With all the struggle there had been in getting to Oxford (one miserable university scholarship for the whole county of Cornwall, where today things are made all too easy), with my determination to get there, little help and no comprehension from a working-class family, practically illiterate as mine was, worry had become an element in which I lived. It was to become a familiar country with me, one way or another, all my life.

*　　*　　*

A news-cutting from *The Times* has refreshed my memory of who the Scholars were who came into residence together that Michaelmas term – not that I have forgotten those who became my friends, and in any case their doings are recorded in the Diary. The senior classical Scholar of our year, who became chief of my friends – at any rate, he occupied a special place in my mind – was Henry Julian Wadleigh, from Marlborough. Half-American, his father was, I think, American chaplain at Merano. Beside him were A. J. Tunnard from the Perse School at Cambridge, J. H. Whitehead from Manchester Grammar School, and L. H. Scott as Exhibitioner from Mill Hill School. For History Scholar there was P. W. P. Gee from Wellington, a rather large, sluggish fellow with an immense mop of plastered hair, and R. C. Langdon-Davies from St George's, Harpenden.

Of these names it does not seem that history has had much to say – with the exception of Julian Wadleigh, who became a headline name in the newspapers in connection with the Hiss case. I fear that our year were a rather undistinguished lot. But there were more interesting and more gifted undergraduates at the House, either Scholars of other years or else commoners. Humfry Payne, who was senior classical Scholar in his fourth year, had a kind of ascendancy in our estimation, remote and aloof as he was. Immensely tall and willowy, with fine gold hair and a pink complexion that could flush like a girl's, he gave the impression of being bored with undergraduate life, and we thought of him as already almost a don. We suspected that he was remarkable, though we could hardly know what a genius for archaeology he would turn out to have, with his inspired excavation of the Heraion at Perachora, followed by his early death. And, indeed, what a mortality there was among those Greek historians of brilliant promise – discoveries or pupils of the master of them all, J. D. Beazley: Humfry Payne, Alan Blakeway, Michael Beaumont, Tom Dunbabin. Of Payne, his widow Dilys Powell has written beautifully in her memoir, *The Traveller's Journey is Done*, which brought those early years vividly back to me from another angle. Yes, Payne was indeed bored with being an undergraduate, was already making assignations to meet up at Carfax with the girl who became his wife – all rather out of our youthful ken. In his lofty way he was rather kind to me, most junior of the Scholars.

Another classical Scholar, a year senior, Robin Burn, became a good friend. Full, even in those days, of fascinating and original ideas about early Greek history, he was also a devoted mountaineer, and, for want of better in term-time, was for ever climbing about the roofs of colleges. Roof-climbing was a regular sport and had its devotees. Since Burn's father was Dean of Salisbury, Robin had a mountain of a cathedral to climb over in vacations. Among commoners there was Roger Makins, with whom I went to tutorials with Feiling and Masterman in our second and third years – taught together, we were also elected Fellows of All Souls together. Nor have our paths wholly diverged since. David Cecil was two years senior, but in my second year suddenly appeared in my rooms and made himself my friend: rather difficult to follow as I found him at first, I have known no one whose conversation, when understood, was more rewarding in ideas, more original or suggestive, or more humorous. He is a born (and devoted) teacher: I learned more from him than from anyone.

On the next staircase was a bird of brilliant plumage – Harold Acton. Almost every undergraduate generation has its bird of paradise, exerting a kind of fascinated ascendancy by its plumage, if not by real gifts – there always are some, even if that for publicity is uppermost. In the days before the first war there were Belloc, Max Beerbohm and Guedalla, as there was Rupert Brooke at Cambridge; in the days before and after the second war there were such talents as Sidney Keyes, Peter Brook, Kenneth Tynan. But never can there have been *such* undergraduate réclame, such publicity, such a peculiar ascendancy as that exerted by Harold Acton in his day at Oxford. He was the recognised leader of the Aesthetes; everything that he did was news. He had the advantage of a very recognisable figure: tall with black hair already balding in front, there was the odd affected carriage of himself with which he shouldered and minced his way through the mob. As if that were not enough, he was inseparable from a carefully rolled umbrella – attendant spirit or, at need, a weapon against the Philistines. In addition, there was his way of speaking English with a strong Italian accent, pressing every emphasis out of the consonants. 'Oh, my deah, I've been so mis-er-able *a-all* the day,' he said to me one day when he had caught a cold. When I came upon the careful accentuation in Evelyn Waugh's *Brideshead Revisited* – that portrait of just our Oxford generation, more particularly of the Aesthetes – in Anthony Blanche's 'Oh, my deah – sip-sip-sip, like an old dowager', it all came so clearly back to mind again.

Innumerable were the stories told of Harold, endearing the exploits. It was said that a gang of rowing men at Worcester, at any rate of hearties, expressed a desire to meet a bevy of Aesthetes. The meeting was arranged: in came Harold, pouter-pigeon-breasting his way, umbrella on arm, followed by a deputation of simpering Aesthetes, Harold (never at a loss) saying: 'We are so dec-a-dent, and they are so in-no-cent.' It was all very funny and affected, innocent in its way and added to the gaiety of life. On my terrible principles, fanatic as I was, I should have disapproved – and, indeed, I thought they were rather wicked. But somehow I never could find it in me to disapprove, though plenty did. For weren't we both against the Philistines, and we had literature in common. Harold produced a volume of verse in his first undergraduate year, *Aquarium*: there it was in Blackwell's shop-window, in all the panoply of canary yellow, pink and puce. I could not afford to buy it, but I was deeply impressed – and so ingenuous that I did not perceive that, beneath the undergraduate sophistication, the poems were no better than my own. Shortly, both Harold and I were contributing to *Oxford Poetry* and *The Oxford Outlook*, and I came to know him a little, never well – that would have been going too far; but well enough to perceive that under that exotic exterior there was kindness of heart and sweetness of nature.

Of my opposite number at Balliol, Peter Quennell, who was elected to the English Literature scholarship there at the same time as I was at the House, I saw not a glimpse – unless it is of him that I have a fantasy-memory, a golden-haired young man with a girl, who was being tugged along by a beautiful large dog on a lead, outside Parker's bookshop in the Turl. Peter Quennell was already a name among us for his poetry, published in *Public School Verse*, in which my first poem had appeared, though mine was no Public

School. Richard Hughes had been the sponsor of this scheme in those blithe days of new beginnings after the war, and there the names appear that have become familiar now, among those totally forgotten: Peter Quennell, Graham Greene, Christopher Isherwood, W. H. Auden. Peter Quennell's verses were so much more sophisticated than those of the rest of us, and three lines of his from a poem called 'Procne' have remained with me all my life:

> So she became a bird and bird-like danced
> On a long sloe-bough, treading the silver blossom
> With a bird's lovely feet ...

There must have been some incantatory power in it to have remained in the mind so long: a good poet was lost with his 'Retreat from Parnassus'. He tells us in that that his 'only reason for adopting free verse was that I had never learned to scan' – and here was I, laboriously, secretively, conscientiously, under the surface of reading hard for Schools, subjecting myself to the discipline of regular verse, only to have my poems disconsidered as old-fashioned. For thirty years the new idiom of Eliot and Pound has been poetic orthodoxy – all my working life in fact – and my poetry has been out of it, disconsidered, myself discouraged. And yet, paradoxically, I received more encouragement, more warmth and helpful criticism more friendliness and personal help in becoming a writer from Eliot than from anyone else. And, paradox within paradox, I have always felt – he once admitted as much – that my discouraged verse, poetry of sensibility, defeat, despair, was much nearer his than his more fashionable (and publicised) followers'. They really had a wholly different spirit from his.

Anyway Quennell parted from Oxford, or, as his autobiographical *The Sign of the Fish* charmingly says, Oxford parted with him. He went off early to live the literary life in London,

> But came to Oxford and his friends no more.

I saw more of Graham Greene, for he edited *The Oxford Outlook*, was encouraging to my poetry, and made me a member of the Ordinary, in which we contributors, the writing folk, sometimes foregathered. There are the names: Basil Murray, Gilbert Murray's scapegrace son, who figured in early Waugh novels and died young; Gyles Isham, actor and baronet; Robert Speaight, actor and author; Robert Birley, Eton beak and public mentor; Claud Cockburn, creator of the shocking, scandalous, salutary, anti-Appeasement newsletter, *The Week*; Rosalie Glynn Grylls, fellow Cornish Celt, who became later a close friend. There was I, on the side lines, uncommitted, disengaged.

Two other luminaries of my generation I never knew, Cyril Connolly and Evelyn Waugh, though both of them were intimate friends of Richard Pares, whom I knew through the Labour Club. For, when it came to politics, I was anything but disengaged.

For one must remember the atmosphere of *that* post-war world. The grim experience of the first war had reinforced the strength of idealism. There was a real belief, not only in my ardent and ingenuous generation, in bettering the world. 'It must not happen again' was our attitude to the war; the sacrifice of the generations before us must not be in vain. A better world must be built up, internationally through the League of Nations, at home through the working-class movement and the progressive parties. We were all in favour of good causes, always collecting for famine-relief, some of us, such as Ralph Fox, went off abroad on relief work. The idealistic force in religion had not evaporated: the Oxford Student Christian Union, 'Oscu' as we called it, was in full swing. So was the W.E.A., the Workers' Educational Association, which, though secular and nonsectarian, had really been launched by the religious zeal of those eminent Oxford Anglicans, Bishop Gore, William Temple, R. H. Tawney.

We were, I fear, very ignorant about the true causes of the war and the malign forces within Germany which were inveterate and would come back to make yet another attempt at the domination of Europe. We thought, misled by Keynes, that Germany had been badly treated by the Treaty of Versailles – with no thought of the kind of treaty, witness Brest-Litovsk, she would have imposed if she had won. We of the Left were specifically mis-directed by the pro-German books and sentiments of Bertrand Russell and Goldsworthy Dickinson, H. N. Brailsford's *War of Steel and Gold*, E. D. Morel and their like. Not until I went to live in Germany and saw how things were for myself did I recover from the pernicious rubbish in which I had been indoctrinated.

Those were years of hope, however, in which it was not foolish to hope: there still was a chance of influencing the course of events right up till the late 1930s. Britain was still in a position to exercise leadership in Europe: we took that too much for granted, and, in the event, our leaders proved themselves unworthy of it. We did not know, young and ignorant as we were, full of good will, what malignity there is in the world or how limitless is human folly in the sphere of politics.

Such, at any rate, was the liberal atmosphere of the time, and such the background to my story.

*   *   *

What an advantage it is, for the historian, to have kept a diary, not only to get the record straight, the atmosphere right. The memory is not only a selective but a shaping instrument. I find that I was much more sociable, had many more friends, than I had remembered. In subsequent years I formed a picture of myself as a shy recluse, living much to myself in my rooms, not taking much part in general activity. What this must indicate is that it was the inner life to myself that I really valued, and this is what had stayed with me. At the time it surprised me that my Public School friends, conditioned to constant gregariousness and no privacy, could not bear the solitude of their rooms: they were always in and out of each others'. I had always been conditioned to being by myself, so that I enjoyed being alone in my room: always plenty to occupy me, reading, writing notes or poems, diary or letters, thinking my thoughts or even occasionally looking out of the window.

My little self-made engagements book corrects my memory, and shows me how frequently I was asked out and, surprisingly, how frequently I had my friends back to tea (I couldn't afford to ask them for any other meal). One curious thing about Wadleigh was that he never entertained anybody much, though he could well have afforded to – much better than I; but he was hardly a domesticated animal. With a powerful gorilla-like frame, spectacled and short-sighted, already very hirsute, he shambled about the place in a gallumphing manner, occasionally giving vent, without any nice sense of humour, to something between a snort and a roar. What ever can have attracted me to him? I suppose it was his indubitable masculinity and rough good will. He took me out with him to buy a bath-towel: he commanded a large brown towel of the roughest material obtainable. I was much impressed. But there was more to it than that. He was very serious-minded, taking the world gravely, and so was I. Moreover, was he not the senior classical Scholar of the year, with a sort of precedence, pupil of the famous Cyril Norwood at Marlborough, which had signalised itself by getting seventeen scholarships and exhibitions that year at Oxford and Cambridge, more than any other school? Then, too, for all the uncouthness of his manners, Wadleigh was a gentleman, which I was not; and I should add that, at bottom, he was a good sort.

We had met on the staircase, involved ourselves in an argument and he came into my room to hold forth about Shelley. He already fancied himself as a budding philosopher, and upheld Shelley's superiority to Keats as a poet on the ground that Shelley was both poet and philosopher. I did not know how to deal with this, though I knew that Keats was the better poet, and was much put out. (Even today, forty years after, it makes my hand tremble to write it.) I don't need to go into the argument now, for it is obvious that Shelley's superiority as a philosopher does not prove his superiority as a poet: the test must be an aesthetic one, in terms of poetry in and for itself. I use this simply as an illustration of what Oxford did for one. When I came up I was largely a creature of feeling and sentiment – and I considered this rather feminine; though I felt very strongly about things, I was very uncertain how to set about defending my position intellectually. After hammering away at argument, morning, noon and night, at the end of my undergraduate time I felt that I could defend myself adequately, or almost any position I wished to take up.

This dialectical question entered very much into my relations with Wadleigh. He was so much better educated than I: a classical scholar – that aroused feelings of inferiority. (I have always hated not knowing Greek: not to know Greek is to be an uneducated man.)

Wadleigh was going on to do Greats, and was already thinking in terms of Greats philosophy. Practically all the ablest scholars in the humanities in my day were classical scholars, brought up on the old traditional Greats grind: Latin and Greek literature and history, ancient philosophy – metaphysics, logic and ethics. Though a modern historian myself, as a good Oxford man I have always accepted the superiority of the Greats training over any others: nearly all the best people have come through it.

Now that the philosophers have abnegated their transcendent claims and confine themselves mainly to logical analysis, the other disciplines have come into their own: we historians and literary people can think what we like, provided it is in keeping with correct methods of thought. The great cat away, the mice can play. In my day it was not so: Oxford philosophy claimed an overriding authority over other, sectional and disparate, disciplines.

Wadleigh was the heir to all this, and the fact that I secretly accepted it made it all the more irritating. He was older and more experienced; he assumed the superiority of a Greats man. This made me jealous of him, so that there was a competitive element in my relations with him from the first. But also I admired him. Masculine men are very unobservant: I don't suppose he saw that my attitude was a contingent one, in the long (and not very long) run entirely under my own control. Marlborough, the Classics, Greek, ancient philosophy, and the rest of it! – he was up against someone cleverer than himself when it came to the point.

The situation reminds me of the devotion George Santayana entertained all his earlier years for Bertrand Russell's scapegrace brother, Frank. And later on the poor philosopher discovered that Earl Russell had not even remembered his devoted admirer's Christian name. I don't suppose that Henry Julian remembers mine – I never called him by his; to me he was always Wadleigh – and I had finished with him long before his name became notorious through the Hiss case.

Nevertheless, we jogged along together in harness; he was important to me, he was my first convert to socialism – whatever that meant – and through him I managed to recruit a considerable number of Public School men to the Labour Club. When I came up, there were two supposed socialists in the whole of Christ Church, not a very promising recruiting ground. One was a timid, good-hearted, somewhat battered old sheep of a Yorkshire woollen-worker, who had come up with a W.E.A. scholarship, and couldn't say Bo to a goose (there were many geese about); the other was a roaring upper-class eccentric with a hardly intelligible manner of speech. Wadleigh and I had a recruiting drive which fetched in a membership of over a score for the Labour Club – larger than any other college; so that during all my undergraduate time the club was dominated by House men, who provided the bulk of the officers, chairmen, secretaries and so on. All this took up a good deal of my spare time – but indeed I had no spare time. Often I didn't know what to do for time, what with writing my weekly essays for tutorials, lectures, reading, writing, organising for the Labour Club, meetings, committees, visiting and being visited. If it hadn't been for the vacations I don't know how I'd have got the interminable reading for the History School done. There was an advantage here in not being able to go to Scotland, or Switzerland, or wherever so many well-to-do House-men went. I always went home and worked solidly all through the vacations.

Perhaps politics, after all, was a better option for a growing youth with a passionate temperament than the New Psychology, which was all the rage in the early 1920s. As an undergraduate wit put it, those were the days when

> Bliss was it in that dawn to be a Freud,
> But to be Jung was very heaven!

Those were the days of George Edinger's marvellous fake-lecture in the Town Hall, with a lot of senior members of the university present, given in a strong, German accent, in the familiar German jargon, on neither the Conscious, nor the Sub-Conscious, but the Co-Conscious.

For my nineteenth birthday, 4 December 1922, I had received a parcel of cake and buns and Cornish cream from home, so I had a tea-party: Wadleigh, Whitehead, dear Tom Lawrenson (a Geordie from South Shields, mathematical Scholar, who had specially learned to smoke a pipe in order to come up to Oxford, as I had specially tried to learn to like coffee), and David Low, who has made himself a name as a scholarly bookseller. 'Afterwards we read Arnold's "Scholar Gipsy" and "Omar Khayyam", until through sheer boredom, I suppose, the first two had more or less of a scrap.' Classical Scholars, too! I watched the furniture being thrown about and my room disarranged, until I could stand it no longer and put an end to it. All the same, here was my circle being formed: we all became members of the Labour Club.

Next day:

> I have come back from a meeting of the Essay Club where a paper was read on Auto-suggestion. It is strange that so much attention is being paid by undergraduates here to the New Psychology: one would never have expected it. There are continuous [sic] meetings at which Psycho-Analysis is discussed with its kindred subjects. Only the other day there was a meeting at the J.C.R. [Junior Common Room], addressed by Dr William Brown, who is Wilde Reader in Mental Philosophy.

This beneficent Wilde, I fancy, was not the sainted Oscar, after whom the chair might more appropriately have been called, considering the subjects dealt with by the Reader. He was a practising Harley Street psychiatrist, but the idealist philosophers of Oxford would not allow that there was such a subject as psychology. So the Wilde Reader in Mental Philosophy gave advice on what young men have to put up with. How expect any other with a lot of vigorous and virile youths mewed up in a college, with no outlet supposedly permitted to sex?

For myself, the Diary records a greater state of 'purity' at Oxford than I had found possible at home, and I was bent on making this absolute. I did not approve of all the talk about sex: 'I tire of the continual round of sexual affairs: everybody talks of sex, everybody thinks of sex, the accursèd thing enters into every moment of our lives.' I, at any rate, wouldn't have it. What a prig I was! and what a further strain my over-developed will imposed upon me – provoking, too, for a youth with an erotic temperament, I was determined on absolute Puritanism. Somebody sensible should have introduced me to the facts of life; but nobody dared. Dundas, the Senior Censor, was notorious for the sex-talks he imparted to all likely undergraduates. Emlyn Williams's book, *George*, has a perfect rendering of such an encounter. Years later I once asked Dundas why this privilege had been denied me, and he answered, I think truthfully: 'Much too frightened.' His intuition was right: however well-intentioned, his worldly wisdom would have been coldly, or perhaps even hotly, received. On another occasion, too, he renounced an encounter with me in one of his brief, mumbled phrases: 'Too complicated.'

Henry Julian, however, took his troubles to the sage and regular counsels of the Wilde Reader. This was rather disapproved of by me: I objected to his habit of 'for ever having his heart out on the carpet'. It seemed to me too vulgar, too Oxford Student Christian Union – as it would become too Buchmanite and Groupy. Whatever one had to put up with was best kept to oneself. Perhaps this was too inhuman a doctrine, but I have often thought of the line of affiliation between the heart-out-on-the-carpet and the confessions in the Hiss case. I express no disapprobation other than an aesthetic one.

So my first term rushed excitedly by: tutorials with Masterman, breakfasts with Dundas. It was the custom of the dons to ask one out to breakfast, after Roll-call or 'Rollers' in Hall: a barbarous habit, and I remember the difficulty I had in knowing when to take my leave, longing to go but fearing to be impolite. But teas, in the Cornish way, were my chief times of entertainment. On lunch I had to economise: I often had nothing but soup, and bread with strawberry jam for dessert. In fact I had so much of it as an undergraduate that I have never liked strawberry jam since. There were teas with everybody – Carpenter from Truro (his father was vicar of St John's), with Cleverdon at Jesus (subsequently a well-known B.B.C. producer), with Pelham Box, a graduate student who had already published a book – it was very nice of him to take me up. I used to think he had a Cavalier appearance, with his refinement of feature, delicate colouring and upturned moustache. He had some chalky condition of the bone, which meant that he was for ever breaking an arm, and he died young. And, indeed, it is touching to think of the wastage among those young fellows who were at Oxford with me – quite apart from the second war, so many of them died less than half way along their course. A much higher proportion than among working people: I suppose they lived more exposed, more highly strung lives, took more chances. Some died, quite young, by their own hand.

What a medley of persons I knew and had forgotten: the Baron de Gunzbourg, a French Rothschild who lived at the bottom of my staircase; Maycock and Fellowes-Browne, embryo Anglo-Catholic priests who went regularly to Pusey House or the Cowley Fathers, one of them on coming back used to run his fingers through his hair to collect the scent of incense – I didn't think very highly of that when he told me. There was a rhyme that went:

> The rather-rathers
> Go to the Cowley Fathers;
> The whole hoggers
> Go to St Alioggers –

i.e. the Jesuit church of St Aloysius, as opposed to the Anglo-Catholic church of the Cowley Fathers. These things interested me less than they had done: I was loosening myself in mind from the Church, that had nevertheless done so much for me and played such a part in my early life. Once I did go to High Mass at the Cowley Fathers and heard a sermon on 'God is Love', or rather the beginning of it; for neither term in the proposition meant anything to my mind, and, furiously indignant, my nose burst out bleeding, so that I had to rush from the church.

Two clerics did their best to retain me. Chavasse of St Aldate's, son of the second Bishop of Liverpool and himself to become Bishop of Rochester, found me exploring his uninteresting Evangelical church across the way from Tom gate, in my first days still proudly wearing my Scholar's gown. He asked me in to lunch at his vicarage, later to dinner, and was always extraordinarily kind. I liked him and was grateful; but his brand of religion had no message for me. I was more affected, and in fact disturbed, by the appeal of Rawlinson, Tutor in Divinity, later Bishop of Derby. He was an intellectual, a High Churchman and a clever man, and was kind to me. He was not disinterested – as was only his duty – and appealed to my ambition: one day might I not be Dean of Christ Church? He never gave up hope and never quite let go of me, for all that I had found in politics a substitute religion, at any rate a fanaticism. The inner struggle gave me a nightmare or two in which he figured; but I was always grateful to him for his kindness and his interest.

He would have liked to be Dean of Christ Church himself; but he was not even a canon. Much cleverer and livelier than the rather sleepy lot of sheep who were the canons, slumbering all over the place in their roomy mansions – somebody called Tom Quad an 'ecclesiastical desert' – Rawlers used to say of Kill-Canon gateway that led out of it into Peckwater Quad, 'Kill-Canon gate: would that it would function!' It was said of him by some colleague, with the familiar spice of clerical malice, that beginning as a Pragmatist (he must have imbibed his philosophy at Corpus from Schiller) he postulated a universe and found that that worked; he then postulated a God and found that that worked; he then postulated a Church of England (he had begun as a Nonconformist) and found that that worked best of all.

Actually his preferment in the Church was rather retarded. He had a formidable rival in a rotund, and even cleverer, man, N. P. ('Nippie') Williams, chaplain of Exeter College. No one could make out whether Nippie was burdened with much belief, but he wrote a masterly book on the Doctrine of the Fall and of Original Sin, on which he was an authority. Nippie had a pink, perspiring, oleaginous countenance, and marched about, like a character out of *Barchester Towers*, the image of clerical self-satisfaction. Roy Harrod, who didn't believe a word of them, used to make a cult of Nippie's sermons: they were a fascinating edifice of intellectual construction. The election to the Lady Margaret professorship of divinity was a popular one; there was a great whipping up of clerical voters, and of course the less attractive man won – I am bound to add, in justice, the more suitable. 'Rawlers' left Oxford to become Archdeacon of Northumberland. He was a small man with a large wife: it was said that they were once announced at Inveraray Castle as 'the Archduchess of Auckland and a gentleman'.

Our Dean, Henry Julian White – he shared Christian names as well as initials with Wadleigh – was even more diminutive and also married to a large, dominant (in this case, American) female. One sometimes wondered whether the cat might not eat up the canary. White had succeeded a much more distinguished man, Tommie Strong, who as Bishop of Oxford continued to be about the place. Indeed, Dean White wasn't distinguished at all, and he was far too much of a reactionary for me. He one day said to me that *The Times* was nothing like conservative *enough* for him, only the *Morning Post* was sufficiently reactionary. I fancy he was teasing me, but I believed him and wrote him off at once for a fool. Which I don't suppose now he was. The post-war Royal Commission on the universities had recommended the suppression of one of the canonries and turning its funds to more productive purposes, for students, tutors, etc. The canons had apparently agreed to this reform; but the Dean had gone round and made them fall into line to resist it, on the ground that the first breach of the dyke would let in the flood.

The fact was that there was a scission between the Dean and canons on one side, who were top dogs in Christ Church, and the tutorial body, the lay element, who were there known as Students. This meant that the House – the largest and grandest of the Oxford colleges, with the Cathedral establishment embedded in the midst of it – lacked cohesion and integration, and was not wholly satisfactory as a college. We hardly knew the canons; only one of them went out of his way to be friendly to me and invite me to his house – dear Canon Cooke, Regius professor of Hebrew, with the beautiful daughters. Watson, the nattering Low Church professor of Ecclesiastical History, was immensely learned but one of those who could never get round to writing anything. Another canon, Walter Lock, was professor of Pastoral Theology: what did that mean – district-visiting? Then there was Bishop Shaw, Archdeacon of Buckingham, whose house on the north side of Tom Quad abutted on to the foundations of the magnificent chapel Wolsey intended: the bishop's face was as purple as the evening suit he wore dining in Hall on Sunday evenings. Come to think of it, he looked much like Wolsey must have looked himself.

There remained only Headlam, whom I knew to be a reactionary and disapproved of in consequence. Tall, gaunt and big, he was said to have the blood of Oliver Cromwell in his veins, and he certainly had odd facial habits, a nervous tic which made him make convulsive grimaces, while he gnawed his large gardener's hands in turn. In the Cathedral Sunday by Sunday – Scholars who were Anglicans had to attend – my place in the Scholars' stalls (I chose the Cantoris side, where I had sat in all the years as a choirboy at St Austell) was directly opposite to Headlam's in his canon's stall. One day I found those steely, magnetic eyes on me in a fixed stare; I wasn't going to have that, so I returned stare for stare, and went on staring until Headlam, with one of his odd grimaces, gave way and shook himself free. He shortly after left to become Bishop of Gloucester. Little did I know that in later years we should become such friends at All Souls, and last of all he came to share rooms with me: we grew to be fond of each other. It reminds me of dear G. M. Trevelyan, who said that if anybody had told him in his young Radical days that he would one day occupy the Master's stall in Trinity chapel, he would have been scandalised.

Altogether, one may say of the Dean and canons in my time that they were a pretty uninspiring lot. No Gaisford or Liddell, no Pusey or Scott-Holland – let alone a Dean Church, a Bishop Gore or Temple! Our teaching dons were a conscientious body (with one notorious exception), and especially the History dons who were kept hard at it with the post-war increase of undergraduates. All the same, I must say honestly that, thinking back over it, I missed the inspiration of a really great teacher, who could have given one a lead intellectually and helped effectively to form one's mind – such a person as G. E. Moore, Alfred Marshall or Keynes at Cambridge, Gilbert Murray or A. L. Smith at Oxford.

There was among the younger dons one man of genius, J. D. Beazley, and I have always been proud that I was his choice for the English Literature scholarship at the House. But I was not a classic, and could never come under his tuition who, more than anyone, was responsible for that marvellous stricken generation of young Greek historians. Beazley was virtually the creator of the study of Greek vases, at any rate in England, and became the greatest authority in the world on them. With an unsurpassed combination of exact scholarship with aesthetic sensibility, he has written the definitive works on the subject. Before the war, young, he had been the friend of the poet Flecker who had written poems to him; his own verses he had destroyed – one more warning of the conflict between scholarship and literature which engaged my inner mind and emerges as a leading theme in the Diary.

Beazley was married to a remarkable woman of many gifts and talents, of entire originality and independence of spirit: the current of life bubbled spontaneous and free as a spring, but the spring was warm, for there was true kindness of heart besides the vivacity and charm. With the background of Constantinople, the Greek islands and the Levant, what more suitable mate for a Greek archaeologist? Already a gifted pianist and linguist, she made herself into a first-class photographer for their joint devotion – one heard marvels of Jackie's linking together fragments that were physically dispersed from the Czartoryski Museum in Warsaw to Cairo, and from Crete to Chicago. Marie Beazley made an exotic appearance in the 'ecclesiastical desert' of those soporific canons – especially when, fancying herself as Minerva, she got a goose that followed her around the quadrangles, recognising her by the large black-and-white check of her skirt. Alas, one week-end that the Beazleys were away at Cambridge, the goose ate the *Daily Mail* and died of it.

But how kind the Beazleys were to me! – especially Marie. In my first term there came an invitation to lunch – delicious omelette, asparagus and white wine, and once more, on the part of the *ingénu*, the awful problem of taking one's leave.

This made me prefer the simpler entertainments among ourselves of tea and crumpets, especially by my own fireside, when there was no need to disperse and the talk could go on for ever – or, at least, until Hall. There were teas with Weatherhead and Whitehead and Speechley – who was he? I remember a mellow, kind, avuncular personality, on his way into the Church, a recruit of mine to the Labour Club. On another day with Hugh Molson – a nice-natured youth with fish-like gills and a pompous manner of speaking. 'I really *moo-urn* Lord Davidson,' he said to me once, on the death of that Archbishop. Opposite the east front of Queen's, the dark entry to St Peter's-in-the-East afforded inviting shelter to the embraces of lovers. Richard Pares used to tell a story of young Molson looking down from a room there one night upon such a pair, and surprising them with his authoritative 'Stop fornicating' – and they did.

(Montherlant: 'Wherever there are two people who want to make love to each other, there is always somebody about to say, *Non!*')

One night I went to a Town Hall meeting to hear the celebrated Major Douglas, the creator of the Social Credit movement. This nostrum was very much in public discussion, nobody quite under-standing what it meant – in so far as it meant, simply, inflation we have had it and there may well have been something in it. For those were the days of the disastrous financial orthodoxy that led us to the return to the Gold Standard and parity at $4.88. (To think of it now! Would it were possible!) Nobody understood monetary questions then, and Major Douglas's ideas were wrapped in a cloud of jargon from which it was impossible to extract the sense. The chair was taken for him by the egregious Professor Soddy, who had practically given up the subject of which he was professor and to which he had made important early contributions with Rutherford at McGill, namely physics, for the religion of Social Credit. I shall never forget that ass: Soddy took the chair and held forth for three-quarters of an hour, making Major Douglas's speech for him, until we wondered whether we should ever get to the prophet himself.

When Charles Henderson was once played that trick by a boor of a local chairman in Cornwall, who spoke for nearly an hour and then called on the speaker to give his address, Charlie gave his address as 'Penmount, Truro,' and said, 'And now I am afraid I must catch my train.'

* * *

The basic reason for my happiness at Oxford was that there I found my true nature; in spite of my social inexperience, my restricted opportunities, self-consciousness and lack of confidence (where other people were concerned), this environment was more natural to me, i.e. more in keeping with my nature, than that into which I had been born. D. H. Lawrence was quite right: the mental life of the work-ing class is too restricted and cramping for an intelligent boy to endure it. One would perish of inanition; they never understand anything, haven't read anything, or heard or seen anything, could never answer the questions my mind was full of, from childhood on. (What price *their* judgments, then, in the realm of art and literature,

as is demanded in Russia today? A real inversion of values, a deformation of the spirit.) D. H. Lawrence and I *know*, for we belong – as
opposed to the absurdity of an Orwell, seeking enlightenment by
going to the people. It needs an ex-Etonian in revolt to think of
anything so pointless.

This did not mean that I cut my emotional ties with my family
and original environment. So far from that, they were much
stronger than normal – much more so than with most bourgeois,
and probably rather stronger than was good for me. I was deeply
rooted in Cornwall and in my home, and was, moreover, absurdly
loyal. The excitements of my first acquaintance with Oxford did not
mean that I lost touch with my old friends at home. I was a conscientious letter-writer and kept up better than they did, in spite of
all my new activities, interests and companions. My Irish friend
among the masters at school, whom we will call Bacon, wrote that
he was 'up to the ears over this da– play'. This was the play that I had
made out of Q's *Troy Town*, which was to be performed in the
Christmas vacation. Nevertheless, as a good follower of mine, 'I am
following closely the work of the I.L.P. at Westminster. The speeches
of Newbold, the Communist, are intensely interesting. At Election
time here Mr Barritt [the Headmaster] and myself were vigorous
supporters of the Labour policy, especially the capital levy. But I do
think they could have secured a better candidate than Joe Harris –
with all due respect to the man.' I thought so too, and noted this for
future reference.

My Cambridge friends, Jimmy and Dorothy Crowther, kept me
in touch with news of their Left Wing circle. Jimmy had written
that summer, 'Maurice Dobb of the *Plebs* was one of the three to
take Firsts in Economics at Cambridge. Ralph Fox will have been
viva-d for Schools today. I hope he gets a First. [He did.] At the
end of July he leaves for Russia for a year to help the Friends' Relief
Commission.' Dorothy wrote me news of the Left intellectuals. 'Did
Jimmy tell you that B. Russell married his secretary, after his first
wife divorced him, and that they now rejoice in a child and he is
particularly pleased? His present attitude by no means squares with
his chapter on marriage and population in *Principles of Social Recon-
struction*! I have not yet had the book on China.' She had been

staying with her 'Welsh friend who married L. Hogben, and was amused to find her turned into a devoted parent.' Parenthood became a frequent habit: marriage to Lancelot was no sinecure. At Oxford had I seen anything of Professor George Gordon yet? 'I told him about you once, and also sent a message through Mr Tolkien at Leeds. But don't mention him and Q to each other. There is bad blood, I fancy. It seems that years ago Professor Gordon published some original work on Shakespeare, and he thinks Q has used it unprofessionally.'

I think this refers to Q's *Shakespeare's Workmanship*, and I have heard that there was a bone between Q and Gordon. George Gordon, though a gifted man, was an idle one and not much given to publishing anything of his own anyway. He was the favourite disciple of Walter Raleigh, whom I just missed going up to Oxford – most brilliant of lecturers there, along with Gilbert Murray – and Raleigh was bent on Gordon succeeding him. Q was an elector, and favoured the better and more industrious scholar, Nichol Smith. Nichol Smith was assured of the majority, but at the election, Robert Bridges went over to the other side unexpectedly, and Gordon got the job. He held it until he became President of Magdalen, when Nichol Smith very properly succeeded and everybody was happy. Such are the ways of such things: better to earn one's living independently by one's works, as Q and I have done.

I find that I was looking forward to coming home. 'Saturday will see me travelling back to Cornwall and to mother, and to Jean [the girl next door] and everybody else whom I like. My two months in Oxford have been the happiest in my life, but I shan't be sorry to be going home again.' I could hardly wait to tell my mother and father about the grandeur of Christ Church, especially of dinner in Hall: the blazing fires on either side not far from the dais, the dons in evening dress warming themselves at the fire not far from the Scholars' table where we sat. There were the shaded lamps along the tables the whole length of Wolsey's great Hall, the cardinal himself looking down upon the festive scene, raising his hand in blessing, his cardinal's hat upon everything, plates, tureens, dishes, silver, the wash-basins in our rooms. All round the lights gleamed in the glazed portraits of the men who had once been here, even as we – men of talent, men of genius, above all men of power. Here were Christ Church Prime Ministers, Peel, Canning, Rosebery, the formidable eye of Mr Gladstone; here was the lean, gaunt face of John Locke, prime man of genius among them all, whom the House rejected; here were the inseparable Fell and Aldrich, men of music and good cheer; here Ruskin, and there, at the bottom of the Hall, holy John Wesley and the pale, drawn, tortured features of Lewis Carroll. On the opposite wall, among the bewigged, ballooning bishops, lawn sleeves and robes of the Garter, was a fellow-Cornishman to encourage me, Bishop Trelawny.

> And shall Trelawny die?
> Then thirty thousand Cornishmen
> Will know the reason why.

But – it was time for one of the Scholars to say grace: that long Latin grace every syllable of which I can still repeat, so deeply are those nights engraved in my memory, forty years after.

II

Freshman

COMING home for the Christmas vacation I had no difficulty in picking up the threads of my former life. Q once said to me how much he preferred living in two places, and I have so much appreciated the rhythm that recently I have added a third, California. The first thing was the performance of *Troy Town*, which the school had been working at and of which it gave an extremely successful production. The play worked out rather like a Barrie play, as it might be *Quality Street* – Barrie and Q were friends and had much in common. Q came over from Fowey for the first night, white tie and tails – so like him, and took me along with him on the platform. It was all rather memorable, and the play might well have been given further performances in the intervening years, if anybody had had the energy or initiative to do it.

Q also came over to Speech Day and Prize-giving and made a graceful speech, which I evidently thought light-weight. There was a good deal of sparring with Shaw, who had recently said that Eton and Harrow, Oxford and Cambridge should be razed to the ground and their sites sown with salt. Really, what an ass Shaw was, in addition to being a man of genius! Q reflected sadly on the loss of 'the flower of English youth' in the 1914 war. How right he was we had even more bitter reason to lament later, when the leadership of the country rested for two decades in the hands of the second-rate, and the ablest of young Englishmen lay in their graves in Flanders and France. Q himself later told me how much he grieved for Rupert Brooke, whom he had recruited from the classics to carry on the English School at Cambridge, 'which, in a manner of speaking,' he said shyly, 'I invented.'

I resumed my walks to those beloved, sequestered spots that had given me inspiration and renewal in my schooldays, Carn Grey and Luxulyan, high up in the hinterland above the bay, moorland country all granite boulders, bracken and gorse, intersected by streams and the tracks of the former miners, to whom my father's people belonged. It was all so intensely Cornish, unalloyed by strangers coming into the town and its spreading ugly suburbs in the coastal plain below. There were the names the old vanished people reaching back to antiquity had given the places where they lived. Some of them I walked through I could interpret. Tregonissey, in its original form Tre-cunedwid, meant the hamlet of the tribal chief, really the head settlement of the lower area – not unnaturally, for it had the best soil. Carclaze, the big claypit in which father worked, meant the green camp; the workings had a long history, reaching back as a source of tin to the Romans – or, as local tradition said, to King Solomon. Today, as everywhere up there, tin had been succeeded by china-clay. Evidently Carclaze had been dominated by a prehistoric camp. I walked through Trethurgy, a curious hamlet scattered around a bowl of earlier tin-workings: the hamlet of the water-dog, i.e. otter. The tin-works were frequent in those names: Penwithick Stents meant the tin-works at the head of the little rise. Rescorla, pronounced Rescoller, meant the moor of the sheepfold; but what did my favourite Methrose mean? – it seems, the cultivated land in the heath, appropriately enough.

There, in from the road, among its fields, enclosed by granite hedges, lay the little Tudor manor-house where John Wesley used to stay on his visits this way. I never knew of its existence, four miles away from home, until I went to Oxford and read Wesley's *Journals*. Only then did I venture up the lane to intrude upon the good farm-folk, the Higmans, and be shown the little walled court, the one-storeyed medieval hall, the parlour beyond which once had a fine carved oak chimney-piece, with coats of arms – sold off by the dispirited and dispiriting baronet of Prideaux, Sir Colman Rashleigh, to America. (Where is it now?) And so on to beloved Luxulyan, i.e. Loc-sulyan, the place of Saint Sulyan, with his holy well: target, terminus, paradise of all these walks. For there was the romantic valley, with its great rocks and high climbs and waterfall, and the splendid aqueduct, Treffry's Folly, our version of the Pont du Gard.

One day I walked with my school-friend, Len Tippett, to Carn Grey and Crinnis: we had so much to tell each other, he about the Imperial College of Science where he now was and I about Oxford, that for once we failed to argue. How much we enjoyed our arguments! – he the older, something of a mentor, steadier and more prosaic, with more common sense, I led away by ideas and poetry, almost intoxicated by them, the air, the walk, the excitement of life at nineteen – never have I known such ecstasy as those walks when young, in that upland country! Another day I had an argument with Bacon about the Catholic Church that lasted all the way to Luxulyan. 'Tea in the inn there: saffron cake and cream. After which a long walk back through the Valley and Biscovey in winter twilight and darkness. Moonrise as we were coming through Holmbush.'

At New Year I received a nice letter from my namesake, R. G. Rows, the blind sage of Helston and G.O.M. of Cornish education, whom I had been taken to see by F. R. Pascoe, the County Secretary for Education, that summer. I was wrestling with Mill's *Political Economy*, a little out of my depth; I was assured that

> his style is, I think, first rate and his matter, though perhaps in some respects out of date, keeps its place among later economists. You need not fear that you will assimilate too much of Mill ... In your intercourse with Oxford graduates and undergraduates never forget that 'a man that hath friends must show himself friendly,' and that you are likely to get back from your brethren in study the echoes of the tones you send out. Your three or four years at Oxford will, I have no doubt, lay the foundations and build some of the superstructure of a character which will be the joy of your life.

Rows had been a celebrated orator in his day and, I fancy, a revered Wesleyan local preacher. But what an odd idea that one's own *character* should be the joy of one's life! No Anglican could possibly say such a thing: wasn't it an indication of the indefeasible Nonconformist smugness?

One way and another I received a lot of good advice, not all of it welcome.

At New Year came a rocket from my beloved old headmaster, 'a letter the like of which I have never read before, and never wish to see again.' But, indeed, I well remember it. He had apparently written to recommend me to the attention of his sister-in-law, widow of a scientist Fellow of Exeter. The poor lady, however, had heard from her charwoman, my former landlady on scholarship expeditions, that I had become a Bolshevist, and 'under the circumstances [sic] she did not feel disposed to make my acquaintance.' Little did this prudish bourgeoise know how loftily I sat towards making the acquaintance of anyone. I certainly had no desire to know her; but what gave me a furious headache was that my beloved A.G.J., to whom I owed so much, should have been upset. This was the only cloud in our relations in over forty years. Anybody else would have received a frightful rocket back; but he was sacrosanct, I merely took no notice of the unfortunate letter.

But the Diary is full of it: I had regrettably lost an opportunity, for 'people of her kind are the essence of the university, your Socialist crowd are only the froth.' I wasn't sent to Oxford to become 'a ranting Socialist' (my headmaster was a reader of the *Daily Telegraph*), but to acquire the culture of Oxford and 'to have the stamp of Oxford on me when I leave it'. To this end I should 'worship humbly at the shrine of Oxford's greatness' and I should 'jump at the chance' of knowing people like his sister-in-law. (I never 'jumped at the chance' of knowing anyone, except Churchill.) If Wadleigh were a philosopher, perhaps he would 'keep me stable'. There was something comic in the idea of Wadleigh keeping me stable, and I never to my knowledge set eyes, from either Christ Church or All Souls, on the Widow Jenkinson.

I was even at the time half-inclined to laugh, when my headache was over; but indeed these perpetual irritations from stupid people became no laughing matter. They built up a resentment which I have no desire to overcome, and they fortified me in my conviction – which everything that has happened since in the world's affairs confirms – that in political matters, as in all matters involving general thought, human beings are idiots. And that, in time, undermined the foundations of any beliefs, or even wishes, in regard to them. This is the wisdom of no illusions about them – at any rate the wisdom of Montaigne and Hume, of Swift, Voltaire and Gibbon, of Tocqueville and Burckhardt, of Henry Adams and George Santayana, of the sages who speak specially for me. The education this Cornishman received from his fellow human beings all the way along was not inappropriate for an historian. To Talleyrand's 'Surtout point de zèle', one may add, 'Above all, no illusions about them.'

My headache was confirmed by what Barritt told me: that at the County Council meeting at which their one university scholarship – so generous a provision – had been decided, a note was passed up to Q while he was speaking for me, which read 'Do you know that this boy is a Bolshevik?' Q tore it up and went on with his remarks. 'What else could any sane human being have done?', the Diary innocently enquires. 'I cannot imagine a writer of such a note, outside the lunatic asylum.' Alas, I well can now.

These were years in which people were scared by the mere word Bolshevik – years when they were terrified by the scarecrow of the Russian Revolution, when it was in no condition to touch them. Nor would it have made such advances, if these people, by their confused idea of appeasing Nazi Germany as a defence against the Reds, had not let themselves in for the second German war and the Russians into the heart of Europe.

* * *

Back at Christ Church at the end of January, I admitted that 'as usual I felt rather weepy at leaving home, especially when mother cried.' She must have had more feeling than I had remembered, and I have done her an injustice in my memory. She certainly had iron in her composition, but that may have been a front she put on to the world. And, in fact, our family life was one of warmth and affection, made all the more so by my frequent illnesses, beginning from now on: there was an emotional security that gave stability to my agitated life, with the sharpened sensibilities, the one skin too few. There was an inner citadel for me to inhabit, all the stranger – like that of T. E. Lawrence's family in the Polstead Road – because cut off from friends and from having much to do with other people, and, I suppose, for a similar reason.

However, 'once I have arrived, come up to my own room with the fire burning warmly and my own books on the shelves to welcome me, I am content.' There was all the joy of welcoming my friends, and a week later there is a passage attempting, in vain, to describe the ecstasy of the enjoyment of life: one of those moments of return upon oneself when, in all the rush of activity, there was a sense of suspended life in contemplating the trees in the Meadows, as the day before I had been arrested at Wytham by the sudden outburst of song from a bird in the fields on the right answered by another on the left. 'I felt the happiness of a life-time all in that one passing moment.' I knew those moments of apprehension well, in which one seemed to pierce through the envelope of the universe to the heart of things. But I had never said anything about it to anybody, for I thought no one would understand. I remember that Wordsworth had given expression to the experience in 'Tintern Abbey'; in time to come I would discover that this same experience was at the core of Ruskin and Proust, who gave the most extended account of it and erected it into a system of thought, as did also Joyce in *Portrait of the Artist* and Bridges in *The Testament of Beauty*. Perhaps it was the experience that was at the root of all poetry; as a system of thought it meant that life was redeemed really by its apprehension as beauty, the only eternal value: this was the way one saw things *sub specie aeternitatis*. Under the surface interests of my life, excitements about politics, ideas, people, under surface appearances coming and going, this was the real religion of my life. The paradox was that the contemplation of surface appearances was the way into it, but under a suspension of time, when time seemed, but only seemed, to stand still. As this spring Sunday morning at Trenarren in 1963, with the insistent onrush of the sea upon the shore below, and the daffodils gold under the sun in the garden.

At Oxford at the end of January 1923, 'I have written to mother this afternoon: hope she is all right.' Then off to a meeting in the parish room across the way at St Aldate's, to hear Bishop Temple of Manchester speak about C.O.P.E.C. I fear I have forgotten what the initials stood for – one of the innumerable well-intentioned organisations created in those sanguine years, full of good will, in this case by the dear Church of England trying to keep abreast with the modern world. I was very much taken with Billy Temple, as many people were in those years: 'a splendid and inspiring man' – there was a great deal of him. This came after 'a three hours' discussion of socialism and all that it implies, at Weatherhead's … The result is that I have been in a state of excitement throughout the evening.' There was our little group gathered together: Low, Speechley, Weatherhead, Tom Lawrenson, above all Wadleigh: I had 'gradually influenced Wadleigh, who is the greatest convert among undergraduates here that the cause can have.' Perhaps we might do something comparable to 'what Wesley and his friends accomplished in the eighteenth century?' I omitted to notice that they didn't accomplish much until they went out into the world.

Wadleigh and Tom Lawrenson went on to the Cathedral, to the ten o'clock service held on Saturday nights.

> I wished that I had gone, when I left them and came up to my room. It might have been a help. And yet, I don't know … I cannot make up my mind about religion, or about Christianity. It is a long time since I have prayed, and I do not feel the need of prayer. And it is only when such a man as Bishop Temple or Bishop Gore speaks that I feel touched at heart by the Gospel. I wish that I knew Greek in order that I might study the New Testament; but the teaching of Christ even in the English I must know better and more deeply. Tonight, for instance, I heard a profound interpretation put upon the words, 'I am the way', and others of Christ's answers to people who wanted help from him.

Ingenuous youth: 1923, age nineteen.

I thought that I was losing the love of poetry. 'In Wadleigh, too, the same thing has happened during the last few months. Something of greater value has come in its place: the desire to put things right in the world. I don't know when I first gained what has become a new religion to me. Reading Ruskin at the end of 1921 made me into a socialist.' (Prescribed for me for the Cornwall County scholarship – if only those sage gentlemen of the County Council had known what they were letting themselves in for!) In fact there always remained the inner, esoteric impulse from which poetry is born. '30 January: I am feeling strangely elated and restless tonight. I cannot settle down to work: there is a well of excitement in me which calls me forth to go down the dark lanes near Merton Street.' I wonder how many know the medieval derivation of the name Grove Street there, with its indication of the purpose it served for restless undergraduates of nineteen?

No such outlet was open to me: I had already experienced a rebuff in that line which ended the matter. 'A letter tonight from a girl at St Hugh's whom I have met but twice – once in a tailor's shop, where she came up and asked me for a lady's cap; and again at Mrs Wright's, where I was telling the story to two undergraduates, of whom she turned out to be one. She wants me to go to their play at St Hugh's.' I feared that this would be an evening-dress affair, and when I got there, to my horror, it was. There were all the girls in evening dress and their attendant young men in dinner jacket and black tie or, more often, as in those days, white tie and tails. There was I 'in my poor old Sunday coat of blue; Miss G. herself in a black muslin thing that was half dress and half not – at any rate, it did not appear to cover her shoulders. I never want such an experience again.' And, sure enough, next day I heard about it in the quad – the kind of thing young asses would attach importance to; I wondered whether the rumour had gone all round the College. For me, with my absoluteness of temperament, it was a liberation: no more experiments in that direction; the time that other young men wasted that way I had other things to do with. Still, I have often wondered what happened to the girl, what kind of life she made of it. Nor have I ever forgotten her name: she was a Grosvenor. I did not hear from her again.

As for work – I must have given the impression that I was not working; I fear my tutors sometimes got that impression too. In fact I was working for History Previous, an examination to come at the end of my second term; I cannot remember what it entailed – some indication where my heart was. However, 'something today has been accomplished: a two-hour paper on Mill's *Political Economy*. My speech at the Labour Club is still on the horizon.' There follows an account of a really busy day.

February 2nd: Got up at eight, had breakfast and worked rather desultorily until ten, when I had to go to a lecture on Rousseau's *Contrat Social* at Hertford. At eleven a lecture at Christ Church on St Simon [another socialist: what could the dons expect?], after which I wrote an essay. At one o'clock lunch – bread, cheese, marmalade and water for drink – frugal to a degree; after which I wrote another essay – took all the afternoon over it. Tutorial at five; another lecture by Barrington-Ward at six; dinner at seven thirty. After dinner, a meeting of the Labour Club, which Gallacher was to have addressed. Another Communist turned up in his place: an efficient and sincere man. My impression of the thing is one based really upon fear of revolution: I am subconsciously fearful of what might come about once capitalism has been destroyed, or even in the process of its destruction. It seems very hard to make all one's life-work the well-being and happiness of the people, and yet actually cause them all the more suffering by the very bringing about of revolution. And my mind isn't even made up as to its desirability: in my present mood I am an opportunist and all for expediency. Principles [I meant doctrines] which are going to cause suffering to others are a soulless thing, which I do not love.

So much for the local idiots who thought the boy was a budding revolutionary. In fact, what is noticeable about the statement, under its innocence, is its common sense. The sentiment expressed at nineteen seems to me valid at fifty-nine. There was a good deal of talk about revolution in those years dominated by the Russian Revolution, only six years before, and it still had an immense appeal to men's idealism at that time. But what was the point of causing so much indubitable suffering for hypothetical gains? Even if we allow that some material gains have been achieved, what is that to the nameless millions of dead who perished in the process, and at the price of a deformation of the human spirit?

'I came away from the meeting in a state of tense excitement,' and our little circle of friends went on to Low's rooms to carry on the discussion. In the end poetry broke in, and Lawrenson read (rather badly) a poem of Rupert Brooke's. Hardy much praised, especially *Jude* and *Tess of the D'Urbervilles*. Coming back from Peckwater, we reached Tom Quad as the bells were all chiming midnight. For a moment we allowed our imagination rein. I suggested that we should not walk straight back to Meadows, but should walk around the cloisters. In the straggling moonlight and amid the shadows we tried for a while to carry ourselves back into the past.

I still remember frightening myself by peering through the dark and ghostly slype (now blocked up) to the little graveyard at the end where the old canons were buried; one saw the patch flickering in the fitful moon. 'Outside now, the elms are swaying in the wind. The night is rather a rough one. I must take myself off to bed now: it is getting on for one o'clock.'

Poetry and politics – or was it politics and poetry? – such were the two sides of my tense, full life.

* * *

At this point a decision, very important for my future, was made for me by the dons at Christ Church. Trustful and confiding – then – I would have fallen in with anything they decided for my good. The point was that I had come up as a scholar in English Literature and was expecting to take the English School. The Christ Church dons did not think very highly of the English School – they thought of it as rather a soft option, mostly taken by women, as it was; they had not even a tutor in the subject. The History dons may have wanted to capture me for a potential First – certainly the History Scholars of my time were not a memorable lot and did nothing to signalise themselves. This was a decisive turning of the ways. If I had gone on to take the English School, I suppose my lot would have been cast with poetry and literature; I might even have become a critic. Taking the History School fortified my interest in politics, it even provided some equipment for a part in it; it opened other doors – for example, an All Souls Fellowship, and the accent and conversation of that unique institution redoubled my political interest.

I took to my Diary

in order to clear up my ideas a little with regard to it all.
Masterman wants me to change over from English to History
Schools. It is evident that he has given some thought to the
subject, and is very kindly considering what will be the best
thing for my future. And I think that on the whole he is right.
History is a much wider field for work, and it will all the
better equip me for life itself. I have sentimental hankerings
after the English School, not unmingled with a lazy hope that
literature after all is a soft option. It is so much easier and more
comfortable to be reading literary criticism and Shakespeare
plays than to be sweating blood over economic theory (especially where Mill is concerned!) and political science. However, it will be of more use in the world if I do the latter, and
that settles the question whether my future is to be in politics
or in literature. My mind is at bottom made up; but I am in
danger of falling between the two stools of politics and literature and of getting nothing accomplished in the end. Perhaps,
however, I shall seat myself on one stool, and make an attempt to
support my feet on the other.

It seems to me now not at all a bad summing-up, it forecast rather
what came about: politics the external activity, writing the real and
constant inner concern of my mind. Precisely because I was an
introvert, essentially concerned with the goings-on in my own
mind, far more full of the juices of life, I wanted to round myself
out on the other side with some extrovert activity. I had plenty of
private life, coping with myself and my many interests of mind;
I thought I ought to make a contribution as a social animal –
particularly after I was indoctrinated in Aristotle – in the realm of
politics. Precisely because I wasn't very good at action, organisation
or anything practical, I considered I ought to try and become a
better-balanced individual and make an external contribution.
Writing was my private devotion, my indulgence, my consolation,
my life; politics was public duty, ministering to the sense of self-
importance, ambition. A tell-tale circumstance is that in all the
volumes of the Diary, when I was actively engaged as a political

candidate, very much taken up with all sorts of Labour activities, there is little about it. I really grew to hate it; it never yielded anything to the spirit, save envy, hatred and all uncharitableness; it was nearly all a waste of time, energy and health, a waste of breath and of the precious hours. One gained something, no doubt – and of use for the writing of history – in the understanding of human beings collectively. But what a deception! One learned, what Hitler and Mussolini, Stalin and Khrushchev – and Mr Baldwin – understood all too well: that collectively they are quite irrational, at best children, and what foolish children!

The point is that the Diary has very little of all this, for my real life was elsewhere. Were the dons then, was I, wrong in turning to history? No point in discussing hypotheses now, or what might, alternatively, have happened. As dear Jimmy Neale, Grant Robertson and so many other historians would say, the die was cast.

Henceforth, for my three years as an undergraduate I found the immense amount of reading for the History School – much of it laboured and dull and ill-written – a fearful burden. (One of my exact contemporaries, the Brackenbury Scholar at Balliol, Cyril Connolly, found a way out in turning his back on it.) Here was I, who found constitutional history particularly heavy going, in time ploughing through the whole of Stubbs, the whole of Maitland and, believe it or not, the whole of the interminable Tout, who was then coming out in many volumes on administrative history. Great seals and privy seals and signets were quite the thing, not to mention pipe-rolls and liberate-rolls and close-rolls. If I had known it at the time, I should have enjoyed Raymond Asquith's 'Epitaph on a Tired Statesman', as it might have been his father:

> He hated affairs, he loathed the State:
> He wrapped his lunch in Livy;
> He threw the Great Seal into the grate
> And the Privy Seal into the privy.

It was all much weariness of the spirit. I used to think I should never get my head above water; after all, I had not been brought up to this sort of thing at school, unlike the Public School boys. In the end, just in time for Schools, I did get my head above water and was able to see the lay-out of things. I even felt my intellectual muscles flexed by all the effort – the confidence that I could cope with it. But this was not until the end of the course. It had been an awful grind, a good deal going against the grain. I don't think my tutors thought I was going to make it, with so much else (and far more interesting) going on. They sometimes seemed rather disappointed; little did they know that underneath the excitements of the Labour Club, becoming an officer and helping to run it, the Essay Club at Christ Church, literary clubs in the university, writing for undergraduate papers literary and political, writing poetry and keeping the Diary, I was in fact ploughing through the heavy mass of reading for Schools.

Here are my juvenile feelings about Mill.

> I have made several attempts to read Mill – the chapter on 'Taxes on Commodities', which is inconceivably dull. Mill is a wilderness to me. The vast mass of his work is laboured, intricate and barren; but occasionally one comes across a fertile place blossoming in the wilderness. In some passages there is real eloquence, and a foresight that astonishes. On the whole I prefer him to Nicholson: he is more imaginative and more human, even if he is not so lucid.

Today I should merely add of Nicholson, lucid – and unreadable.

Henceforth, too, there was a conflict between the claims of history and literature, added to my other tensions. How on earth to find time for both? I was afraid that poetry would get squeezed out – as in a year or two it was with the more promising and mature Quennell; indeed, it was hard to find time for it, even in the vacations when there was so much history-reading to catch up. One day in May, I find:

> No work have I done for days. On Thursday, true, I wrote and read an essay to Feiling on the Danish Invasions and kindred interesting questions. But not a word have I read of Vinogradoff, Maitland and other worthies on this early period. Instead I have written a review of *Aquarium* for *The New Oxford*: not a bad piece of work, though it tails off to a weak conclusion. I must

revise it and copy it out for Graham Pollard. Then I must write a note on the second number of *The Broom*, a review copy of which Acton gave me a few days ago. On Thursday night I read *Deirdre of the Sorrows*; last night and this morning, *Heartbreak House*. Shaw's Preface is a tremendous thing: the play, too, despite its diffuseness and atmosphere of unreality. Perhaps it is just this that is its strength: it makes the whole action take place in a mad-house. And that is, I suppose, what England and Europe at large were in the pre-war days.

As if they have ceased to be since! There follow some very juvenile comments on 'the old diplomacy', which was a prime target of the Left Intellectuals of those days – as if the diplomacy of the inter-war period were any improvement on that of pre-1914! I was being initiated into this way of thinking by Ralph Fox of Magdalen, who had paid me a visit, and was on his way to Communism. 'A talk that I had yesterday with Ralph Fox, when he told me a little more than I had known about the assassination of Jaurès, and the sinister character of Isvolsky, has sickened me more than ever of the old Europe. Upon the new Russia now I base my hopes, whatever happens to me in the future, whether I declare myself a Communist or not.'

I transcribe these sentiments not for any intrinsic value they have, but simply as so much evidence of the atmosphere of the time, the hopes there were of a new and better world after the war of 1914–18, the hopes that were placed on the Russian Revolution, and the cruel deception they underwent – far more sickening and barbarous (naturally, in the circumstances of mass-civilisation) than the deception of Wordsworth, Coleridge and Southey in their hopes of the French Revolution in their day.

Ralph Fox gave his life for Communism, or rather had it thrown away for him, as we shall subsequently see, in the Spanish Civil War. (There, as I write – now in Oxford – are the bells of his college ringing out a full peal across the grey roofs of the city and the pale-green foliage of the trees this hard, reluctant spring: testimony to more lasting values, more refreshing to the spirit.)

Only a few days before I had met him for the first time.

Ralph Fox and a whole crowd to hear him dispute with Wadleigh assembled in my rooms last night. Afterwards I had a talk with Fox alone which lasted till after midnight. I like him very much: Wadleigh does not give him credit for what he is, but seems to expect him to be philosophical. That, thank heaven, he is not. He is a pure artist by nature, and like me goes through the world observing and noting things, rather than with a specially thought-out philosophical theory to which all life's experiences are fitted. I shall like Ralph Fox, and hope to see much of him this term. His play *Captain Youth*, written mostly at the age of sixteen, I must get and read.

Actually, Wadleigh was right. Ralph Fox *was* by nature a pure artist, a sensitive and rather feminine creature, who – if it had not been for the accursed time – should have been a writer and had nothing to do with politics. I can see him now – that slight figure, sufficiently tall, the well-modelled head, slenderly poised, the dark hair brushed back, close-cropped as befitted a faithful Communist *à la Staline* (Stalin did for him all right), lambent, expressive eyes, mobile Adam's apple, refinement and sensitiveness in every line. Reading literature as he did – he was a natural linguist – Ralph had no intellectual position of his own, and so gave himself to Marxism. He accepted it: he did not work it out for himself. (Precisely the same thing happened to Christopher Hill later.) Ralph once admitted to me how much he regretted that he had not read History at Oxford – it would certainly have given him a more informed, a securer and more critical basis for understanding politics.

In default of this, he gave himself: he became a dedicated man, living the truncated, puritanical life of a full party-member, as described in Whittaker Chambers's autobiography. Ralph made a fearful sacrifice of himself, for it meant the deformation of a personality, the suppression of so much of his true self, the artistic and literary, the sensitive and observant. As the horrors of the 1930s closed down on us, our relations became more and more exacerbated. Every time he came to see me in Oxford I would inveigh against the criminality of Communist policy in Germany in the early 'thirties, actually co-operating with the Nazis in order to destroy Social Democracy. There were the Communists in 1931 co-operating with the Nazis in the tram-strike in Berlin against a Social Democrat government. 'Can't you see,' I would shout at him, 'that it isn't the Communists who will come out on top of this, but the Nazis?' Time after time he would trot out the old Stalinist line: the Social Democrats were the enemy. I despaired of human intelligence – as I have learned to do more fully since: the experience of the 'thirties was illumination enough for one lifetime.

In the end Ralph did see, or rather, had seen with one side of him all along: an intellectually honest man, he could not close his eyes to all the facts, put up with the lying beyond a certain point, the regular inversion of truth turned into a system by the Communists (as by the Nazis), the 'double-talk' and 'double-think' so precisely described by Orwell. What the world does not know – but I have the evidences, the documents – is that, before the end, Ralph Fox was through with Communism. On his very last visit to me he wanted to give up and for me to get him a job at Oxford, to retreat from it all. I made enquiries both at my own college and at his, but of course there wasn't the ghost of a hope. He was ordered to Spain by the Party, which wanted martyrs for the cause. The English contingent on the Cordoba front was left isolated and unsupported, in a forward position, by the valiant Spanish workers, and there they were machine-gunned and cut up by the Nazi planes. That was where and how Ralph Fox died: so much for co-operation between the Communists and the Nazis! But Communism had its martyr all right – its martyrs were to be numbered by the million. In those years Ralph Fox's was rather a famous name, perhaps forgotten now: as an historian I merely state the facts of his case, as of so many nameless others.

But this has led me far ahead of the sanguine 'twenties, and our youthful, hopeful years.

III

Spring and Summer, 1923

THE Diary brings back scenes I had totally forgotten, along with those I had not. On an evening in February 1923, in the middle of some woman's address at the Labour Club,

> Ramsay MacDonald and his son came in. Immediately, great excitement, and a prolonged round of clapping. Enthusiasm was intense, and before the meeting closed Ramsay Mac. had to get up and say a few words. Then we sang 'For he's a jolly good fellow', and 'The Red Flag'. The latter I had never heard before: nor had I realised what a noble thing it was. The whole evening was inspiring. I must write home and tell them all about it.

My family, though working people, had not been Labour folk, until I came along with my nonsense: they didn't understand a thing about politics and had never taken any interest in it – a healthier state of affairs. At election times my father had voted Liberal, like all the other china-clay workers; and on top of the kitchen-clock at Tregonissey stood a little plaster-bust of Mr Gladstone. (I wonder what has become of it now? Broken? discarded? thrown away by me? – a symptomatic fate.) My mother, because she went to church, was made a member of the Primrose League. A fat lot she knew about it, one way or the other. And as the result of my youthful enthusiasms, my poor father became a great admirer of George Lansbury and Gandhi – whom he pronounced to rhyme with 'eye': not much of an improvement on Mr Gladstone. These were his heroes.

I recall from later years at All Souls Sir Edmund Craster's telling me of an old aunt, who used to say to him, 'I really believe, my dear, that Mr Gladstone is the Evil One.' Class for class, so much for ordinary people's political understanding.

People can hardly appreciate now – after the debacle that over-
came his reputation with the treachery of 1931 – the extent of the
hero-worship that MacDonald received from his followers. There
was something romantic about his personality; he had a very handsome appearance, with the dark, greying mass of wavy hair, the
flashing eyes, the Celtic temperament that was capable of arousing
his audiences to enthusiasm (a word that was frequent on his lips,
with his curious, contracted pronunciation of it). He had the addi-
tional appeal to our hearts of having only just emerged from the
persecution and misrepresentation of the war-period as a traitor.
(He may have been wrong, or at least confused, in his attitude to the
war, but he certainly was not a traitor.) He had only three months
before, 21 November 1922, been elected leader of the Labour
Party, against the uninspiring, pedestrian Trade Unionist, Clynes:
here was complete rehabilitation, a national leader, in line to become
the head of the first Labour government we hardly dared hope would
come about so soon.

MacDonald's son, Malcolm, was up at Queen's – another thing
that helped to bring the leader near to us; for everybody liked
Malcolm, a charming, unassuming, nice fellow, who gave himself
no airs for all his considerable intelligence and even greater prestige.
At this time he had rooms in Drawda Hall, along the pavement
from All Souls, where one could hail him, for he was frequently
visible, being very sociable and always popular; but we juniors regarded him with proper respect. His tutor was Godfrey Elton, who
followed MacDonald into disgrace in 1931, and was promptly made
a peer. Whereupon Namier made one of his inimitable *mots*: 'In
the eighteenth century peers made their tutors under-secretaries;
in the twentieth under-secretaries make their tutors peers.'

Towards the end of June there came a visit to the Oxford Union
which I have not forgotten: Lloyd George himself, only a year after
his fall from complete ascendancy in Britain, still the most famous
figure in Europe and throughout the English-speaking world. He
had come to defend the Treaty of Versailles against a Scottish
'Wee-free' Liberal, the upright Mr Pringle. I remember it all: the
famous leonine head of hair, the diminutive figure, those wickedly
glinting gold pince-nez with which he made play; above all, the

beautiful, caressing Welsh voice, the purity of the vowel-sounds, the way he purred words like 'peace' into 'pee-ece', the seductive intonation enough to 'charm a bird off a tree'.[1] In those days before radio and television, such things meant so much more: speaking and writing were all in all. I remember the way he taunted the highly ethical Pringle, who had not been able to see one 'scintilla' of justice in the Treaty of Versailles. Lloyd George took up the unfortunate word and used it again and again to put the screw on the Pringle, who writhed and turned white with passion under the torture. It was not an edifying spectacle, and it boded no good for Liberal unity, just being talked about after the split caused by the war-time Coalition.

What I had forgotten was the violence of my reaction to the scene. I had taken the infection against the Treaty propagated by Keynes and spread by the Left Intellectuals; I was in no condition to recover until a better knowledge of the historical background and acquaintance with Germany opened my eyes to where the responsibility really lay. So far from being prejudiced in favour of Lloyd George, I thought he was 'morally in the wrong' and his successful defence all the more deplorable.

I have never been so disgusted by such a spectacle. The man laid himself out by all the means he has at his disposal to the vote-catching process so comparable to the 1918 Election. He deliberately skidded over every point: the most slippery charlatan in politics. And this the man whom hitherto I have admired for the magic of his personality, the electrical vibrance with which he inspires whole masses of people. Ugh! What ugly things crowds are; how all the worst things come out in mob-psychology: it is to this that Lloyd George appeals. The patent obvious ways by which the Wizard drew his audience, and worked them up to his solemn peroration about the memory of the 900,000 glorious English dead!

Such was my reaction to this oratorical triumph; I have always thought oratory rather a bastard art (with Churchill, for utter sincerity, an exception): it is plain that Lloyd George would have

[1] Sir Winston Churchill's phrase.

done better, with one member of that audience, to be simple and sincere. For there follows a passage of outraged contempt at the mob that had been so lured on: 'a mob all the same, though of Oxford undergraduates, hailing from middle- and upper-class homes, and from the Public Schools ... no more intelligent than a crowd of clay-workers in Cornwall or of coal-miners in Cardiff.'

I never set eyes on Lloyd George again until that day in the late 'thirties, not long before the outbreak of the second war, when I spent an afternoon and evening in his company at Criccieth and watched those spectacles flash wickedly again, this time at the inanity of Neville Chamberlain. 'I have had many ministers, some of them competent, some of them incompetent; but the only minister who totally and completely failed at his job – that man was Neville Chamberlain.'

In my first year I used to go fairly frequently to these gladiatorial shows at the Union, and be impressed by the unbearable brilliance of the speaking. In May Hilaire Belloc came down. 'Bandaranaike and Nicholson, both House men, were good, but were quite outshone by A. M. Clark and a man called Henson from Wadham. Even Belloc didn't come up to the standard of these two. A rather ponderous man – I didn't expect him to be Chestertonian in that fashion. Quite obviously he hadn't prepared his speech, but nevertheless took the House by storm. Tremendous receptions for everybody.' How guilelessly enthusiastic we were! I recorded some of the *mots* friendly Christopher Hollis had collected, with which to encrust his Presidential speech: on the U.S. Senate's attitude towards the League of Nations, 'like an inverted Micawber, waiting for something to turn down', and the cynical Frenchman contemplating the Statue of Liberty: 'We also erect monuments to our heroic dead.'

In my second year I went less to the Union. Edward Marjoribanks – Hailsham's half-brother – made a kind attempt to recruit me to speak there; but the truth was that I was much too shy and nervous to speak in so worldly an assembly. And, also, I thought the atmosphere was not for me: I preferred the serious-minded, not to say simple-minded, sincerity of the Labour Club, to which I would devote all the energy I had to spare for politics.

There were interludes from serious-mindedness. Here is one such.

Mrs Beazley took me along to the Stables to see her Shetland pony: a sweet little creature, shaggy and untamed, harnessed to a diminutive cart, with furs, rugs, biscuit tins and provisions all packed in. Mrs B., her daughter with two school-chums, in red gipsy head-dress were going off on a Bohemian trip. Mrs B. is driving, the girls walking, and they intend to put up at small country inns over the week-end.

But how to get the erratic little Shetland out on to the roads? This is where my experience with Neddy at home came in.

I volunteered to manœuvre the pony and equipage safely down the High and out of Oxford. The queerest sight: the tiny pony going its own way, sometimes running, sometimes stopping, mostly tripping along in an irregular and inconsequent manner, until I seized hold of his bridle and forced him to run all down the High – with Mr and Mrs Chaundy capering on behind, and Mrs B. vociferating and gesticulating in the trap. All the population were amused: I forgot all about dignity, and thoroughly enjoyed the thing.

It must have been the oddest spectacle since Lady Ottoline Morrell used to drive exotically in from Garsington, hair dyed red-gold, Habsburg prognathous jaw – as in the John portrait – and advance up the High in her phaeton, no doubt thinking herself Juno.

There was plenty of social intercourse, friends one ran into at every turn. One night in March I heard the Christ Church bells for the first time. Hung in the tower over the Hall staircase, they could not be heard to advantage in Meadow Buildings, so I walked out into the town to hear them:

up the Turl and into the Broad, down Holywell and into the High; instead of coming in by Tom Gate again, I walked down St Aldate's into the wretchedest poor quarter that there is in Oxford. From Christ Church to Folly Bridge it is squalid enough; but turn into the courts and alleys that run out from the street and the place is worse than one would think possible:

dismal shanties with roofs all askew and walls cracking, no drainage, no gardens, all the washing hung out on lines across the alleys. I met Chavasse on my way back; he told me that recently three girls about eighteen had been taken to hospital to be treated for venereal disease; that a woman from one alley had been killed by a bus and had left a family of five illegitimate children, the father of whom he was trying to discover. Another wretched woman across the road was taking lads of sixteen down the towpath, teaching them sex at a shilling a time. And so on. The poor fellow looked quite disheartened as he told me of the horrors which that filthy slum bred.

Chavasse was a good fellow and a hard-working parson; but actually he rather liked this kind of talk in those days, not long out of the war and by way of showing he was modern-minded, I suppose.

For myself I find I didn't relish all the talk about sex. No such talk was to be heard at home: not a word on the subject passed my parents' sealed lips, at any rate in front of us children. Here was Oxford full of such talk. I went to see a dreary proletarian play, *Hindle Wakes*, at Ruskin College, a working men's college supported by the trade unions, and –

> Oh, the ugliness of such lives! Even the honest and well-meaning mill-owner. What unreality, amongst them all what narrowness of vision! To think that just because a fellow has gone off with a girl for a week-end at Blackpool, he is bound to marry her ... I tire of the continual round of sexual affairs: everybody talks of sex, everybody thinks of sex, the cursed thing enters into every moment of our lives. It would be well if only I could rush away from the thing and become a priest like Manning and the others whom I admire.

The puritanically-minded adolescent omitted to notice that Cardinal Manning had at least had the experience of marriage *before* he dedicated himself to celibacy.

Rawlinson as Tutor, and therefore our mentor in morals, provided a subject of amusement by his declaration in favour of 'relative celibacy' as his ideal. We wondered what 'relative' meant, and what

Mrs Rawlinson thought of it. A little later, when the twittering Mrs Lindsay, wife of the Master of Balliol, came out with a book on Birth Control with a Foreword by the Master – or was it a Postscript? – it was obvious from his contribution (a) that he hadn't read the book and (b) that he was not in agreement with his wife on the subject.

Everywhere one met people of interest: one day at the Rawlinsons'

a fellow named Parkes, who invited me to dine at Ripon Hall. A nice little place: altogether life there seems rather like that of an old-world family. We dined in a long room at an oak table, candles burning in silver candlesticks. About a dozen and a half were there, two being guests. I sat at the right hand of the Principal, who turned out no less than the celebrated Major, against whom the attack was launched for heresy. Major appeared to be a kindly old man, very deaf, but not wanting in wit and repartee, of a rather noble countenance, fair hair, shaggy brows.

I was much impressed by Parkes, a good deal my senior, who went on to become an authority on Judaism and its history, author of many books.

At the same tea-party I met a lawyer named Strauss.

He and I had a formidable battle over Socialism, in which I got beaten to the teeth. At the end I could hardly say a word, his legal and precise arguments being not so much unanswerable as intangible. He seemed oblivious of anything but the lawyer's point of view: like Balfour's description of Sir John Simon, 'great on little points, small on great ones'. However, despite my poor showing, he came to call on me after I had left the Rawlinsons': was very kind and left me his card, inviting me to call on him whenever I was in London, offering to take me out to dinner when we could continue the argument.

I thought this great luck; but, of course, I couldn't afford to go up to London. And now I wonder which of the Strausses he was, who was so kind? Could it have been Harry Strauss? It could hardly have been George Strauss, who himself saw the light and became a Labour Minister.

Better than all the talk about sex were the country walks that I loved. At the end of Hilary Term I stayed up to take History Previous: I looked forward to being alone

> after the incessant company of term-time. After our last paper in the Schools I was so happy that everything seemed new and desirable. In the afternoon I went for a walk with Benson to Shotover, a glorious place that reminded me of home and Carn Grey: a high ridge overlooking the Thames valley to the Berkshire downs, for the most part still open common, with clumps of trees and dingles with gorse running down the slopes. Up there the breeze is like the breeze at Carn Grey. I was so elated with everything that I just ran down the paths and over the springy turf. We visited the church at Horspath, and went to an inn for tea – a country tea of sandwiches, bread and butter, home-made jam. Walking back to Oxford in the evening was splendid. A day that I shall remember.

Nor have I quite forgotten it still, that day of release, when nothing at all happened: I have remembered its inner savour, when so much that was just external events has gone.

One day I walked to Iffley with Weatherhead and a Japanese whose name was, I think, Ohta, whom I found quite inscrutable. 'All the time I walked with him, I wondered what was going on inside his mind, what he thought of us and of the world. There was no solution to the problem: he remained an enigma, speaking little and, when he did speak, showing a cast of mind so different as to be incomprehensible.'

Next term, Ohta brought along a young Japanese professor of English literature, with whom I immediately clicked: Kochi Doi. He had already translated some pieces of Japanese literature into English, and produced an Introduction to the study of English literature for Japanese students. The summer before he had spent at Harvard, and was as well read in American as in English literature. Just appointed Assistant Professor in the Imperial University of Sendai, he had been sent to England as a preparation for taking up

3

the appointment and also to get an Englishman for the professor-ship. He gave me the impression that I could get the job if I wished. 'What a glorious chance! A salary of £1,000 a year, and the oppor-tunity of becoming a Lafcadio Hearn, or a Robert Nichols.'

For a couple of days I saw myself contingently in the part: the contingency being a second class in the Schools and the prospect of teaching in a secondary school. But I was determined on better things. I told Kochi Doi all I could about Q: characteristically for a professor, he knew only his work as a literary critic. I told him about Q's creative work, his novels and short stories, work with the juices of life in it, which, for all that it is underestimated now, is of more lasting value than most criticism. Next day 'Ohta and Doi came at about four, and the three of us had tea in the J.C.R. A rather un-orthodox thing, I felt the others thinking, but just the sort of thing for that Bolshevist to be taking Japanese into the holy of holies.' I became more and more interested by Doi and his conversation about literature. He gave me a copy of the Shelley Memorial volume by members of the English Club at Tokyo University, and expounded to me the theme of his essay: that love of humanity and the idea of beauty in Shelley were closely connected, and when the first de-clined in him the second faded too. 'What this notion of his is worth I can't tell at present: perhaps not much, though his knowledge of Shelley is as extraordinary as his knowledge of English literature in general.'

Kochi Doi promised to send me a copy of his latest book, a trans-lation of three diaries of court ladies of early Japan – I rather think one of them being the lady Murasaki, author of the classic *Tale of Genji*. This book I still have, a memento of my brief infatuation for Japan – those two dream-days I spent as if in Japan. I excused myself with 'still everybody experiences something akin to it. Doi told me that reading *Aylwin* had made him long to visit Wales and Cornwall. I am served the same trick when I read about Provence or Touraine or Brittany. Lines came into my head like –

> O you with face inscrutable
> And slantèd, mocking eyes ... '

Instead of going on with them, I preferred to indulge my dream.

In fact Kochi Doi and I kept a sketchy contact for a few years. I reproached myself that I had nothing with which to requite his kindness but conversation and promises. However, when Tokyo was struck by the earthquake of 1931 and the university lost its library, I did send the best book I possessed: a second edition of *Gulliver's Travels*. And I wonder what has happened to my kind Japanese friend, with whom I enjoyed such sympathy of mind for those few hours, in the vicissitudes of our time? As I wonder, too, what became of my Indian friends of those early days – Swamanathan, of whom I saw a good deal and have enquired of from Radhakrishnan at All Souls in later years, and Kuppuswamy.

There were the new pleasures, for me, of club-life. Rather to my surprise I was elected to the Pandemonium Club, a kind of junior Essay Club in college, and shortly I was having to read a paper on my beloved Hardy, who had been such an influence in my last year at school. I was already fairly well read in him, but was now reading *Tess of the D'Urbervilles* and *A Pair of Blue Eyes*, with its background of North Cornwall. There remained the *Collected Poems*, a dreadful expense to buy. 'I had long made up my mind to expend this 8s. 6d., though I can little afford it: a proud moment when I came out of the shop with this book my own.'

One February morning I was asked to breakfast by Graham Pollard and Richard Pares at the Hypocrites Club. This place, the haunt of aesthetes and sub-aesthetes, had rather an unsavoury reputation to my innocent mind. I went with some trepidation to the tumble-down house in St Aldate's, up a tortuous staircase and along twisting passages to a room still filled with the atmosphere of beer, stale smoke and the nameless goings-on of the night before: it quite came up to my expectations of wickedness. Not for me membership of such an establishment. However, the meal provided the interest of a tremendous argument between Pollard and an American called Edwards, 'about the economic basis of the working classes' discontent', while Pares and I talked about poetry and *The New Oxford*, 'of which he wished me to join the editorial board next term.'

The Diary shows that I went on writing poetry, though how I found time for it heaven knows. I stuck mostly to the discipline of writing sonnets, or at least in regular metre. Eliot's influence had

not yet made itself felt; and my verse fell naturally into the idiom of
the Georgian poets, whom, along with the Irish, I much admired:
I think chiefly, Yeats, Bridges, de la Mare. As such, it was no better,
and no worse, than other undergraduate poetry of the time. Here is
the beginning of a sonnet, inscribed to H.J.W., which at least recalls
the scene from my window in Meadows:

> All is at peace now in the moon-plashed glade:
>   Nothing moves, save a little rippling wind
> That stirs the elm-branches faintly in the shade;
>   And on the town, where all day long have dinned
> The noise of traffic, workshop-sounds and cries,
>   The calm of night has fallen. Fair as a dream,
> Like gems among the trees and in the skies,
>   The stars shine; and o'er all the moon's supreme.

There are occasional poems in free verse, like one on Armistice Day,
1922, which used to be solemnly observed every year. These poems
read rather like bad Whitman; but, then, a great deal of Whitman
reads like bad Whitman. I did not respond to Acton's kind of poetry,
which I suppose he derived from the Sitwells:

> The lantern fruit glow succulent and gay,
> Blue-veined grapes in massing pendulous,
> Small raisins, oranges acidulous
> Contracting eyelids till the features wince;
> Towering domes of pineapple and quince
> And apples like a film of virgin's breath,
> Strange berries (you would think they bleed to death),
> Piled pappy plums opaquely amethyst,
> Pink furry peaches like a morning mist ...

All this sounded succulent and juicy recited in Harold's declamatory
Italian accent; but I cannot now see that his verse was any better
than mine, though he was all the rage and I never had fashion (or
luck) with me. Pares described Harold's poem as merely philo-
gastric zeal, and considered the poet not very clever. I thought him
outrageously brilliant, but was apt to be scandalised. One night,
after seeing a big ramshackle American friend – who rather alarmed

me by talking two and a half hours about sex and showing no disposition to go – off the premises, I called in on Harold on the way back. 'The poet was going to bed: he appeared at his bedroom door in a kimono of dark-grey silk. It seemed he had been spraying his face with Icilma or some such stuff. The fragrance that issued from the room was overpowering.'

I think I can see better now, so many years after, something of the function that the Diary performed for me. All these people that I was now meeting, young as they were, were years ahead of me in experience, sophistication, maturity, from their Public Schools, their social background in middle or upper class, life in London, about Britain, on the Continent or in America. I must have been a great innocent to them – as indeed I was. They also had their backers, their literary acquaintance in London, who set the standards, could provide them with models, advice, openings. Acton had the Sitwells – but indeed he knew everybody; Cyril Connolly had Desmond McCarthy, as he tells us; Quennell and Waugh had their fanciers, their literary acquaintance in London; David Cecil, the formidable Mrs Woolf and Bloomsbury. I had no one, and in consequence had to learn everything for myself the long way. So the Diary, with its constant versifying, its habit of reporting, of criticising books I read, plays I saw, of arguing with myself, became a means of self-education, of learning to write, as well as a record of the process. Not for nothing have I given the overriding title to the various parts of this book, written and to be written, *The Education of a Cornishman*.

Before I went home for the vacation I had my first talk with my new tutor for next term, Feiling. Here are the first impressions of the youth of nineteen.

Feiling has an enormous room over the J.C.R., looking out over St Aldate's, so large that it seemed bare and empty, despite the bookcases, leather chairs and massive furniture. He himself is a kindly, nervous man; below middle age, but already very bald. His eyes are grey and pleasant, but when I was with him he wore heavy horn spectacles of the light yellow colour which always make me feel sick. His face is intellectual rather than strong, tapering down from a wide skull to lean jaws and sharp chin. It appears that he is writing a book, and all next week dictating to a typist. He has a frequent stutter – one would think that on account of it he would find it easier to write his books rather than dictate them. He was very kind to me, so that I felt well disposed to him.

Such was the well-known historian who left more of a mark in my life, in a rather unexpected way, than perhaps with any other of his pupils.

*   *   *

When the grand young men of the House scattered to their stately homes, their professional parents' residences in London, to their castles in Scotland, their villas in Italy, or wherever they went on the Continent for the Easter vacation, I went home to my old friends and familiar haunts. My first visit was to the school, when nobody was about on Easter Monday, to see if I could recapture the sense of ecstasy I had often felt in roaming alone around the playing fields. I was afraid that in going to Oxford I might lose something of the inspiration I derived from loved places. They seemed to shrink in size; so 'at one spot, I knelt down to diminish my height and so to recover my old vision of the field when I was much shorter than now.' All was well – but what a curious boy, always backward-looking, nostalgically loyal to everything that was past! Perhaps the historian in embryo.

I went on with my general reading – Q's *Old Fires and Profitable Ghosts*, Hazlitt, Carlyle, Matthew Arnold, all so much more congenial than Vinogradoff, Tout and Oman, of whom Belloc wrote:

> O Professor Oman,
> Does it never strike you –
> The more we see of you
> The less we like you?

(Dear Oman, whom I came to know well at All Souls later, the exact converse was true; but reading him was rather a different matter.) I walked to Porthpean with my friend Bacon and a book, and 'sat on the turf at the top of the cliff overlooking the beach', reading Hazlitt. My schoolmaster friend was now studying philosophy for a degree, and scholastic philosophy moreover.

The completeness of this system gives me a feeling of revulsion; I once went so far as to say, on our way back from Trenarren, that I suspected all such logical systems. Then, after fearing acutely the consequences of thus suspecting human reason and condemning its futility, I was glad to find support in Carlyle. 'The healthy Understanding, we should say, is not the logical, argumentative, but the Intuitive; for the end of Understanding is not to prove and find reasons, but to know and believe.'

That passage ended with a comic picture of the Schoolmen gyrating round and round like spinning dervishes, making no real progress but ending where they began. Of course, at that age I could hardly be expected to see through Carlyle's self-approbation or that his intellectual position was (like most people's) but a generalisation of his own temperamental preferences.

Arnold's *Study of Celtic Literature* provided more lasting food for thought. I learned of Arnold's descent from pure Cornish stock on his mother's side – Penroses and Trevenens: he turned after them in physical type. Here was a clue to his difference, his marked un-Englishness noticed at the time, the contrast with rugged Dr Arnold, the son so much more congenial to me. I raced through his work for traces of Celtic interest, and they were not difficult to find: in 'Tristram and Iseult', 'St Brandan', 'Stanzas at Carnac', 'The Forsaken Merman', a legend from all round the Celtic coasts. What was no less striking was Arnold's complete unconsciousness of this, so like the Victorians, and, unlike Hardy and Tennyson, he had never been in Cornwall. Yet his grandmother Trevenen, on leaving Cornwall to get married, got out of the carriage to kiss the soil she was leaving for good. In Brittany the family noticed the resemblance of Uncle Matt to the racial type, himself unaware. How curious, and yet there were his expressed sympathies, along with his distaste for English characteristics, English coarseness, English Philistinism. I was much taken with Arnold's phrase on the 'adverse destiny' of the Celts, which seemed to sum up their history.

There all round me were these haunts that could not be more Celtic: up Trethurgy hill blazing with gorse for my walks to Carn Grey, outlined like a Druid's altar against the skyline. The quarry at its foot, a ribbed granite amphitheatre, reminded me of a *plan-an-guary*, the ancient playing-places of the miracle-plays, like those left at Perranzabuloe and St Just-in-Penwith. What a place it would make, suitably trimmed, for outdoor meetings, political and religious, for services or, better still, for performances of plays. (Like the natural bowls, one may add later, in the vicinity of Los Angeles, Hollywood Bowl, or the Arroyo Seco in Pasadena.) My mind was liable to brim with such thoughts, projects unexecuted and unexecutable, schemes, plans, themes, ideas for books, poems, plays which would never be written.

My friend Bacon warned me 'against fooling myself too much with ideas and plans which are never carried out. I quite see the danger inherent in such an attitude.' I had a suspicion that it was all a question of insufficient energy! It never occurred to me that it was all too much energy seeking natural outlet. 'There is nothing for it, if I am to be of use in the world, either as writer or speaker, poet or politician, but absolute and ruthless continence. That I can attain to in Oxford; it remains for me to make sure of myself at home as well.' It would be cheap to say, what a contrast, I fancy, to so many of my companions at Oxford; but, all the same, it strikes me now as extraordinary. For here was, in fact, a youth with a passionate temperament – so far from wanting in vigour, someone who didn't know what to do with it all; determined, so far as possible, to do nothing but drive it into other channels. Here was an exceptionally sensuous, not to say sexy, temperament confronted by an abnormally developed will. The spectacle, I now understand, must have been provoking to those who were attracted and understood, better than I did, what was what. But for me the tension was constant; it generated immense drive, but it took it out of me physically and in other ways.

Here was a night in April, for example, 'sitting at my table with Keynes's *Economic Consequences of the Peace* between me and the lamp' – when other young men were up to quite other things.

I can hear Jean and Oscar laughing and talking next door.
For a moment I felt jealous. Jean and Oscar; or is it Dorothy
and Ian? ... I have tried to recognise the voices, and still cannot
be sure. I can hear the clear, laughing, inviting tones of the
girl, and the answering laugh of the boy. What a world: everybody at the same game: dogs, birds, mankind. Moreover, it is
spring. Everybody except me; and whatever temptations I
undergo, I must say No. Self-consciousness, still more –
knowledge, keeps me back from a thing which at this age I
ought to experience. But making love doesn't come naturally
to me: I should despise myself for letting such a patent and
obvious trap catch me.

The trap that Nature lays for ardent, but ambitious, boys was
obvious enough with the girl next door. She was a nice, healthy
girl, herself ambitious and (moderately) intelligent. We used to go
for walks together; we wrote each other, I lent her books, encouraged
her education – the usual steps to the altar. On one of these walks
Jean made the mistake of expressing the characteristic female self-
confidence that a woman could always get her man, if she made up
her mind to. I recognised this for what it was – perhaps true enough
in general; but I was shocked, not so much at the sentiment as at the
self-confidence it revealed. I concealed the shock, but combated the
sentiment. Poor girl, she hadn't a chance really. There was always
the instinct to warn one: No. On another occasion when she came
up against a similar resistance, I overheard her – in the horrid
proximity of the Council houses where we dwelt – say from the
next window, 'I could smack his face'. There was the bitch-element:
she was hot-tempered. When my father said, on the only occasion
when he dared to mention such a subject, 'I don't want that girl
brought into this house', though I said nothing whatever, I registered,
'Little you need worry. I've a mind of my own.'
The girl's elemental instinct was right enough: she made a
marriage that began unhappily, but produced a child who has
become a promising writer in her own right. It merely happens that
I don't have much sympathy with very elemental instincts.
Meanwhile my friend Bacon, brought up in a seminary for the

priesthood, had the inveterate heterosexuality of the Irish and was beseiged by the desire to probe the mystery of women. As if there were any, beyond what men created about them! They were no mystery to me: I felt that I knew as much about them as they know about themselves. My school-friend Tippett was at home for Easter from the Imperial College of Science, and I enjoyed walks with him much more on which we did *not* discuss 'Sex, Marie Stopes and the whole sickening paraphernalia' as with the Irishman. Len and I 'talked of things more truly intimate, nearer our hearts, and of much greater importance' – our plans for the future. He was rather dissatisfied with the Imperial College, where the professors appeared fossilised – if only we could get him to Oxford! Straightway my mind careered off on plans: we were to write a book together of Cornish portraits, he to do the scientists, I the literary and historical figures. There I was chasing will-o'-the-wisps of my imagination again: another of the innumerable ideas for books which I have never got round to.

When we got back to the house Len stayed to supper – oddly enough it was we, much less well off, who seemed to have done all the entertaining of my friends.

> Father was in great form, and told us all about the curious 'shivarees', or wedding junketings that used to take place in Tregonissey. When mother and father came back from their wedding, the windows of the house were white-washed [that had its suggestive significance]. Uncle Harry and Polly had their door nailed up when they returned from theirs. It was quite usual to block up the chimney [for it to be unblocked, of course: anthropologists, please note].

A special show was put on for Eliza and Enas Kellow, for the bride was twenty years older than the poor bridegroom. A barrel of beer was broached in May's cow-house; two fellows impersonated Eliza and Enie, marching up and down the village to the accompaniment of mouth-organs, comb-and-tissue paper, beating drum, tin-pan, the rattle of bones. Singing went on all through the night, till three or four next morning. This was the last 'shivaree' – a custom which was as well known in America and, I dare say, has its counterparts in darkest Africa. One perceives that human society is more susceptible of anthropological, rather than rational, let alone intellectual, investigation.

I was pleased with father, usually too silent (for he was very deaf), that evening. I told him that I meant one day to write up the characters of the old village, many of them dead and gone, whom I knew and appreciated better than those living there today. 'When he was getting his candle ready to go to bed, I said that these things once written down and printed, were saved: no danger of their passing into oblivion.' Some of them were written up in *A Cornish Childhood*; there is more to come.

Before going back to Oxford I went out to see my grandmother at Tregrehan (which means, the hamlet on the sand – the Par estuary originally came up here, before the detritus from tin-workings and china-clay filled up the valley). With her I carried on the same habit as with father, observing, collecting memories, noting phrases. Her head, she said, was as 'maazed as a sheep'; she had often come home from market 'laden like a bee'. All these phrases, 'black as sin', 'dark as a crow', called out for a Synge, I thought, to put them in proper setting. Grandmother had an irresistible impulse to part with whatever anyone she liked admired. That evening I praised her pretty jewel-box – cardboard with shells around the base and encrusting the lid – and at once she said I must have it: it contained her medicines and phials. I was rather a favourite with her – she had a respect for 'book-learning' – and was the only one of her numerous progeny who could stand up to her and wasn't afraid of her. To all the rest of the tribe she was a tartar, with her quick eye and sharp tongue. She ruled her immense family extending in every direction more or less as her near-contemporary Queen Victoria ruled hers. Apart from her dynasticism, for I eschew families and family life, I take very much after her.

I chose to walk out that April evening by the by-lanes through Bethel, the fern-fronds uncurling in the hedges, both the ordinary variety and hart's-tongue shooting up from the grass. The gorse on the mine-dumps was thicker and richer against the red sandstone refuse thrown up by the workings. I hung round Wheal Eliza, the last of the mines to be worked, right up to the late 1880s, thinking of the hum of machinery and men, their voices and footsteps where all was silent and desolate now, they and their sons scattered to America, South Africa, Australia. Father told me that his father was the first to use the telephone from the bottom of the shaft to the surface at Wheal Eliza. (Wheal or Bal means mine in Cornish.) He was chosen as a good singer to sing a favourite song of his into the mouthpiece. How oddly it comes to mind, to think of the great Lord Salisbury contemporaneously at Hatfield, personally installing the telephone and testing it with

> Hey diddle-diddle,
> The cat and the fiddle,
> The cow jumps over the moon!

A last walk to Luxulyan with Bacon disappointed me in him. Spinning his internal cobweb of scholastic philosophy, with occasional divagations in the direction of the female sex, B. had no eye for the beauty of the Valley. Yet I took him to the most beautiful and secret recesses along the higher tracks to the waterfall. There were the pools of light upon the holly leaves in the thicket. The oak copse was as yet bare; but the silvery grey of the trunks rising from the blue mist of bluebells down the slope filled me with delight. The waterfall was on, with loops and streamers of water scattering and splashing down among the boulders. Nothing had changed. All was as it should be in this secret temple of my devotion. I had a dream of living there in summer, sleeping *à la belle étoile* on those rustling slopes, or staying in a little granite cottage in the gorge, writing my book. Nothing came of it: when summer came I was otherwise engaged.

Another old friend from church-choir days came back to St Austell for the holidays, my pious friend Booth, who took me firmly to church. I was much put off by long and tedious Lessons, prayers for King and Establishment and, *pour comble de tout*, a sermon by the dear, dotty Vicar on the mystery contained in the number 153, the supposed number of fish taken by the Apostles' net out of the Sea of Galilee. From this we went to the significance of the fish in early Christian art, another 'heavenly mystery', and thus to the persecution of religion in Russia – a subject which displeased me even more. I resolved not to go again.

Of course, I was reading all the time: not only Acton's *French Revolution* and Carlyle, but Balzac's *Eugénie Grandet* and *Le Curé de Tours*. And also Galsworthy's *The Freelands*, of which I have remembered not a thing – tribute to its literary quality. Of writing, I accomplished a prose sketch, 'The Carver in Wood', based on some craftsman and his shop I had observed at Lostwithiel, and published in *The New Oxford*; and a little poem, 'Night and the Shadows', which was printed in the next volume of *Oxford Poetry*.

This vacation, too, I noticed the presence of an intermittent companion who became more familiar than any of them, and never left me completely alone for the next fifteen years: Pain. What with one thing and another, the frightful strain it had been in getting to Oxford at all, the worry and tension it had set up, I must have started an ulcer by the time I was nineteen. In my last school-year I had had an acute appendicitis attack, was terrified – as working people were in those days – of an operation, and put down my stomach-troubles to 'indigestion'. Again, as with everything else, there was no one to advise one or tell one – my family was about as helpful here as with one's education, their attitude inert and uncomprehending. But from the Diary an intelligent look tells one that these recurring bouts were symptoms of the periodicity characteristic of duodenal ulcer. Too great tension: too much secretion of acid: growth of scar-tissue, which ended by almost completely blocking the food-channel. This was some years ahead yet, but I was well started on the way, not knowing what was happening to me.

The general reader must pardon the clinical details that may be inflicted on him – he is at leisure to skip them. But some part of the use, if not the appeal, of this story must lie in what it has to reveal of the psychology of pain and illness. I have been encouraged by a saying of John Strachey, of all people, that there is something dramatic in the story of a great illness, in the end overcome. As it got worse and worse into the late 1930s, I often wondered whether I should overcome it – a prime reason for my preserving so much material in the way of diary, documents, letters. For I was much under the influence of the lines quoted in this same volume of Journal,

> When I have fears that I may cease to be
> Before my pen has gleaned my teeming brain ...

As the 1930s went on, the onrush of political disasters increased the sense of

> Time's wingèd chariot hurrying near.

One way or another, one was always under pressure: one could never let up.

In the 1920s there were long and blissful intervals when the disease left me alone: the ulcer was quiescent. One of these grand inter-missions, fortunately, was during the summer when I took my Final Schools – or I do not know what would have happened to me. Fancy, having to be grateful – at twenty-one – for mere intermission from pain! What luck! What rotten luck! When people sometimes tell me nowadays how lucky I am, I reflect that they do not know at what a price it was purchased. The only real triumph of my life has been to survive.

Naturally all this immensely increased my resentment at the handicap and impediments of the original circumstances of my life. To have been born in a working-class family in those days was bad enough – doubly so for anyone with my tastes and ambitions. But I was prepared to work hard and work my way out of that, into something in keeping with my real nature, let alone gifts and aptitudes – and then to find myself winged, crippled, my life en-dangered, in consequence of the struggle I had had. It was too bad. I cursed my luck.

It was, however, not all loss. One consequence of it was that nothing ever turned my head: I knew too much about the other side of life, the struggle of it all, the contingent sense, that it was all on sufferance. Even pain itself was not all loss. There was a stimulus in it. I observed it and wrote it down, as I observed and wrote down everything. I didn't write it all down, or perhaps even much of it: there *was* too much, and it would have been intolerable. But it became a part of my life; and there it is, even in those early days when I didn't know what it was, noted, the accompaniments observed, as matter of some psychological interest.

'19 April: Two days of indigestion and moping indoors. At night uneasy sleep mingled with dreams.' Even so, I turned my time in bed to account:

The quiet glow of fire
  Within the room
Suppresses all desire
  To ordered gloom:

Save where the flicker-falls
  Of candle-light
Upon the further walls
  Meet with the night.

Beyond, the veils that mark
  The sky and sea:
Illimitable dark –
  Eternity.

21 April: Another sleepless night, and sickness too. I was awake
and half-awake from one o'clock till four. A funny thing I have
noticed several times on sleepless nights lately is the way my
brain works. It seethes with the most varied and disconnected
thoughts and imaginings – just as if a machine continued working on its own when the control was shut off. Last night I half
thought and half-dreamed the most ghastly things: like being
in a cinema with pictures rushing across the screen in no order
or sequence, while I watch from a back seat, astonished at the
rapid motion.

22 April: Last night one of agony; I feared that appendicitis
was coming on: all the symptoms were there, and I was expecting the pain. A long fight against it, lasting till four in the
morning, and ending with sleep and victory. Down from bed
at midday.

24 April: A day of reading and indigestion. Tea-time was
agony for me, and the racking pain lasted all the way to
Tregrehan and most of the time I was there. A little peace, for
which I was grateful, on the way home.

The fact that the pain came on at the end of the process of digestion should have indicated to any competent doctor that it was
probably duodenal. But I hadn't got a competent doctor, and it
was years before I discovered one. (Another reason why I loathe

incompetence in people.) In the middle of this bout, I returned to Oxford for the Trinity term.

Sunday, 6 May: I have been in Oxford over a week now, and the indigestion has gone steadily worse. For three days I have not been able to keep my meals down; I am not comfortable after dinner until I have vomited. Today and last night the pain in my stomach has been excruciating: I have hardly known what to do with myself, or what position to put myself in a place of ease.

I feared another attack of appendicitis, as the summer before. In fact, it looks as if the ulcer, leaving its scar, had healed up for the time, leaving me free to enjoy myself for the term.

Enjoy myself I certainly did, the moment I was free of pain. Oxford in bowery May, apple-blossom, pear-blossom and all the white blossoms of Spring out in the gardens; blue of aubrietia under grey walls, the coloured tulips standing all arow; wind-flowers white and blue along the paths, the scent of balsam-poplar blown across the pastures as one walked; and shortly the chestnuts beginning, best of all the red-candled ones in Merton Field and Magdalen Walks. May-day with the bells pealing from Magdalen tower and over meadows and waters, the punts crowded under the bridge, ready to set off up-river to breakfast at Godstow. To be nineteen, and pick up with kind friends again, in the morning of the world! In the Meadows I ran into Rawlinson, with whom I circled the Meadow again: he was going to St Ives for the long vacation, to write a book he had in mind. (Not so good as Nippie's on Original Sin!) Jimmy Crowther and Ralph Fox came to see me, and I went to tea with Ralph. At the American Club I heard Birkenhead speak: 'a most brilliant speech, exact, polished and perfect. Never a false step or unsatisfying note.' I remember still the grace of that faultless elocution, the well-turned phrases: he was Lord High Steward of the university, 'an office as to the duties of which I am uncertain'. I walked with David Low over Shotover to Wheatley, tea in an upper room of the *Merry Bells*, where the only books were a couple of the Methodist novels of my countryman, Joseph Hocking. Immediately I found the phrase I had remembered from one of them since my boyhood: the R.C. priest entering the church with a boy carrying before him 'all the insignia of his office'. *O sancta simplicitas!* I went with Low to see *Patience*, most of which I remembered from the score that hung about the piano at school, and from which Bacon and I used to sing bits, myself accompanying. 'I have just written and sent £2 to mother. I have £20 from my County Scholarship to come: I can't think why there has been such a delay.' I went to see Sybil Thorndike in the *Medea*; I stumbled out dazed in the afternoon light after it. I should have wept unrestrainedly if the young man who had taken me hadn't spent the whole afternoon gazing 'dotingly in my face throughout the play': vexation alone restrained my tears.

Meanwhile, what about work? Oh, dear: work and the summer term at Oxford are rather incompatible. I was hard put to it.

24 May: A day of ferocious, headlong work. An hour's reading of Oman, two lectures on early English history (rather much of a muchness: I am getting sick of township, burgh, hundred, and shire with all their infernal and inexcusable courts). Lunch and all the afternoon spent in writing an essay on the Anglo-Saxon Church. A hurried tea in the J.C.R. during which I tried to re-read my essay, condole with Box who has fractured his elbow, carry on an argument about the lack of ability in the present Conservative leaders with a rotund person, whom I imagine to be Shaw-Kennedy (one of them). All at the same time.

Just as I was finishing writing my essay I had a visit from Pollard,

who turned up in a most disreputable state, dirty red handkerchief around his neck, slovenly coat and trousers, heavy knapsack of books on his back, slouchy soft hat, untidy hair and unshaven face. He hadn't been to bed the night before: he looked it. He had got interested in a volume of that gorgeous edition of the *Arabian Nights* that he has, and just couldn't find time to undress and go to sleep.

Let that stand for a pen-portrait of the eminent bibliophile in his unregenerate youth.

Next morning I spent with him, supposedly over *New Oxford*

business, in that big room of his, that looked more like a book-seller's shop, over the gateway at Jesus. We chatted and

> read poems out of the 1651 edition of Cartwright and equally
> early editions of Habington and Carew. He has a glorious
> collection of books. Nothing much done for *The New Oxford*.
> There followed two lectures, one of Urquhart's at Balliol, and
> Professor Gordon on the medieval Arts of Poetry at the Schools.
> The afternoon wasted in turning over the leaves of books at
> the Library, and playing the fool with Wadleigh. A hasty rush
> to the river, where I was due for tea with John Garrett, but
> failed to find the boat-house and came back in high dudgeon.
> Tea with Wadleigh. A long wrangle with Pollard over the
> *New Oxford*, in which I poured forth my soul about its present
> and future. Things very unsatisfactory: Pollard lethargic and
> unbusinesslike. Perhaps now that I have got a certain ascendancy,
> I can keep him screwed up to the point.

I suppose that is how I must have been in my unregenerate youth. Early next week:

> Tuesday, 29 May: Wadleigh is here, and Pollard has just been.
> Everybody is worried and harassed, and I am haunted by a
> hundred spectres of work at once. That damned paper I was to
> write on 'The Old Diplomacy and the New' the Secretary
> wants me to write for Tuesday. Booth will be here for the
> week-end, and I haven't begun to read for my exam. in Greek
> History and Literature yet. Then Pollard has just been for me to
> write the political editorial for the *New Oxford*. What a world!

Instead of reading Greek History, I was reading *Mrs Warren's Profession* and George Moore's *Confessions of a Young Man*. Pollard was lending me the plays of Synge, and that afternoon I went off to tea with him, the editorial – I suppose – done.

Before the end of term I had written my paper on Hardy, with which I graduated into membership of the senior club in college, the Essay Club: 'my paper at which I have been working for the last week was very well received: everybody kind, and I was much cheered at such a reception' – since I was still a fresher and they were seniors. Henceforth, I was an active member, took my turn as secretary and chairman; my first little published book, *On History*, originated as a paper for it. Then, amid all the delights of June: 'I am feeling just a little lonely and unhappy. Wadleigh has gone out again with Crafthole-Jeffers: he seems always to be with him now. Lawrenson, too, whom I expected to find in his room, has gone out for the afternoon, probably on the river with Whitehead. I have only been back an hour from Chavasse's, where I had a talk with the Bishop of Truro after lunch.' This was Guy Warman, whom I rather took to, in spite of his being an Evangelical. It took me by surprise that he had been on the County Education Committee that elected me to my scholarship. Running unexpectedly into our cranky old Vicar from home, I asked him along to tea: 'I shall have an opportunity to talk with him about things at home. Would I could look in on them all now – George and Hilda, too, whom I have not written for so long. I will write to mother before I have tea; that will ease my homesickness a little. It will be like talking to them once more.'

One other worry assailed me before going home for the long vacation: my finances. How was I to manage over the next four months?

Not that I am on my beam-ends, or anything like it: I have managed my resources so that at present I have a balance of £17. Some of that will vanish, however, in the expenses I shall have to meet before and at the end of term: buying necessary books, tipping the scout and his assistant, railway fare and so on. That would leave me with no more than £10 to last for clothes and other things until the middle of October. But the real fact I must face is that I haven't a moral right to go home and expect to be kept by father's two pounds a week wage.

It seemed that it wasn't so easy to get a part-time tutorship as I had imagined, or, perhaps, with my views, I wouldn't qualify. In those days it wasn't thought of for undergraduates to take on a manual job, postman or waiter or factory-hand. In any case I wanted to devote the whole vacation to work, to make up for the multifarious activities of term-time. *Que faire?*

One of the classical scholars put it into my head to approach the Senior Censor, who had got him a grant of £20 for the vacation; true, Manchester was more expensive to live in than Cornwall, but his scholarships amounted to more than the £200 a year that mine totalled. With £20, I might give mother £10 or £15 for my keep during the vac.; 'that would be sufficient backing for me to get on with my work without worrying. That is what I cannot do at present. In the first place I haven't clothes enough; I have to think twice about buying a book that costs more than 5s., and so on.' I put off the fearful ordeal of approaching the Senior Censor as long as I could and, when I had an appointment, I hesitated for ten minutes or a quarter of an hour before I ventured up the stairs. When I got up there, Dundas was as nice as could be, asked me to sit in the window-seat with him while I explained the situation. It transpired that I ought to have put the case to him earlier in the year, when college grants were made regularly as a matter of course. Anyway, the Dean had a private fund, from which I was to receive £10. 'It has made me insanely happy all this morning: I went and had an ice-cream and some chocolate on the strength of it.'

Sagely I laid my plans.

I shall go home now feeling a certain independence. That £10 I shall let mother have: that will pay her at the rate of £1 a week for the ten weeks of the vac. Not enough really: but it will all go to help. I needn't at least be ashamed to go home, as if I were to live on father's wage. That side of my troubles is now solved. It is true that there is little likelihood of my having a holiday away, in beloved Brittany, for example, that haunts my mind. Never mind: all the more opportunity for work. And perhaps I shall be able to allow myself that week on Dartmoor with Booth that we talked about.

That did not eventuate: an operation took its place.

* * *

I went home in high fettle, remembering my last day as a fresher, the last day at my desk looking out on to Meadows, 'both windows wide open, and on either side the roses which Mrs Beazley gave me.

I put them into mother's little blue jars.' (Where are those now? I find I have totally forgotten them.)

Arrived home, I resumed my accustomed routine: no Brittany or even Dartmoor for me, I went my well-trodden walks to Carn Grey or on to Luxulyan, to Porthpean and Trenarren. No farther afield, for I couldn't afford money for train-fares. I must have been a familiar object along those roads – indeed I had been from a schoolboy. I halted as of old at the farm-gate at the foot of the new school-field, looking up to the trees of Menacuddle farm that fringed the sky-line, waiting for the experience, the moment of enlighten-ment that did not fail me. It yielded a nice little poem, published in the *Oxford Magazine*, the dons' paper, later. Much as I enjoyed the companionship at Oxford, these solitary experiences yielded an intenser pleasure.

Setting out alone for Carn Grey I wanted company; but 'once on the journey up the hill, all longing for a companion vanished. New ideas and plans thronged into my head.' I hardly know now whether to agree with my schoolmaster-friend, Bacon, that this was self-indulgence. But perhaps the Diary provides the answer.

Sunday, 22 July: It is very rare that these solitary journeys fail to come up to expectation. My mind works never so actively as when my limbs are swinging along the road to the tune of the winds off the moor. The lanes about Knight's clay-work are heavy with the scent of honeysuckle, the lower hedges bright with foxglove and shepherd's smock. On evenings such as this I walk in a fervour of imagination: the plans, ideas, visions that throng into my head! And what is more, they are not of and for the moment alone. Some day they will be drawn upon and used in my work. At present I can content myself with only an occasional carrying-out of an idea for a sonnet or a prose-sketch; all the other ideas are accumulating into a vast store to draw upon in the future. But if I were to die before giving expression to the things I have been storing up in my memory! ...

It is curious to observe this unquestioning confidence with regard to the future when the present was so rugged, full of frustration and often discouraging. Even within the small lamp-lit circuit of my own 'work', I often couldn't get the poetry to go as I wished. The idea was there, but I couldn't express it to my satisfaction; and I dared not spend too much time over it, for there were always Stubbs and Maitland and Tout waiting for me round the corner. Oh, if only I could only bring all my cattle home one day – I used to think – bring all my ships safely into port!

Sometimes the idea itself was at fault: the sentiment would turn into inveterate sentimentality. I started a sonnet about the Cornish miners in exile, who were so much in mind as I walked about their disused mine-workings – I listened till I could almost hear their tramp, the murmur of their voices underground. But I could not get the sonnet to go right:

> O all you stout of heart and strong of limb,
> O you, my brothers, who in former days
> Have set your feet upon the pathless ways
> That lead unto the distant marge and rim
> Of earth ...

No good: how to go on? 'I have read through the two drafts of that last sonnet of mine, and I feel that the second draft is, if anything, worse than the first. I have deliberately ceased composing any more, because at this time of night my brain can't be at its best. The last sonnet was so poor because it was written so late at night.' I suppose the best of the day was going into Stubbs and company: I had spent most of that same day reading his *Lectures on Modern History*, finishing Fletcher's *Introductory History* in bed. Not until years later, with 'Invocation for a Cornish House', in *Poems Chiefly Cornish*, did I manage to express what I felt about the old mine-workings and the vanished miners.

Anyway, verses were usually relegated to the night-time, when the day's work was over. Hence –

> A day of ceaseless wind and rain has passed
> And now the comfortable lamps are lit
> Within the house, and by the fire we sit
> As long as oaken log and embers last.
> The wingèd hours of night slip by in haste
> As moths a moment round a candle flit

And flutter, ere they sink into the pit
Of darkness, dazed and scorched, whence is no fast
Emerge to light and life. On such a night ...

I rather think that this effort was published, unexpectedly, in a subsequent volume of *Public School Verse* I do not possess. But what was
the point of writing sonnets anyway, and making things even more
difficult for myself by following the Italian model with its more
complicated rhyme-scheme? Eliot was giving the *coup de grâce* to
this sort of poetry, and sonnets becoming as disused as the mine-
workings I was trying to celebrate. It took years before I found a
satisfactory way of describing them – in free metre with irregular
rhyme – in 'Winter Heliotropes' (I should have called it 'Camp-
downs', the name of the place), in *Poems Chiefly Cornish*.

The household next door was distinctly gregarious: always somebody coming and going, laughter and high spirits, sometimes singing the songs of old Scotland, and regularly the pull of the lavatory
plug, the flushing of the cistern, as each member of the household
made ready to go off to bed. Besides Jean and her mother, there were
two sons: one had been in the Army too young and come back a
ne'er-do-well, irresistible to the girls, the other about my age more
attractive to me. For Ian was both serious-minded and spirited,
ready to respond to my enthusiasms, good-looking with expressive
lambent eyes, with the ambition to improve himself. The sister,
naturally, was looking for a husband.

Sunday, 22 July: All day Jean appears to have been waiting
round in the hope that I might offer to go out with her. Yesterday afternoon, too, she was equally disappointed. The truth is
that, however much I may like a girl (and I like Jean as much as
any other girl whom I know), I prefer my own company. If I
want to choose a companion for a walk I should choose a man –
and not any man, but somebody like Tippett or Wadleigh, or
sometimes Ian ... Surely it is natural that I should want someone
with whom I can talk on equal terms about books and politics,
art and life, not a person who can open out only upon such
topics as gardening, the weather, girls or young men, as the
case may be?

On the other hand, I was much afraid of being thought stuck up, just because I was going to Oxford. 'It is terribly snobbish to make people feel that you don't want their company; they immediately react with "Too proud: thinks he's too good for the likes of us." ' I made a note to ask Bacon 'if he finds that I am altering much as the result of being in Oxford. He once threw out a remark to the effect that I was, which rather alarmed me. On the whole, I think that Oxford has made precious little difference to my outlook and character.' No wonder – after only a first year there, and considering the resolution I had made at Oxford 'to keep myself inviolate, not to allow myself to be sucked into the stream and carried along with it. My individuality I must preserve and keep untouched; there must be no prostitution of my energy, no wastage of it upon base ends and unworthy people.'

Now, forty years after, I can only wonder where I got these ideas from – certainly not from anybody else – and I marvel no less at the extraordinary will-power for a boy. Can it have been good for him? Life, or the life-stream, had ways of taking its revenge. There was the attraction of Ian, for example – more appealing to me than Jean; and he *was* more attractive, too. One evening Bacon was with us à trois, and rather in the way. 'He talked for three or four hours without stopping and in a very aggravating way, about Marie Stopes, the union of the sexes, sex-impulses and such-like. The man has a monomania.' (Little did I suspect that, years later, I should be the recipient of fan-mail from the celebrated Marie Stopes: 'two or three headlands in Cornwall belong to me' – spiritually, of course.)

One evening Ian came back from work overdone and unwell, and I had to go up and sit with him in bed all the evening. I was much touched by the neat, spare figure under the counterpane needing affection, and wondered if he suspected how I felt. I thought not, fancied myself on masking my feelings as and when I wanted to. Wadleigh, who professed most to be able to read my emotions, had no idea of the moments when I felt hostile to him or the converse. Nor, I thought, had Jean, for all her fancied feminine intuition. 'With Jean at Trenarren twice lately there has been the same division of myself: one side of me behaved in the conventional manner of a young man towards a young woman; the other side held aloof, surveyed it all from the outside – and found it very silly.'

With such a divided frame of mind the trap couldn't close, as with most young men; the purposes of nature were defrauded.

All the same, *en revanche*, there follows a very Whitmanesque poem about Ian, worse even than most Whitman, and as sentimental. In those very same days I read Shakespeare's Sonnets as a whole and realised for myself – what no one had ever told me at school – that the greater part of them were written to and for a young man. This was a revelation. Naturally, I thought they were love-poems –

> Shall I compare thee to a summer's day?
> Thou art more lovely and more temperate –

as in a sense they are. But it is only in the last two years that I have been able to establish the precise sense – platonic, not sexual at all – with my biography of Shakespeare and my edition of the Sonnets. No inkling then what my summer-day's reading of them would lead to in the fulness of time.

Great are the advantages, as well as the rewards, of ambivalence; and I have all along been in favour of keeping all options open. This book itself, all my books, are so many evidences of the advantages of keeping open the bridges between history and literature, not to opt exclusively – is there any need to? It is possible, indeed probable, that life was establishing preferences for one, under the surface, especially when fortified by a cautionary 'No' in one direction. But though the dons had chosen History for me, I never said 'No' to literature.

This July, for example, I was mingling 'Stubbs's ponderous Lectures on the Medieval Kingdoms of Cyprus and Armenia' with Hazlitt's *Table Talk*. I read the whole of Hardy's *The Dynasts*, several volumes of Anatole France and Charles Lamb's *Letters*. I was charmed by his last letter, recalling his supper with some friend, and inquiring 'if that book I have lost be not found, I shall never like fried tripe any more'. Even mother, who was not much given to literary appreciation, appreciated that when I read it to her. '3 August: I did about four hours' reading of history yesterday';

but I washed this down with De Quincey's *Reminiscences of the English Lake Poets*. Sometimes I read along the roads.

De Quincey's *Confessions of an Opium Eater* I took up as I was setting out for Porthpean, and, going along the roads slowly, taking no notice of the crowds of people hurrying by (for it was August Bank Holiday), I read several pages. In the evening I spent two hours reading on a cliff between Porthpean and Trenarren; I found a comfortable coign by a bank, and with the green pastures behind me and the illimitable plains of the sea before me, I was happy.

At this time, as a consequence of repression, I suppose, I was much interested in exploring the sensations of fear. I don't know what the psychological propulsions were, but the motive was to give them literary expression; and next year they produced several poems better than any I had yet done. One Sunday evening from Carn Grey I explored the curious gaunt place Garker below: 'how the name suits the place! It is nothing but a gully cleft in the hill, the surface of the land torn and scarred with streaming for tin through the ages. Half-way down the hill, at the bend, is a deserted house – such a place as a murder might have taken place in: grey stone, with a single red-brick chimney, the windows blocked up or stopped with wood and rags.' I suppose now that it was a deserted miners' lodge; nothing would persuade me then but that it was murderous. I left the road to explore a deserted track up through the bed of the valley, to where a mass of 'burden' had fallen away and blocked it. In that shut-in hollow it was oppressively silent; the moor-wind swept over the higher levels, hardly stirring the bracken here. It was so quiet that I had the familiar sense that I was being watched. By what? No rational calculation that the burden might fall away again occurred to me; it was the tense atmosphere of the place that made me rush out of the hollow. I had succeeded in frightening myself.

As I had frightened myself in my room at Oxford by reading Hardy's poem aloud late at night and reciting over and over,

Who's in the next room, who?

It was midnight; everybody had gone to bed, and all round me was a living, listening stillness – suppose one were to puncture the envelope of experience and enter it: what would one find? I was almost afraid to go to bed. But I collected such experiences. The twittering art-mistress told me of one, which I duly savoured. She was staying in a lonely, rambling farmhouse at Colan, near Newquay. The farm-people had given her a room at the end of a long passage, away from the inhabited part of the house, and looking out on a gloomy plantation of firs. A thunder-storm came on at night; and in the flashes of lightning she saw perched on the window-sill four owls in a row.

Always on the look-out for this kind of thing, I would get father to talk about the men of the Higher Quarters – a name of respect, not unmingled with fear – in the old days. Then, there were intense local rivalries: Mount Charles, Tregonissey, Penwithick, Stenalees, Treverbyn, each had its band of wrestlers and fighters. They met in unofficial fights as well as in the regular contests at feast-time. 'Father thinks the men now are like sheep, compared with the roughs of those days.' But they had left in their hundreds to swell the mining-camps and towns of Hancock and Houghton in the Upper Peninsula of Michigan, to Grass Valley and Nevada City in California, to tough, fighting Butte, Montana, let alone South Africa and Australia. Anyone who knows the story of the early mining-settlements in Michigan or Wisconsin will recognise that the Cornish miners took their primitive ways with them. At home there were the local insults each parish had for the other: at Roche 'they do knuckly down 'pon one knee' (we may imagine for what purpose); while St Stephens' people 'tried to hedge in the guckoo', etc. In my childhood a stranger coming into one of those remote upland villages might well have been stoned: the stones lay all round ready to hand. It was exciting to hear about: it sounds like the uplands of Sicily as reported by Giuseppe di Lampedusa or Carlo Levi.

More exciting anyway than the small round of local life open to me. '24 July: To Porthpean where the School Swimming Sports were held. Mrs Petherick had invited me to tea with the staff and governors – an honour, for which I put on white flannels for the first time and felt a fool.' What a splendid existence to live in a house like that, I thought – a charming Regency and early Victorian stuccoed house with terraces and lawns sloping to the sea. *There* 'one would have inspiration for the very best work and, what is more, accomplish it.' However, clumsily expressed in the Diary, I find the double vision at work – which might have led one on to novels, if it had not been for the formidable presences of Stubbs and Maitland and Tout. I was quizzed by the disagreeable Chairman of the governors about one of the nicer young mistresses having gone out in a boat the week before with the handsomest (and maturest) of the boys. It seemed that the girls were all jealous, said that they hoped they would drown and had tattled. 'I tried to pour oil on troubled waters by suggesting that Miss S. was a modern-minded young lady, and the girls' dislike of her might be merely sour grapes.' That seemed to stop the old Governor; but here were ordinary social amenities, the interests of ordinary people. Insupportable!

The afternoon soured for me, until at tea-time I was taken under the wing of a charming old lady, Henrietta Treffry, who talked books to me. She discovered that, though I knew about Lewis Carroll at Christ Church and had read some of his rare tracts, I had never read the Alice books. I felt rather ashamed: the reason was too obvious – there never had been any children's books in my childhood, or indeed any books at all in the house. (Perhaps I have somewhat over-compensated that today, with a library of over twenty thousand at Trenarren and at All Souls.) Mrs Treffry must have asked me to tea at Place, that historic house with its gathered towers and turrets looking down upon the narrow streets of Fowey and with its water views across the harbour and out to sea – I have written a little of its history in books later, in *Sir Richard Grenville of the Revenge* and *Tudor Cornwall*. And so generously, she had Lewis Carroll's *Alice in Wonderland* and *Through the Looking Glass* in sumptuous, gold-edged Macmillan editions for me. The books are noted in the Diary, but not the tea-party: I just recall the painted beams of the big dining-room and the utterly silent presence of the old squire in the background.

For my enemy had caught up with me: a perforated appendix and peritonitis.

*   *   *

I don't remember much about it, not even the onset – apparently it was my third attack; but I do remember a sense of comfort in being carried down the stairs so carefully on a stretcher to the ambulance. Others who have known the experience of peritonitis will recall the curious sense of comfort, after acute pain, as the poison spreads slowly through the system, dulling the consciousness as one is passing out.

I woke up to find myself in our comfortable, small Cottage Hospital, in the men's ward, with the screens drawn round my bed as a bad case. Dr Panting, one of the surgeons to whom I owe my life, had come up specially from Truro to operate, and apparently 'mother and father had a fearful time of it, as the doctors wouldn't give much hope and told them to expect to be called to the hospital at any hour of the night.' Poor dears, I fear I must have given them a great deal of worry one way and another before I was through. However, I came through this examination 'like a brick' – rather better than I had done History Previous. And I have retrieved one or two memories that give me pleasure. I was possessed with a longing for the clear, delicious cold water that we used to fetch as boys from Phernyssick; and on his first visit my father brought me a bottle of the coldest water from the deepest working of the pit at Carclaze. It tasted to me better than the waters of any Bandusian fount, or even of Helicon – certainly than champagne, of which I should have disapproved.

My second memory is of an early morning when I was recovering, for I was sitting up in bed to wash – I caught sight of the woods of Pentewan valley in the distance, and was suddenly overcome with the revelation of the beauty of life, that kind of return upon oneself when something seems waiting for one round the corner, and it is life itself. I was recovering, but it had been a near thing. I overheard the matron say, one morning, 'he's been rather worse than he knows'; certainly when I caught a glimpse of the incision being dressed by her hard, competent hands – which I rather feared, she was so ruthless and quick – I regarded my ruined belly with disgust and registered, 'like a stuck pig'.

She was a most competent woman, tall, stringy and astringent, who bossed the doctors as well as the nurses and ran the place like clockwork. I dare say she had to be like that; but she was decidedly unsympathetic. Exceedingly sensitive and aware, I gathered that she didn't like me: though I hadn't done anything to her, I suppose she expected that the Oxford boy would be rather above himself. So far from that, I was very grateful for all that they were doing for me and, when I was able to get out of bed, I was particularly careful to go round emptying people's bed-bottles for them as they had done for me. Rather comic, really: it reminds me of Alington's sermons at Eton to the effect that Eton boys should be careful to be particularly nice to boys from other schools.

I find that my mother kept a pencilled note from me from the hospital, when I was recovering: it is all about the awful Tout that I was clamouring for, for my spell in hospital had put a foot through my intended history reading.

> Tout: *Political History of England*, vol. 3. A big red book which reposes on the trunk beside the armchair in my bedroom. Tout: *France and England in the Middle Ages*. A small black book, about No. 12 in from the left second shelf from the bottom of big bookcase. Perhaps those will be enough to keep me going all the time I am here. As I don't read much yet, but shall be glad to do more when I can sit up. Tell Ian that in last Sunday's *Observer* there was an article by K. Feiling – that is my tutor at Christ Church. I wouldn't have missed it for anything. Please thank him for sending on the *Herald* – it helps to remind me I am still in the world. As for me I am getting better and better. And I eat quite a lot … I hope you will come up on Friday as well as on Sunday if you can. My love to Aunt Bessie and Len and you all. Love XXX.

Altogether I enjoyed my time in hospital. There was a little boy in the next bed to me who used to ask if I had sand to play with in my back garden, and I used to have conversations with him about sand-castles and mud-pies. (None of the Matron's apprehended superiority about this. I had come across that attitude of jealousy on the part of middle-aged women towards forward youths before, and I well recognised the symptoms. She came round a little before I left, but only just perceptibly. On the other hand, I admired her –

and also understood.) Then there were rigs of fun with the nurses, and making up limericks about them. When I came to leave, after a month in the place, I was quite nostalgic about it. 'Hospital was an entirely new and different world to me; all its inmates moved in a round with which I had never come in contact.' When I went home, I missed the camaraderie of it all. '14 September: Last night I felt quite homesick for the hospital. I thought of everybody with much sentiment, and very little more would have reduced me to tears. There was Gerry, with his excited, quick ways, his many kindnesses and as many obstinacies.' There follow thumb-nail sketches of my companions and my hospital-limericks.

I came back home not to read Tout, so far as I can see, but to read *Vanity Fair*, of which I have a couple of pages of criticism, according to my habit with important books. (I didn't criticise the historians.) I wasn't completely well: '25 September: Several days have passed during which for the most part I have been unwell. Today, after an unbroken sleep of twelve hours (rare thing for me) I have got up with renewed energy – something like the old vigour.' I had gone to bed at half past seven, but 'thought it wasteful to be sleeping at such an hour. So I turned on the light and read *Travels with a Donkey* again with all the old delight.'

But all was not well.

17 September: A dismal meal today; altogether I have spent a depressing hour or more. The black mood was brought on by the fact that father has only one pair of boots that doesn't take water. All the others are no good when the winter comes on, and he can't afford to wear his best boots. I have just had a pair soled, and he has had to wear those. I ought to give them to him for good, but that and a rather worse pair are all I have.

There follows an outburst against our luck, understandably enough.

This is the sort of thing that appears likely to increase during the next two or three years – as if I hadn't enough of that already in my life! Lack of money has handicapped us all from our earliest years. And one can see how it affects all families around one. But it is a new experience to feel that we are approaching rock-bottom. Mother and father, after more than twenty years in the shop at Tregonissey, retired with a fortune of £100. That was two years ago; they now have £40. Everything depends on my life. If I had died the other day, all hopes of a comfortable old age for mother and father would have been blasted. Nothing would have remained for them but more hard work – harder work, father says, than when he was a younger man – and increasing poverty. Both George and Hilda have their own way to make in Australia and America; and a pretty tough struggle I expect it is for both of them. Whatever else happens, I hope I shall live for this necessity, if for no other.

I forgot to consider, thinking of them, that the operation would make a hole in my careful finances too. But at this black moment an angel descended from heaven – a letter came from Q, noblest of men, to put things right. He may not have heard of my illness, for he says nothing about it; but the letter is so full of his delicate consideration, sensitiveness and tact, that I reproduce it in full. I think it is the first letter I ever received from him who was so much my hero and a living inspiration to me always; I treasured it and often pored over the deliberate, careful phrases of the conscious artist.

I have been asked by three friends to make myself the conduit of the accompanying three £5 notes, and risk the rebuff with which, if you are as generous as I believe, you will not hurt me. I suppose they chose me for the risk knowing that I had once on a time been at Oxford and not too affluent, and guessing that it might come with the less chance of rejection if offered by an elder brother (so to speak) who has been through the noble mill and known the pinch, at times, of the machinery.

I need say no more except that (a) the sum can be increased at need: but is purposely kept low that you may feel a residue being with-held from you to help other Cornishmen of whom we are proud: (b) that it is sent quite unconditionally and (c) – if you'll allow me to say it as a friend – that to accept so trifling a gift is (in my experience of men) a finer thing than to reject it. So I plead that you don't hurt the feelings of three anonymous persons who simply regret, with me, that Cornwall doesn't do more for the sons who increase her credit.

And now, less formally, let me say how much I envy you. To be young, and *there*!

> Tanagra, think not I forget
> Thy beautifully storey'd streets –

E. K. Chambers once stole that quotation from me *à propos* of Oxford. But he can't steal the affection for the place which I want *you* to bring back in your turn. The sneers of dons and cheap wits are negligible. Only bring back to us the essential Oxford, and you will help us when the time comes.

With good wishes believe me,

Yours sincerely,

ARTHUR QUILLER-COUCH

What a noble letter! I can only say that, in addition to all his gifts, his genius, Q was the greatest gentleman I have ever known.

My Diary registers my feelings. '*Jubilate!* My excitement at seeing three five-pound notes of the Bank of England was intense' – I had never seen one before; mingled with a spasm of disappointment that 'father was more phlegmatic than he ought to have been'. But how to reply to such a wonderful letter, which I was even more proud to receive from my hero on literary grounds, than on financial. Q making himself a 'conduit' – I loved that, and have often recalled the phrase. Hurt him by rejecting the proffered help? – I should no more have thought of it than of taking the hint that 'the sum can be increased at need'. Indeed, I never remembered that phrase: it passed completely out of my head.

With my worries resolved, I could go back to Oxford for my second year in good heart. On no motion of my own I found that my £80 scholarship at the House was put up by £25 a year. So that altogether I had the grand total of £225 a year on which to live and make do. Within these margins I managed so well that I completed my undergraduate years without a penny in debt, outside the family.

4

IV

Second Year: Testing Time

SECOND year is a testing time for young men at the universities. The freshness and excitement of first year are over; it is time for them to grapple with themselves, to get down to work – or not, as the case may be: for decisions with regard to the future, how things are going to work out for them in life, are being made, often without the active co-operation of their will. In consequence, many students suffer from what may be described as 'second-year trouble': there is no name for it, but the phenomenon is easily recognisable.

Here was my friend from Manchester Grammar School, who had had the advantage of the classical grind at that famous institution, which we held properly in respect, and a classical Scholar of the House, unable to cope with things in his second year. I had come back from my vacation of illness and inadequate reading in consequence, full of good resolutions to amend.

29 October 1923: Today I have done eight hours' solid work, not to mention miscellaneous reading of papers and periodicals. But I have had to spare myself the change from reading I was looking forward to: W. came in, depressed and in a sad state of mind. He can't work, he can't make up his mind; his examination will be upon him and his syllabus unprepared. Oxford he hates, and almost regrets he ever got a scholarship here. I could do nothing for him. What little experiments in the way of sympathising I have made with Wadleigh are of no great effect. So I have fallen back on the advice to these people to help themselves. Nobody else can effect their salvation.

What was wrong with W. anyway? He was perfectly healthy; he hadn't the enemy in his guts that I had to contend with. Wasn't

Oxford good enough for him? (I don't know what happened to him after he went down: I have never heard of him since – probably a happy little *petit-bourgeois* family life, in a happy little Manchester suburb.)

'I am tired out with my work, and this last hour attempting to comfort W. And I haven't written to my mother and father, brute that I am: I know how mother must look out for a letter from me by every post; and I haven't written. That for tomorrow morning, then, without fail.'

Here was another function that the Diary fulfilled: a kind of confessor, a moral pace-maker, keeping myself up to the mark.

Before I left home for Michaelmas Term at Oxford I had been questioning the value of keeping the Diary at all: too much that was trivial in it, I considered I should devote myself more to thoughts and ideas. 'Many things have been troubling me during the last few weeks, since I came out of hospital. Perhaps even before and during that time. I don't know where I stand. I don't know what to believe – I scarcely know how to think. The world is a whirlpool.' I was particularly agitated, in these early years after the Russian Revolution, about the way things were going to go with society: no one to tell one, no one to help. I couldn't make up my mind which way to go in relation to them.

So, a perturbed youth of not quite twenty, 'this afternoon, 1 October 1923, I set out on a walk with the deliberate intention of thinking out my position. I even formulated articles which might serve as a basis for future action.' But they did not satisfy; I reproached myself with having no definite philosophical position. Perhaps I ought to read philosophy in order to define a position I could hold to as true? The expectant young man accused himself – 'I cannot construct a complete creed; my beliefs are scattered hither and thither throughout the world of my mind.' The afternoon's walk served to precipitate a most inadequate series of 'articles' or propositions, all tied to the consideration that

all the signs, economic and religious, political and literary [remember that this was the world of Bonar Law and the rule of the business men: Keynes's 'hard-faced men who had done well out of the War'], point that we are moving in the direction of the strengthening of social bonds; in so far as we loosen instead of drawing closer, we fail and man's well-being suffers. Our aim must be to draw the bonds closer, to knit them together in a firm social order. The present order is loose, top-heavy and artificial. Therefore we must build an order that is firm upon the basis of the soil. All must work: the number of men employed in direction and administration must be small in proportion to those engaged in primary work. They should be the summit of a pyramid; the present order gets more and more like a top, only kept upright by perpetual whipping and spinning.

Here was 'a case for a republic of Workers and Peasants'. But, arrived at that, 'why bother about man and his future? What is my philosophy?' I recalled a passage from Gorki's *Diary*: what the poet, Alexander Blok, said when tired of Gorki's philosophising: ' "All this is boring," said Blok, shaking his head. "The thing is simpler; the fact is that we have become too clever to believe in God, and not strong enough to believe in ourselves alone. As the foundations on which life and belief may rest there exist only God and myself. Mankind? But can one believe in mankind after this war, and on the eve of inevitable, still more cruel, wars?" '

Here was a poet's intuition at work; this was pretty perceptive of the true nature of the twentieth century, then not very far advanced on its hideous course – far more so than the glib optimism, the facile promises, of the politicians.

Already my intuition told me that Blok was right. 'Here is put into words exactly what I have felt lately. I have no faith in man; I have ceased to believe in God. There remains only myself. Can I so order and discipline my life that faith in myself will be justified?'

That was written forty years ago, when I was not yet twenty. It has remained and come through as the dominant position that has carried me through life – not a bad position either, certainly not an ineffective one, in a world falling about our ears. One is so much less dependent on external circumstances, on the contingencies of life, the insecurity, the undependability of friends, the way human beings have of so rarely coming up to expectations, of hardly ever fulfilling what little they have in them to achieve.

Later, when I read the whole of an even more congenial, lonely spirit, Newman, I was struck by his conviction that 'there were only two luminously self-evident beings, myself and my Creator'. And what happens when the whole human construct of a Creator collapses as simply superfluous?

*   *   *

Back at Oxford I was content with my simple things around me. 'I am installed once more in my very own rooms. It is tea-time: the cups and saucers, cakes and tea-pot are set out on the little table before the fire. I have drawn the big arm-chairs to each side of the hearth and am awaiting the arrival of a friend to complete the picture. It is delightful to be back once more, for the sake of the place itself, not only because of all my good friends.' M., whom I had been brought up to regard as my aunt, in fact my half-sister (living in my splendid isolation, with my head in the air, I was the only member of the family not to know), 'has let me have her marble clock, and I find its tick-tick friendly. The clock and the reproductions of the Mona Lisa, Hals and Rembrandt have helped to fill up the empty spaces of the sideboard and mantelpiece: everything looks more comfortable. At last the fire is burning up, the kettle is singing, W. has arrived.' This picture of domestic simplicity may be compared with that given by my contemporary Evelyn Waugh in *Brideshead Revisited* – which offers a more coloured parallel of the exotic life of the aesthetes of our Oxford generation than my simple, serious-minded circle – with its slightly contemptuous dismissal of his friend 'Collins', the scholar set on his way to becoming a don, and his innocent *décor* of Medici prints, etc.

Shortly I encountered my own form of second-year trouble. 'I have been unhappy lately, in spite of circumstances, which aren't quite so forbidding as usual. I believe it is dissatisfaction with this barren swotting of history and accomplishing nothing worth accomplishing.' The truth was that I wanted to be writing. 'After coming back from an evening at the Labour Club, I took down the book with Verlaine's "Après Trois Ans" in it, and translated it into verse. It has taken about two hours, and it is now getting on for half past one in the morning. But I feel that I have done something well, and I go to bed satisfied.'

Now the ineffable Wadleigh came to disturb my equilibrium, only achieved with difficulty by the aid of poetry.

Wadleigh and I have had a conversation about the change that Oxford has brought about in us both. Me, Oxford has changed for the worse, he says. I don't believe it. It is true I no longer have the same spirit of indignation over the wrongs of the people. But they have the opportunity to help themselves, and – they prefer pubs, football matches and cinemas. Nor do I hope any longer to convert Oxford young men to my view of things.

After all, most people only took the opinions of their environment; these people came from a totally different environment and couldn't be expected to see things as I did.

My diagonal course across English society led me to appreciate the silliness of different classes' illusions about each other. My working-class brother, for instance, believed that the physique of upper-class men was inferior to that of working men. Conversely middle-class Left intellectuals are apt to overestimate the intelligence, or at least the rationality, of the people – or they pretend to, for there is a real insincerity in the *New Statesman* point of view all along.

As to my own work, I had been going at it

fairly hard lately. Yesterday more than ten hours altogether. Today not so much; yet I have read Plummer's book on King Alfred and enjoyed it (except for some flatulent expressions of imperialism to which I replied in the margin). It has been on my conscience that I have written so little poetry. Nor have I thought much about it ...

Several times Rawlinson has been to talk to me lately. I like him very much, and yet fear him somewhat. I know what his aim is: it is to get me for the Church; and he knows that I know it. It makes him wary, but all the more pressing. I feel touched to the heart at his appeal. And yet, on my part, it is pure sentiment: a feeling which, if I am strong, I shall distrust. For, though pessimism about the world becomes stronger and stronger in my mind (as R. knows), yet I do not feel that need for religion which he is counting on ... And how can I possibly believe doctrines of the Church which fly in the face of all common sense? A more possible creed, intellectually, would be that lack of creed which is Quakerism: as to that I have not so much an active dislike as a temperamental incongruity.

Rawlinson's pressure had a curious consequence: it affected me so much that it gave me a nightmare I have never forgotten. I dreamed that I was being strangled by an enormous snake – the first, but not the last, time that I have had that nightmare – with my arms pinioned behind me (I must have been lying on my arm-muscles), and the snake heavy across my chest.

After this, I did not go in for any more discussions with the kindest of the dons, and perhaps the question between us was thus decided. It was a lucky escape.

Nevertheless I was much perturbed, and could not express what I felt; Hardy said it for me:

> Has some vast Imbecility
> Mighty to build and blend,
> But impotent to tend,
> Framed us in jest, and left us now to hazardry?
>
> Or come we of an Automaton
> Unconscious of our pains?
> Or are we live remains
> Of Godhead dying downwards, brain and eye now gone?

I thought that I too regretted coming to Oxford: 'it takes away one's hope, and saps that vital thing in a man which might have accomplished something. I am not sure even of myself. And I feel very much alone in the world.'

There follows a sonnet for Armistice Day, which always affected me in those years – when I went on to All Souls and lived amid the portraits of the young Fellows who had been killed not so long before, I developed a cult of that lost generation:

My brothers, who in distant places sleep
And whom unending night has wrapped around
In an eternal silence ...

My old friend, H. B. Booth, came to stay with me and we all
went to the Playhouse to see Ibsen's *The Master Builder*. The old
Playhouse at the end of the Woodstock Road, round the corner
from St Giles's, comes back to me now with its extraordinary dis-
comfort, its draughts and frightfully creaking chairs which numbed
one's bottom as the evening wore on – yet what excitement it gave
one for a half-a-crown! One saw Synge, Strindberg, the early plays
of Robert Nichols and Richard Hughes, a great deal of Ibsen and
Chekhov; I believe that a whole school of distinguished actors
emerged from that simple school with its minimal funds and
apparatus.

I didn't know about that side of things, for I never had any contacts with the theatre – alas, for I might have written a play; but I
and my friends were faithful supporters so far as our exiguous funds
allowed. The Diary has the habit of criticising the plays I saw as of
the more important books I read. *The Master Builder*, however, left
me without any capacity for criticism. 'Perhaps it is due to my
extraordinary unsophistication.' That seems a good shot: I had been
so little to the theatre that I gave myself completely up to the play,
was absorbed by it, lived it. 'Halvard's problem is in one way very
like the problem which has put something between Wadleigh and
me. Halvard had been unwilling to sacrifice everything to his life's
work: if he had been wise enough to avoid the entanglements of
human loves and relationships, his work would have gained all. He
attempts the impossible and fails.'

The end of term left me alone again on my staircase, and 'after
the incessant companionship of Oxford, I am more susceptible to
loneliness than I used to be. When I first came up from Cornwall,
I rather welcomed any momentary relapse into solitude such as I had
been accustomed to: it gave me a sense of exultation to be alone.
But now the stillness everywhere preys on my nerves. I am appalled
by the ghostliness of the shadows, and still more by the echoes that
resound, like a hollow cough when I open or shut a door'. Was I

perhaps over-working? 'For there's nothing like a time such as this for reading: I am simply mopping up books' – at such a pace that 'my head was feeling heavy and confused: it is very unusual for me to have a headache – in fact I remember having had scarcely one in my life. In three days I have read Max Beer's *Social Struggles in Antiquity*, F. A. Simpson's *Rise of Louis Napoleon* and an enormous two-volumed *History of the Papacy in the Nineteenth Century* by Nielsen.' For light relief Shaw's *Back to Methuselah*.

Out in the city, 'bells have been ringing at intervals for some time now. I can't think which church it is, but they are very like the bells at home, pitched in the same key and of the same full tone.' They induced a mood of wanting to write a sonnet to dear Tom Lawrenson, my absent friend. 'But my brain isn't free to occupy itself with dreams. I get a keener satisfaction from writing one sonnet than reading a whole history, I know. But I must not indulge myself. Lately I have been coming to the notion that duty has a greater call upon one's energies than one's own pleasure. And yet it doesn't dispose of the difficulty; for if I am better adapted for poetry than for practical affairs, isn't it my duty to devote myself to poetry?'

The problem was to know where the balance of one's capacities and interests lay. 'I have entire confidence about my own capacities as compared with the people whom I meet here. I know my ability is superior to theirs. But it's not good enough, for all that. I have inclinations in too many directions to be best in any one. And now is the testing-time.' I had multifarious irons in the fire. Ahead of me was the obstacle of an Anglo-Greek examination, for which I had allowed only a fortnight at the end of term to get up the required Greek history and first four books of Plato's *Republic*. There was the regular reading for History Schools; and I had just been elected Secretary of the Labour Club, with all the correspondence, making arrangements for meetings, entertaining speakers, looking after college secretaries, which that entailed. Moreover, I was anxious to write a poem for the Newdigate.

Next morning, 17 December, found me 'begun upon my probably endless correspondence as Secretary of the Labour Club. I wrote to Ramsay MacDonald, Maxton, E. D. Morel and Phillips Price. As they were all on the same theme, I had to exercise some ingenuity in the variations. I hope to goodness that they all answer in the affirmative.' Alas, for the infant politician's hopes – not one did; one had to enter on another round all over again. However, the Union would not allow me to borrow J. A. Symonds's *Michael Angelo* for the vacation, so that removed the distraction of writing for the Newdigate from my path. I consoled myself by buying Rossetti's *Poems*, in the Oxford India-paper edition. Next evening when I was settling down to work, B. came and talked: I think this must have been Robin Burn, who lived on the corner-turret staircase, No. 7. 'Together we went out to dinner: the first time I have done such an extravagant thing since I have been in Oxford. Altogether I spent 9s. on dinner and Rossetti: with that I might have bought Trevelyan's *Age of Wycliffe* which I need. Damn money! I get more and more fed up with having to think out what I shall spend, and how to save by going to a shop rather than to the J.C.R.' Damn Greek history, too: I threw caution to the winds by spending time on a sonnet:

To my Friend: T.L.

How great the loneliness when you were gone
I had not thought to find; nor did I know
How fully ran our friendship's even flow
Making rich our lives, as the rivers run
Among the pastures to make rich the plain.
Your absence is a drought upon the land:
The fields of friendship are but thirsty sand
Desolate as a desert, parched for rain.
And I have trod the ways we used to tread,
And waited by the pool we knew of old
That caught the lights when evening turned to gold:
In hope to catch some threads of happiness
Blown with the memories of the days now dead,
Before I came to fear my loneliness.

Hardly any of these early poems were published. The supercilious may say, what wonder? – merely traditional Georgian stuff. What purpose, then, did they serve, apart from giving expression to the pent-up feelings of a boy's life lived too much to itself? Well, it all served as training for the writer, I suppose. I observe the naturalness of the rhythms and phrases – as opposed to the clumsiness with language of some of my juniors in the 'thirties – and the equally natural fall of the alliteration that always betokens the instinct for poetry. Come to that, I am now as well able – so far away – to criticise this verse as anyone else: for all their simplicity and unpretentiousness, these early poems last as well as the more publicised political poetry of the 'thirties. Though they never had fashion with them, they are the more authentic for that.

Back at home for the Christmas vacation, I felt 'disinclined to take up the Webbs' *Decay of Capitalist Civilisation* after Kenneth Grahame's *Dream Days*'. A visit from Mrs M. to my mother induced me to go back with her three or four doors away along Robartes Place, where we all lived quietly and respectably enough, to talk politics with her husband. The M.s were an exceedingly devoted couple, kind and good, indeed hopelessly gone to the good. They were Plymouth Brethren or Christadelphians, I forget which; they inhabited a world of fundamentalist nonsense, they lived on the pleasant slopes of Slades as if in a vale of tears, not holding much converse with their neighbours for fear of corruption from this wicked world. The wife, pleasant enough to look at, was deaf; the husband, with a long and sexy proboscis, had a cleft palate. They were a presentable enough pair, except for the rubbish they thought. And they produced a perfectly normal, healthy, rather good-looking boy. This child was the despair of his pious mother, who confided to mine how strange it was that he did not want to hear about Jesus. Once when the boy was unwell and my mother went over to sit with him, he pleaded with her, 'Don't read to me about Jesus. Read to me about burglars.' Even my mother, with whom humour was not a strong point, saw the humour of this.

Of course, the M.s deeply disapproved of my religious, or lack of religious, views; they even dared to deplore them to my people. When the boy grew up and married away from his home into a normal, sensible environment, he told me how he had been brought up to think of me as utterly abandoned, a lost soul. But, indeed, the good M.s cannot have been anything like so much shocked at me as I was shocked at them for daring to have an opinion on such matters.

Living in a working-class environment there were various religious crackpots who emerged with the sun, like something one sees when one lifts up a stone. There was Mr F., the club-footed tailor, who had an apocalyptic way of talking in the language of the Book of Revelation. It would have been wonderful to tape him, record him – but such things hadn't been invented: it would have been like listening in to the Levellers, or the ecstatic nonsense of the Army Debates of 1647. Then there was Mrs Mingo, an enthusiast who played her sectarian harmonium in the street outside the Town Hall, where we held our Labour meetings, so loudly that we couldn't hear ourselves speak inside. When we pleaded for an intermission, or that she might desist, she pondered and then replied: 'You see the Devil is abroad, and the word of the Lord must go forth.'

All these idiots had votes, and had to be borne with and talked to – though it was a pain in the neck to do so. I felt like Dean Acheson, after a first-class political analysis at Cal. Tech., confronted by the question of an asinine professor: 'What role does Mr Acheson think the Christian Church has in the world situation today?'

Such were the amenities of home life. There were others round the corner. '30 December: This afternoon for a short walk I went to Look-out lane, and saw there a pair of lovers fondling each other on a bank amidst the bracken.' *They* were getting on with life. So too next door; the trap had closed on Ian, he had to marry his girl and get on with life, the new life on the way. Gone were all the romantic dreams of culture, of following me to the university – and my dreams of a helpmate in the cause. Before this, he had been working, after his day's work was over, four or five hours at French and Latin to pass his qualifying examinations. I took this upshot rather more philosophically than I should have expected, even arguing that it was probably as well in the long run – though it was the end of a comradeship.

It was accompanied by a curious episode. Ian had asked me to tell him his fortune – an odd accomplishment to possess, which I infrequently use, for it is apt to get one into trouble with friends. As in this instance – for in the cards I saw what was in the wind, without any knowledge and before I was informed. What was unexpected by me was that Ian was furious: he thought that I knew and was glad at his downfall, by a kind of horrid *Schadenfreude*. It is true that

Queen Elizabeth I didn't much relish other people enjoying themselves, when there wasn't much enjoyment about for her. But, in fact, I was innocent: I had not known. The episode made a difference to our friendship. Nor was it the only occasion when something psychic has happened to me in telling people's fortunes from cards.

There were other distasteful accompaniments to our simple way of life. New Year, 1924: 'Father came back early from work tonight, wet and tired after the day's work. He has just gone up to bed: I can hear mother and him talking.' A new worry was that dear Neddy, the donkey, fell sick. Readers of *A Cornish Childhood* will remember his character: frisky and spirited when young (fed on oats), trotting like a pony, liable to run away under Holmbush viaduct when a train roared over it. He had been a regular companion of my school-days: we were familiar characters along the road going down to his field, Neddy cropping peaceably, while I (with loose rein) had my nose in a book. I was fond of him, and would make off with buns and lump-sugar from the kitchen-table when he came to the gate. He knew my voice and would make a curious hard breathing noise when he heard me about – asking for buns and sugar. I had secret verbal endearments for him too, such as all animals love: there was plain 'Neddy-doon-kay', then more commonly, 'Noddy-dinko', and in a special mood, 'Neddy-dink-caw-caw'. He liked this, or I thought he did; he would put his ears forward and breathe hard through those delicate mouse-coloured nostrils.

Now, 'he's caught a cold through being out in the field in this damned weather. I remember once before we were afraid of losing him, and he's irreplaceable. If Neddy were to die, there's no more money to get another donkey for mother; and as she can't walk out [she was crippled with arthritis], she would have to stay in all the time.' It made me miserable to see the poor animal suffering. 'I stayed with Neddy in the stables a long time this morning; it's more pathetic to see him ill than a human being. We can at least say what we are feeling, but the dumb creatures just bear pain in silence. I hope poor old Ned won't die; last time I remember worrying lest he should, and now I am equally anxious. This evening father thought the best thing for him would be a drench of hot beer or ale.' There followed a curious expression of Victorian respectability. Though I wouldn't have dreamed of going into a pub for myself, 'I would willingly have gone down to the "Duke of Cornwall" for a pint for Neddy. Father and mother wouldn't hear of it: they thought of the bad impression it would create if I, of all people, were to be seen fetching beer from a pub. As if I cared in the very least for what people thought of anything I said or did.' I cared only for the substance of the thing: I wouldn't enter a pub on my own account, for Neddy I would have waded through beer. However, I wasn't allowed to go. Before I went back to Oxford, fortunately the little dear – whom I nursed, arms round his neck, tears in my eyes – got better.

*   *   *

During that December a transformation came over the political scene: the businessmen and the profiteers who had run England ever since the Liberal party lost its ascendancy, with the formation of Lloyd George's Coalition in 1916, appealed to the country under their new leader, Mr Baldwin, and were decisively rejected by the country. Asquith and Lloyd George temporarily made up their feud; the two wings of the Liberal Party joined together for the Election. Birkenhead and Austen Chamberlain tried to get themselves accepted once more by the Tories, after their association with Lloyd George. The exigencies of the War had upset the party system, and the truth was that the ablest political leaders were those who sat loosely to mere party, under the personal magnetism and immense popularity of Lloyd George.

In 1922 he had been overthrown by a revolt of the Conservative back-benchers, led by Baldwin and backed by the Cecils. Lloyd George's small group contained two men of genius – himself and Churchill – and two Conservatives of ability, Birkenhead and Austen Chamberlain, a better man by far than his fatal brother, Neville Chamberlain, one of whose motives in coming back to politics was to keep Lloyd George out. These were men of first-class ability and conscious of it. They could not believe that they would have to submit themselves and the country to the rule of inferior men – as, in the event, they had to. For the next two decades – until the disaster of 1940 forced the return of one of the men tarred in Tory eyes by the Coalition, to save the country in the extreme danger into which years of their rule had led it – Britain was run by those men. Worse still, from top to bottom of the nation's life, in every sphere of it, the country was wanting the flower of its youth and manhood, spilled out in hundreds of thousands to resist the first wave in the criminal adventure of the Germans that has wrecked the twentieth century.

That was not how I thought about it then; but I was young, and I did not know. I was brought up by my Left-Wing friends to think that we were as much responsible for the War as the Germans! Having a mind of my own, it did not take me long – especially after living in Germany, where one could see for oneself what Germans were really like – to think my way through this pernicious rubbish.

There is nothing about the Election in the Diary at the time, though it resulted in the return of the first Labour government – which shows where my heart really was, wherever I supposed my head to be. Mr Baldwin, new to the game of party-leadership, followed his convictions and appealed to the country on the issue of Protection; decisively rejected, he never made that mistake again. Indeed, the dominant political figure in the country for the next fifteen years, he did not seem to have any convictions left, even when it came to the question of his country's safety and very existence – for all that he was for ever talking and posturing about 'England'.

At the Election of December 1923 the country produced five and a half million votes for the Tories, eight and a half million for the Opposition, Liberals and Labour together. That fairly represented the underlying situation of the country during the next two decades. There was *always* a majority in the country against Tory rule; but the Tories managed to precipitate a series of election-scares – over Zinoviev and the Red Letter in 1924, over the Gold Standard in 1931, and with a fake-appeal of standing by the League of Nations in 1935 – which gave them virtually continuous, large majorities in Parliament throughout this period. Until it landed us in a struggle for our very existence in 1939, from which we emerged a second-rate power in the world. I hope the English governing-classes, when they look at what their ancestors achieved for this small island in the world, have a proper feeling of respect for what they have managed to reduce it to in their time.

The unexpected result of this honest Election was to put the Labour party ahead of the Liberals for the first time, with 191 seats against the combined Liberals' 158. We were on our way to seeing the decline and break-up of the great Liberal party, which possessed a much higher average of ability than either of the other two. Unfortunately, it took the Liberals 'an unconscionable time a-dying', and this was another factor in withholding ability that should properly have been employed in the country's service, where it was badly needed. Labour would have gained even more seats, if it had not been for Liberal combinations with the Conservatives in some constituencies to keep Labour out. However, in Parliament the Liberals put the first Labour government in, and maintained it there until it lost control of the situation and, more or less, threw its hand in.

Nothing of all this in the Diary, naturally enough considering my narrow, undergraduate horizons. I find that I was writing articles for a small Labour paper, *The Local Leader*, run by rich Mrs S. at Tonbridge, mother of one of my undergraduate acquaintances. On 2 January 1924, after 'a strenuous day at Penzance' – I think, giving a lecture – I came back to find a telegram clamouring for an article by return of post. So I sat up till midnight, writing a review of a little book of *West Ham Poems*, a kind of forerunner of the proletarian – or would-be proletarian – poetry of the 'thirties.

Back at Christ Church in mid-January, I thought that 'I wasn't so very anxious to be coming back to Oxford this term. All that I love best is at home; and mother and father are getting old. I wonder if I shall get Seconds in my Schools, and have to teach at St A.C.S. after all? From some points of view it wouldn't be a bad prospect: I should be able to live cheaply at home with mother and father, and save money to keep them comfortable. But – it would be the end of all my dreams.' I wondered why I was so fed up, full of vague discontent and obstinate questionings. At Sunday service in the Cathedral, to which as a Scholar I regularly went, the Dean preached on belief and disbelief in God. 'It sounded as if he himself believed in what he was saying; but I felt in a complete morass myself, and unhappy. Then came the Committee meeting of the Labour Club, to which I had to rush. Lunch in the J.C.R., then came back to Tom's rooms to find Wadleigh holding forth about purpose in the universe. For a moment I felt nauseated: it seemed so unreal.'

Far more real to me was the state of the Meadows, now very beautiful under January floods, one big lake over which I watched the sun rising. Instead of worrying to no purpose about purpose in the universe, I set my hand to a poem about the Meadows; it did not work out well. With no sonnet written, and no history read, a Hertford man of crab-like appearance, very dark, crustacean and spectacled, with a curious sputtering delivery, bearded me in my rooms and

> stayed for three solid hours! However, he's an interesting fellow, and knows an immense amount of folk-lore, especially Scandinavian. He has learned old Icelandic and read many of the Sagas. But his enthusiasm doesn't prepossess me: I should prefer the more refined, if decadent, literature of the Troubadours, and the mysterious legends of the Celts. The prospect of learning Icelandic for the English School does not attract me much. J., however, regards me as one of the heathen against whom he wages a campaign. He thinks the Norse peoples have received hard treatment from posterity, and that their whole character has been vilified. But what else, when our opinion of the Norsemen is formed by the literature of the peoples who suffered most at their hands?

And so the argument went on.

'29 January: A hurried note, at a time when I should long ago have been in bed and asleep. It is now half an hour after midnight, and Jones has just gone after an interesting two hours' talk with him.' (This was A. H. M. Jones of New College, to become a friend and join me at All Souls, now the most eminent ancient historian in the country.)

> He went with me to the Essay Club, where Fisher (H.A.L.'s nephew) was reading a paper. I had to open the discussion, and found an opportunity to disagree with the paper over Meredith. Even over Leslie Stephen and Maitland, I couldn't see eye to eye

with Fisher. However, I shall get an opportunity of stating my own view about history and historians, poetry and poets very soon, as Burn wants me to write a paper on 'The Purpose of History' for the next meeting.

This was followed by a humiliating evening at the '19 Club, the shame of which I still remember, the people, the room, the jokes, everything. The '19 Club was a low-brow, rather drinking, club in College which was run by Hillard, Tunnard and Oliff, a rather objectionable crew who were very much the opposite number to my circle, Scholars who did no work, boozed a great deal, and made themselves disagreeable – their form of second-year trouble. At any rate, they were sent down by the College at the end of their second year, and a jolly good riddance. I detested them, all except Hillard, who was a rather fine fellow mis-led by them. But ought one to be afraid of accepting their invitation to enter this bears' den and debate socialism and the new Labour government with them? Certainly not. On the other hand, I was innocent enough to think that they would debate the subject seriously; I hadn't the worldly sense to suspect that they would take the opportunity to bait us.

Wadleigh led off as the senior; he spoke far too long and as he prosed away he lost our chance of establishing a sympathetic, or even a polite, hearing. When it came to my turn, I was baited by a fellow with a West Country name, who wasn't going to let me get hold of people by my usual emotional appeal, interrupted all the way along, and turned the thing into a farce. I was completely put off, and furious with frustration and resentment. They all turned over to the more enjoyable sport of drinking. I wonder if they have had so much fun since? The Diary recognises that I would need a long apprenticeship before I become any good as a speaker. And this was true. I felt that I had it in me to be a good speaker, once I could feel sure of myself, for 'I react quite easily to my audience'. But I was not sure of myself: I was lacking in confidence. In fact, it took years before I gained that confidence. I think it came, largely, as the result of the Election of 1929, when I went home to Cornwall to speak for the Labour candidate anywhere and everywhere, on the soap-box and in the streets. No use flinching there, with a mob around one!

I felt like an infant swimmer, thrown off the deep end into the water, and having to make the best of it. Somewhat breathless I emerged, with some surprise, to find that I was no longer afraid of an audience.

All this incessant talk – not only the formal debates at the Union, the discussions of the clubs, the reading and criticism of papers, but most of all the arguments and exchanges among ourselves – afforded the real medium of education at the university. It was far more important than lectures, of which there were far too many (there are even more today) and from which one learned little: one learned more, in shorter time, from a good book. Reading essays to one's tutor was important, if only because it kept one up to the mark. But I didn't have the luck to have a tutor with a real gift for teaching; one read one's essay, and that was that. When I myself came to teach, I intervened much more actively, not only with regard to the content of my pupils' essays, but with how they were constructed and written. The real process of an undergraduate education at Oxford is that achieved by the undergraduates themselves, a process of dialectic, as the Diary describes in detail such as I had not remembered. The arguments that went on till midnight and after were not loss of time: they formed our minds for us, they hammered out a position, or the foundations of a position, that would serve us through life. (This was where the young Philistines of the '19 Club, resorting more readily to drink, were such fools: they threw away their precious chances.) Here was, and remains, the great advantage of the college system of Oxford and Cambridge: here were assembled some of the cleverest boys in England, in close proximity, constantly in and out of each other's rooms with their thoughts and problems, their fun and jokes.

All was not so serious; there were pleasant interludes. A day or two after our rout at the '19 Club, 'Wadleigh has at last got himself new sofa- and chair-covers for his room. Hitherto it has been so bleak that I call it the "uninhabited island". Now he's got stripey covers, black with green and yellow bands. I wrote a triolet hurriedly this evening to celebrate the event.' Wadleigh was, indeed, hardly a domesticated animal: he had no faculty for creating any comfort around himself; only a woman could do that for him. Whereas Tom Lawrenson and I enjoyed perfect domesticity.

2 February: I am writing this in Thomas's rooms. It's very nice and informal: I am on the sofa with the diary on my knees, and stacks of unanswered Labour Club correspondence by my side. Besides that, Cunningham's *English Industry and Commerce*, for I've got a tutorial on Monday, and my essay still unwritten. Thomas sits before the fire in his armchair and is looking quite business-like over a mathematical tome, but otherwise paternal and pleasant enough. Wadleigh has been here in another emotional crisis. When he gets 'em, Thomas and I will in future cast up eyes to heaven: 'What? Another!' Poor old Henry Julian: not such a deep dog as one would like to imagine. Still, he's very disturbing at times – until one realises that his instinct for playing a part must come out somehow.

One observes the equivocal attitude to H.J.W.: I couldn't help but be attracted by him; but the relationship was not going to be all give on my side, and all take on his. And his very obtuseness brought its reaction on my part: one wasn't one of those who suffer in silence, or indeed suffer at all with impunity so far as the other partner was concerned. I was not a passive type, but always prepared to react actively, beyond a certain point. As for these exhibitions of abasement and self-pity, they filled me with distaste: one put up with what young men have to put up with, without having one's heart out on the carpet in this humiliating Student Christian Movement manner: too vulgar!

Tom Lawrenson and I took comfort in, and derived immense pleasure from, long country walks on Saturdays. This Saturday, out of Oxford by St Aldate's and through Kennington and Radley to Abingdon. We called in at the churches: at Radley I hoped to shock Tom's religious susceptibilities by opening up my umbrella and marching with it like a canopy over my head up the aisle. Alas, I had no such means of electrifying my congregation as the old Cornish clergyman who, at the *Nunc Dimittis* at evensong, would illuminate 'To be a light to lighten the Gentiles' by opening up a pink parasol. (Dear Church of England! – if it didn't exist, it would be necessary to invent it.) 'At Abingdon we had a disappointing tea in a shop looking out on to the Square' – and on Christopher Dempster's splendid Town Hall. 'No boiled eggs as on our last walk; no jug of fresh milk from the landlady's own cows; no vast family teapot to quench two men's thirst after a ten-mile walk.' However, we explored the churches: the fine five-aisled church of St Helen's by the river, prying into vestries and corners to find a piscina here or a stoup there. Then there were the remains of the abbey, with little St Nicholas's at the gate, and John Roysse's Elizabethan Grammar School – an ancient establishment such as I wished I could have attended. And so back by bus, for fear of being late for Hall: even the bus was inviting, as it waited, engines throbbing, in the Town Square. We went on top to a front view: a fine February sunset in the west, through fields and woods to Boar's Hill, whence we saw the lights of Oxford below.

When the week's round began again with cold, inclement, discouraging Monday – for me the days of the week have always had their atmosphere, as for Rimbaud the vowels their colours –

all the other fellows are trooping down the path through Meadows to the ground where the Cupper is to be played; and I am as usual stuck at my desk, with my essay unwritten, looking out of the window and envying them. Not that I want to see a Cupper, but I hate writing history essays ... Had lunch yesterday with the Rawlinsons and the Bishop of Lichfield. I was very pleased to meet yet another bishop. I am getting a considerable acquaintance among them: my early ambition, if not realised actually, is so vicariously. I like Rawlinson more than I can say: he has always been kind and he knows me better than any of the other dons. He has a bond of sympathy with me, I feel; and I sympathise with him because I feel he is unhappy. Perhaps it isn't so; but I have an instinct that I would rather trust than any protestations to the contrary.

It was plain, from the sonnet that follows, that I was not altogether content.

To H.J.W.

My life is like a house that stands alone
Within a garden, buried among trees;
Perhaps a ray of sun or puff of breeze

May stir the darkness and the shadows thrown
Upon the hidden pathways or a wall.
All else is silence, and daylight now has gone –
If anyone should walk there, and should call,
Only an echo, answering, would moan.
But, in the house, the shadows would awake
And stealthily move along the corridors:
Vain hopes and unfulfilled desires would make
Echoes resound as on far phantom shores:
Ghosts would throng and answer at nightfall
If anyone should walk there and should call.

It seems to me now a completely Freudian poem, its innocent imagery recognisably Freudian – the clear reaction to repression. The psychological bearing was obvious enough, though not evidently to the person for whom it was intended. Nobody did come to walk, or was allowed to, in that particular garden; thereby springs poetry. And that was the answer to that.

For the rest, one was immersed in the innumerable activities of term.

6 February: I am suffering a slight reaction after the frantic business of yesterday. Read for nearly four hours this morning, too: perhaps that accounts for the muddled state of my mind. All yesterday morning and afternoon I dashed about Oxford making arrangements for meetings and rooms for the Labour Club. I was thoroughly tired out by the end of the day, and the half-a-dozen or more letters that remained to write even at 10 p.m.

It seems that I must have written a great many letters and done a lot of donkey-work for the Labour Club – as the Minute Book would show, if it survives. 'Well, Thomas has just arrived from the barber's, his head shorn of the immense mass of wavy brown hair that made him look more like a poet than a mathematician. There is a grey-blue mist creeping up the Meadows, and hanging about the trees and housetops nearby.'

The Beazleys, who had migrated to the most beautiful house in

St Giles's, did not forget me. This was the early Georgian Judge's Lodgings, with its elongated windows along the *piano nobile*, its formal approach to the fine doorcase, originally built as the Marlborough family's town-house in Oxford.[1] I was bidden to tea in the splendid room that filled the upstairs front, and observed the entrance hall running right through to the green lawns at the back. I suppose this was an early instance of an experience that became familiar enough later – falling in love with a house. The Diary has an ecstatic description of the old china and screens, the tapestries and white-painted furniture, the views out over gardens and towards St Giles's, sun setting over the roof-tops during tea. 'Very light and airy conversation, such as does not suit me. Mrs Beazley as wonderful and charming as ever. Her daughter Mary and her daughter's friend Josephine as affectionate as young girls could be. With Harrod I made no contact.'

But I was immensely impressed at meeting H. W. Nevinson, the celebrated Left-Wing journalist of those days, famous for reporting the Balkan Wars and for his pro-Boer sympathies. T. B. Causton had kindly asked me to dine in Hall with him and his eminent guest, and afterwards to 'a coffee-party to which all the brilliant Balliol people came: Montague (C.E.'s son), D. R. Gillie, Wynne-Jones and others'. I held Balliol and her intellectual repute in much respect, and unpatriotically wished rather that I had been a Balliol man. We had 'a splendid time. I took up a strategic position in an armchair at the back of the room, whence I could direct the conversation.' In the event, I found that the Balliol men were not unbearably brilliant, and I mastered my nervousness sufficiently to take more than my share in the discussion. Nevinson's talk was 'alive, keen and satirical; his experience of men and affairs of the most extensive', and with an angle of its own. But I was saddened and distressed by a despairing streak, verging on cynicism. 'He's a fine intelligence apt to look on most men as fools, and perhaps at bottom dissatisfied with the small amount of influence it has had upon men. He might have been something better than one of the three greatest English journalists alive. It left me with a feeling of hopelessness on his part: that the

[1] It is described as an Inigo Jones house in Harold Acton's *Memoirs of an Aesthete*. But an aesthete should know the difference between Inigo Jones and Queen Anne.

problems (we ranged over them from the Ruhr to race-problems in South Africa) were too knotted and complex for us to solve.'

I can recall Nevinson still, with his fine, slanting, sculpturesque head (rather like Smuts), piercing bright eyes and ruddy complexion, with his little pointed beard that gave him a Cavalier appearance. I got involved in an argument with him about the Bolshevik treatment of Georgia, about which I knew nothing and Nevinson everything: I had swallowed the Russian propaganda on the subject. Self-determination for small peoples, indeed! The Georgian people, its separate nationality, had been thoroughly steam-rollered. But there was an historic revenge upon the Great Russians to come: Stalin, a Georgian by birth, had no bowels of mercy, consciously or unconsciously, for the Russian people.

Next day, Sunday, 10 February, was no less filled with varied interest and elation. Here is an average Sunday in my second year.

> This morning (except when Splurge of the International Labour Office came to see me: a not very prepossessing individual with pale face, lank hair, horn-rimmed spectacles and spats) for two hours I worked at my paper for the Essay Club. Lunch at J.C.R. A walk round Meadows with Bainbridge. Return to work right up till 5.30. Made tea and sat by the fire drinking hot tea and eating cake (not very nice) and biscuits (rather dry). I was as happy as a lark, however, for my paper was finished; and life is worth living when something, however little, is accomplished. Went to evensong at the Cathedral, and was buoyant enough not to be depressed at the row of shrivelled mummies, the canons, in the stall opposite me.

I gave myself up to the enjoyment of Dr Ley's organ recital, though the transcription of the slow movement from a Vaughan Williams symphony puzzled me by its strange and disquietening sequences. Don Carter, already arrayed for dinner in Hall with an enormous fur-collared coat on top, sat in the stalls opposite. My fellow Scholar thought he was trying to look like a peer, I thought more like a profiteer; in fact he succeeded in looking like his own lazy self. He wasn't puzzled by the Vaughan Williams; he grew more and more restive, making no effort to conceal his distaste, and saying out loud at the end, 'Thank goodness.' That put one rather in favour of Vaughan Williams: my first introduction to the work of one of the greatest Englishmen of the century, whose music came to speak specially to me, with its inner bonds in the liturgy and the life of the Church, its sources in Tudor polyphony and folksong, its revelation of an inner world into whose beauty I could enter all the more poignantly because I could not share its faith.

'Then came Hall and, between eating ham and veal and not eating horrid spinach,[1] I talked against both Fisher and Byam-Shaw, advocating my pet theory that poetry should be short to attain intensity of emotion, and that intensity of emotion is worth more than extensiveness of conception. It is an argument for "Kubla Khan" rather than *Paradise Lost*, and a pretty perverse one.' I remember now that provocative line: it was, of course, a generalisation from my own aptitudes and preferences. It has led me to say, on occasion, that I would rather have written 'Drake's Drum' than *Paradise Lost*! From Hall I went on to my rich American friend, L., who had a large suite of three rooms in Canterbury Quad *plus* a grand piano which he allowed me to play. Thence we proceeded to New College chapel to hear Palestrina's 'Missa Papae Marcelli'. Here, sitting practically on the altar-steps with that mysterious Kyrie Eleison stealing upon the crowded silence, I was in a heaven of ecstasy, until L. informed me in an interval, quite loudly:

'That's William of Wykeham's crosier there.' I said: 'Yes, I know. But people will hear you if you talk so loud.'

L.: I don't give a damn for that.

Later, when I whispered a few words for friendship's sake,

L.: This is the first Perpendicular church in England.

R., laughing: How American of you!

L.: What are you laughing for? (After a pause) Aren't you interested in architecture? All Americans are.

R. (nettled): Well, if you want to know, Perpendicular architecture was developed first at Gloucester Cathedral.

I wasn't sure whether it wasn't fan-tracery, but knew that L. wouldn't know. I was irritated by his presence, preferring always to

[1] I have changed my mind subsequently about spinach – a working-class dislike – as about other things.

hear music alone. But I rather think he had brought me and reproached myself with being 'most unfriendly'. Poor L., a good deal
older and larger than I, had a heart palpitating with sentiment; I fear
it wasn't any use, he received nothing but discouragement.

That week I duly read my paper, 'An Interpretation of History',
to the Essay Club, and attended a symposium of the 'Ordinary': this
was a group of contributors to *The Oxford Outlook*, pivoting upon
Graham Greene and Patrick Monkhouse, who edited the yellow-
covered periodical. This printed the early works of Cecil Day-Lewis,
Robert Speaight, L. A. G. Strong, Emlyn Williams and such who
have become well known since, and others who have been forgotten.
At the end of the week Harold Acton gave a tea-party, 'a novel
affair, for his aesthete friends and Montagu and Clark of the Cambridge Labour Club who came to debate at our meeting last night.
A strange experience for me.' I felt completely out of the talk, which
was all about 'the Sitwells, Pirandello (whoever he may be), D. H.
Lawrence and homosexuality'. This was much too advanced for me.

Worse than this, they talked of the obscurer Victorian painters
and artists: Acton is the apostle of pure 1840. Everybody
admired a stuffy tea-caddy [or did I mean tea-cosy?] that he
had placed under an early Victorian print. And then someone
would say that he had a precious drawing by Sandys or Etty
or somebody that might do for Acton's exhibition, which has
been forbidden by the proctors, who 'could not see that it would
serve any useful purpose'. The trouble was that everybody was
so knowing. Once or twice in my particular corner we got
going on some less esoteric person of interest – Ernst Toller or
Bertrand Russell. Where I knew something about the man, as
in the case of Russell, it was easy to see where their knowledge
came from – the reviews.

All the exquisite bits beyond verbal description I came back
and acted to Wadleigh: how Acton minced about with arms
swaying and long fingers extended. There was the comedy of
the kettle, which had to be refilled and placed on the fire with
languid grace. But the fire wouldn't burn for a big lump of
unbroken coal; so the poet had recourse to the fire-tongs, which

he handled with the delicacy with which he had handed the tea-cups about, and gave the lump of coal two caressing pats. After this he retired from the contest, until some more mundane person took the fire in hand, or we wouldn't have had any tea till morning. Meanwhile the poet floated off to a group to talk art-shops of Florence and theatres of Rome. We were all pro-perly improper; I came away with my head buzzing with phrases like, 'Oh, a charming man: he has a chapter on the coition cry of gold-fish.' I suppose it must have had something to do with D. H. Lawrence. But I'm completely lost.

It was fairly evident that this was no world for me.

Simpler fare was more congenial. André Maurois' *Ariel: ou la Vie de Shelley*, not long out. 'Two nights ago I read that book until half-past two in the morning. I read it to the end, but was starved with cold, and haven't been well since. Must go to bed early tonight, and recover some of the sleep lost. It is getting darker and darker. The bell is ringing to call the people in from the Meadows.'

A few nights later: 'Have just come back from Hall with Wad-leigh, after a walk to Merton to look up a person I can never find at home.' This must have been some Labour Club college secretary whom I had to chase up for subscriptions. I had finished reading R. B. Merriman's biography of Thomas Cromwell, and found it 'an absorbing book: nothing of that sodden soil to plough through of Stubbs or Tout'. Was history gaining on me? Or was it more my kind of history?

'This evening I have been so much excited as not to be able to contain myself – and all about nothing. Nothing has happened very much, except that things and people seem to get friendlier. At Thomas's, before Hall, the spirit moved me to write a poem in the manner of "General Booth Enters Heaven". It was quite a success: I recited it with all the "Booms!" and "Rum-tum-tums" up the staircase where there was an echo.' I was soon brought back to earth, however, and the facts of human nature.

Tunnard has just passed by to his rooms, introducing his friends to my door as 'the abode of the bloody Socialist ...' How the devil he got his scholarship here, I don't know: good coaching I expect. And he has a facility at what Wadleigh calls the decadent art of turning plain English into elegant Latin. At the Perse School Dr W. H. D. Rouse took considerable interest in him, and presented him with a book called *Boche and Bolshevik*, to which he himself had written an Introduction, for fear that Tunnard with his Liberal tendencies might become a revolutionary! It doesn't say much for Dr Rouse's intelligence. All that Tunnard is fit for is the life of a man about town. He has plenty of physical energy, and this might be made use of in furniture-moving [it was] or unloading railway-trucks. His friends too! – Hillard, Oliff and Jacob, the inseparables. But Hillard and Jacob are Rugger blues and as such looked up to; Oliff is President of the '19 Club. I should think there must be a bridge-party in Tunnard's rooms tonight: one hears many footsteps and much slamming of doors.

This little group of big toughs gave me a good many uneasy moments; in a less tolerant college than the House, or in a smaller one, they might easily have turned into persecutors – indeed Tunnard did egg them on into persecuting me a bit. He must have been morally a coward, for he didn't dare to face me himself. He was my nearest neighbour on the staircase, just across the way. Our first greeting had been friendly enough; after all we were both Scholars of the same election; he came from a school I much admired, then at the height of its fame under my namesake (with whom, subsequently, I was often confused). But our paths immediately diverged: I was an intellectual from the working-class, Tunnard a middle-class type who had no intellectual interests whatever and proceeded to waste his time completely. Very gregarious, he was for ever entertaining in his rooms; and, in his second year, shocked me by installing a barrel of beer in his bedroom, to which there was frequent recourse. When his friends got tight, one had to look out: I would 'sport my oak', a stout black door, and the gang of toughs would shout and scream and beat on it, sometimes attempt to pour water through the letter-box, while I sat it out within, heart palpitating with fury and indignation as much as fear, though it was unpleasant. Once I bearded Hillard, who was a decent big chap, at the door and he slunk off rather shamefaced. But the instigator was Tunnard, a nasty type. I can see him now, all the six feet of him, good-looking, fair hair curly, face flushed, roaring and screaming, a puzzled look lighting up the fine animal eyes. He came to an early end. He was a great fool with his life.

What a different world mine was from my neighbour's only a few yards away! The very next day, having got Bertrand Russell to speak for the Labour Club, I went to meet him at the station. Here are my first impressions of that too-famous man, un-overlaid by subsequent experience and the capacity to criticise. I see now that D. H. Lawrence and George Santayana, who both knew him well, were right about him: on one side, the intellectual, the ratiocinative and logical, a man of genius; on the other, with regard to human beings and affairs and therefore politics, out of touch and uncomprehending, arrogant and often silly. Of course there is a connection between being so very clever at mathematics and logic, and so fatuous about people and politics. Human affairs – as a great practitioner, Catherine the Great, said of the ideologues – do not march *comme sur le papier qui souffre tout*. People do not behave like mathematical digits. G. M. Trevelyan, who, as an historian, understood about human beings and, as a contemporary of Russell's at Trinity, knew him well, said to me: 'He may be a good mathematician – I don't know about that; but he is, and always has been, a goose about politics.' Added to this is the arrogance of the intellectual, prepared to lay down the law about a subject he doesn't know about. (Why can't they see this? I don't lay down the law about mathematics and philosophy: I am prepared to listen to them. On the other hand, I can tell them something about history and politics; and that is where *they* should listen.)

Here is the ingenuous observer of twenty.

At the station I recognised him from the Rothenstein portrait that I once had a glimpse of in Blackwell's. A very good likeness, yet I remember it as quieter and less alert than Russell's countenance actually is. It did not convey the impression of aggressiveness that one gets from the face in the life. What an extraordinary head it is! Most unprepossessing I thought at first: I wondered how any woman would want to marry him. And

Russell's voice! so far from being well-produced or full and resonant, it is harsh and rasping and comes from the throat instead of being thrown forward in the mouth. But I didn't find him hard to talk to, though his remarks were few at first. He was so shabbily dressed that I wondered if he found it a struggle to exist. After all his books can't bring him in much money: they appeal to a small audience. As for the press, very few papers can be open to him for the complete expression of his views.

All this has changed since then. A writer has only to survive, in the English environment, till eighty to be regarded as a sage and listened to with veneration, whether what he talks is nonsense or not – and Russell is now on his way to a hundred. With the loosening of controls – apparently he has forgotten that only a few years ago he actually advocated a preventive war against Russia! – there is such a thing as specific old man's vanity.

In his fifties, then, Russell was kind and courteous to the young men – I was very much his disciple. We brought him to my rooms before taking him on to the Good Luck Tea Rooms (!), according to Labour Club custom, for dinner, 'while I, also according to custom, forgot to take my name off Hall and will be charged for dinner there'. Poor Russell, how bored he must have been! I have remembered to this day his saying that before having to make a speech he always hoped that he might fall down and break a limb or that the earth would open and swallow him up. Innocently, I interpreted this to mean that he felt nervous, and it had an encouraging effect on me thereafter. For I was so fearfully self-conscious that, though I had the temperament of a speaker, I could scarcely make a coherent speech at all. And here was the great man of my admiration confessing himself to be nervous! It was very encouraging.

At dinner Russell opened out, and

one could see from the character of his remarks the character of the man. What he said was so precise, so logical: no muffiness or haziness of thought about him. I should have loved Wadleigh to come and talk with him: B. Russell would have applied a little of the necessary realism to Wadleigh's earnest religiosity.

The things that Russell said later about the Church, Wadleigh would have agreed with; but the way in which he went further in antagonism to what the ardent call 'the very essence, the spirit of religion' would have been salutary for St Julian.

Russell gave us a very good time, 'his speech a marvel of lucidity and insight'. One remark at the outset gave me some pause. 'He had been asked, he said, to speak on the Philosophic Basis of Socialism. But he had a certain respect for philosophy, and wasn't willing to force it into contact with things of everyday life.' I perceive now how revealing that disjunction was, the fatal weakness of having one's philosophical position on one side, and one's view of human affairs on the other: they should be brought into relation with each other, in one coherent frame of thought. The youth's instinct, at twenty, brought up short by this disjunction, was not wrong, though I did not know how to deal with it at the time: there was something fundamentally unsatisfactory in Russell's position. Finding that out was part and parcel of one's education – a process of self-education by experience.

*   *   *

Exciting as the public world was, the inner world yielded more delight and meant more. I find that the motto for this week of 24 February 1924, in my I.L.P. Engagements book was from Carlyle: 'One Monster there is in the world – the idle man.' No one could say that I qualified for that. On the day when the Essay Club was meeting in my rooms at night I find:

A miracle has come about. Ten minutes ago before I sat down to lunch, the sky appeared to be darkening and it was getting still colder. And now when I get up and come to the window, I see the ground and the housetops all covered with snow. My trees stand up black and gaunt against the white background of the meadows, but along their boughs run lines of white where the snow has caught and held. It is all very beautiful, and I hope snow will fall throughout the afternoon. There is such a happy sensation to be got from sitting in by the fireside, when the world outside is white with snow.

In this intense inner life, there were troubles, too. Evidently a second crisis had supervened in my relations with Wadleigh.

> I have felt so desolate all today: as if all the heart had gone out of things. I spent a bitter half-hour with him last night. I felt ill, it is true, and so what he said in all friendliness I detested. And then the devil took hold of me, and I said the bitterest things that came into my mind. Whatever happens, I must not devote my thoughts to him in the least way. Two terms ago I thought I had shaken myself free of that: that was while C-J. [his Student Christian Movement buddy] doted on him, so it wasn't difficult to keep away. I didn't go to his rooms, nor do I much now: he comes to mine. I think I see my way clear. What I must do is what I decided two terms ago, and from which I have deviated somewhat lately. My own life is bound to be lonely, and I have accepted it. The difficulty comes only when I am tempted out of the way of my own making. I shouldn't think of sparing him, or anybody else: do I spare myself?

The next entry reveals something of the process of making oneself accept (or perhaps, not accept – according to view).

> A beautiful evening, with a kind of soft glow from the sun lighting up one side of the tree-trunks, and the mere edge of the stone-work of my window ... But I am not happy all the same. It will be a long process forgetting all about Henry Julian again. I almost did it once before, and I shall have to make myself go over the same path. Henry Julian himself will be oblivious of it all: as usual. I wonder what he's doing now at Marlborough? Sitting out reading somewhere, or perhaps tramping home from a long walk. I don't suppose it bothers him much, what happened on Sunday night: he'll have his girl to think about.

And I don't suppose it did.

I understand the essence of the situation now more clearly, though I think I understood it even then well enough. It was not possible to take for granted my devotion, or even my friendship, and have all the other things in addition. Everything in life had its price: I had learned that the hard way. (It was a help years later, as an historian, in understanding the psychology of the 'inscrutable' Elizabeth I and in writing about her.)

After this, there is not much more in the Diary about H.J.W.: I succeeded in killing that affection. For his third year he chose to move out of college, while we Scholars in general remained in college. Very well; he had chosen: he could not have the best of both worlds. When he came into college occasionally he made various attempts to join in as of old in the quiet companionship of Thomas and me, to come to our rooms as we sat and worked for our Schools. I saw to it that he was not welcome, erected a psychological barrier which he could not get through, in fact excluded him. It was a process not without its moments of rather bitter pleasure: after all, one must have iron in one's composition. He got his inevitable Second in Honour Moderations – he didn't think highly of the process of turning English into Latin and Latin into English. He fancied himself as a philosopher and took Greats with great portentousness. He went on to get a Second here, too.

There were always other fish in the sea, even if they did not mean as much to one. Here was one who sought me out.

After the Symposium last night, G. P. Fisher came round to my rooms and we argued Materialism until 2.15 a.m. By that time all the lights on the staircase were out and he had to feel his way down the stairs and across the quad. A typically English brain, not without grit and tenacity for all its idealism, but slow and rigidly inflexible. I don't think he can be open to any new ideas at all. F. is going to be a pro-consul, his aim the Indian Civil Service. And he somehow works it out that this career is inspired by the idea of social service and self-sacrifice. Why not say that his motive is social service and self-interest? Why these people suppose that making the most of one's abilities is opposed to the service of the community, I don't understand: surely the rational view to take is that they work towards the same end, except with sub-normal and criminal people. It is the man who reconciles his duty to himself and his duty to the social group, and identifies their interest, that will make some contribution to the world.

5

I find in this the germ of the political theory which I worked out later: sketched very inadequately in *Politics and the Younger Generation*, developed more fully in the lectures I used to give in the later 1930s, the notes of which I have never published. The tall, lanky, good-tempered fellow with whom I used to have these arguments comes back to my mind, though I had not thought of him for years: very fair curly hair, gold-rimmed spectacles, blue eyes, long horse-face and jaw. Alas for his idealism and social service, he was killed playing polo in India.

At the end of the week Tom and I had a fine walk, on the first Spring day, to Nuneham and Baldon. What a vanished world! At Baldon we had honey for tea –

> Stands the church-clock at ten to three?
> And is there honey still for tea? –

in a little house where a woman kept shop.

She apologised for the quietness of life there, and the unpreparedness as to food in which we found her. She said all the villages round about belonged to Queen's College, and all the fields. I suppose the colleges make better landlords than the county magnates. The countryside looked prosperous enough, and yet the life of these country people must be near the margin. The woman, I believe, was going to have a baby. It was a pity, for she had a tiny boy who kept her occupied, and she was a little irritable and plaintive. Her house was crowded with furniture, the walls plastered with pictures. She was a fine figure of a woman, big and muscular; but her hair was lank and she had a worried expression. I wonder what sort of a man she has got? They own their house; that makes things a little less difficult.

Already the evidences of the new age, the hideous world that has engulfed us, pressed in upon us. 'The continual stream of cars along the main road distressed us', and at Nuneham we turned off down by-lanes. On the way back I had my first view of the horror of Morris-Cowley. 'What an immense expanse of monotonous corrugated iron and brick walls! Thomas was quite unperturbed about it, and said if I wanted to see industrialism I must come to South Shields. The Cowley works must employ hundreds of men, and yet what an uprooting of the old, placid country life! An old man working in the fields stopped to watch the stream of seven newly-finished cars leaving the shed and taking the road. He seemed to admire; but I wonder if he hadn't some regrets.' (A pencilled note written in 1938, the year of Munich, comments: 'Not he – nor thoughts either.')

The programme I had managed to fix up for the Labour Club that term, in spite of the difficulty of getting hold of Labour leaders now that they were immersed in government, worked out quite successfully. We began with a Dons' Debate in the American Club Rooms at which Malcolm MacDonald and Schofield, a Ruskin College don, spoke; also Stanley Casson, who became a well-known Greek archaeologist and went down in a plane off the coast of Cornwall during the war. In addition to Russell, we had Phillips Price to tell us about the Russian Revolution, of which he had been an eye-witness; E. D. Morel, to put us all wrong about the causes of the war and the Treaty of Versailles; Pethick-Lawrence, sensible old Cornish-man but rather waterlogged with economic statistics; a debate with the Cambridge Labour Club, and a Social at the end of term.

Nevertheless, when it came to electing next term's chairman, I had to take second place to a woman from Somerville, it is true, my senior in the Club. I had a majority of first preferences, and then my particular friends from New College, Jesus and Trinity ganged up to put her in on second preferences. She made an excellent Chairman, with more *sang-froid* than I had. I came in at the head of the Committee with over eighty votes, against other people's sixties and forties – tribute to my hard work for the Club, I suppose. This did not console me: I wanted my third year completely free to devote myself to work for Schools. The prospect would be spoiled if I were to be Chairman in my last year. That, of course, was what came about. When I wanted to be Chairman, it wasn't forthcoming; when I didn't want it, I was elected without opposition. That has been very much the pattern of my life all through, when it has depended on other people.

Before term ended, I had another bout with a nearer enemy,

ulcer-formation: for anyone interested in clinical history – the rhythm seems to have been one bout a term.

10 March 1924: I should obviously be at work on my essay for this evening's tutorial. As usual I can't; and as usual my stomach is in a wretched state. I wonder if it's all due to mental worry? I'm coming to think more and more it is, as these periods of indigestion and sleepless nights occur in the busiest times, just when I've got most things on hand to do. I don't want to be a dyspeptic for the rest of my life. Nor do I want to have to nurse myself over meals, to be careful and slow in eating, and all the rest of it.

I remember once arriving for a tutorial with Feiling, who very kindly offered me tea, but saw that I was in obvious pain. He said, 'If this goes on, I shall have you operated.' But I had had an operation the year before and thought that that had put everything right. Whom to ask? If only I had had a good doctor, it might have saved years of increasing anguish; but I couldn't afford to go to a doctor. I plodded on, hoping all would be well ...

It was in these rather depressed periods that I consoled myself with poetry. I find this little poem at this time:

Evening

A cool and quiet ending
　　To the hot day;
And mists wind up the valley,
　　Blue and grey.

A bird sings in the darkling
　　Boughs of the trees;
And all the noise of the city
　　Now sinks to peace.

O, such a magic moment
　　In days to be
Will be as the green, sweet land
　　After the sea.

I suppose it was written in some mood of release from torment –

there were such, thank goodness, even in these bad spells. And the moment I was better my spirits shot up to the ceiling. Here was a walk with Thomas, along the upper river by Hinksey and Wytham, to the Trout Inn at Godstow, with oak settles and willow-pattern china, and a crowd of arty undergraduates, so that we had to wait a long time for tea. So, while we waited:

> How long do we wait for tea
> In this very aesthetic place?
> What good is aesthetic to me?
> How long do we wait? For tea
> There's no prospect that I can see
> Of getting much more than grace.
>> How long do we wait for tea
>> In this very aesthetic place?

The whole point of a triolet – absurd form – was to break the sense, without changing the words, in the fourth line.

When I got home for the Easter vacation, there were other worries to think about. I had 'flu, but was finishing Trevelyan's *England under the Stuarts* notwithstanding.

Father's at home with a little complaint of his own: I believe it's overwork. But there's no money for him to stop and have a rest. And there's no prospect of his ever having a lighter job, until I can make it so for him. I lose all patience when I think of the position the family stands in, and the handicap it has always been not to have enough money to go round. It's a handicap I am tired of having to put up with. When I go down from Oxford I suppose I shall be all right, whatever job I get. But then all my plans for tramps in Brittany and France will have to go over, if I have to provide for these people who hadn't sense enough when they were young to provide against old age. It's obvious that I am not likely ever to be able to marry. Not that I want to. But to have parents is as much to give hostages to Fortune as to have children.

These last few days at home have tired me out with thinking how to make ends meet and what to do for the future. One night I couldn't sleep for thinking about it. And mother and father never cease to talk about it.

I see now that it was bad for one psychologically to identify one-self so much with them: after all, they were simpler and tougher than I was, and they hadn't so much on their minds. It merely piled the resentment up – not at all good for the ulcer. 'It would have been more to the point if they had done something when they were in health and able. They are getting old and decrepit now. There's no prospect for them, apart from my future. It's unthinkable what would happen to them if I were to die. I've made up my mind to take out an insurance policy on my life.'

A week later my black mood had vanished – for I was working satisfactorily, 'flu over. '2 April: I have just come down in happy mood from that cold eyrie, my bedroom.' I had an uncomfortable, slim, cane arm-chair, into which I fitted myself, rug over my knees, beside the window that gave me a glimpse of the sea between the roofs, and at the end of the road a long view towards Tregrehan and the woods of Trenython. 'For I have managed to stick a whole afternoon at Maitland's translation of Gierke's *Political Theories of the Middle Age*; moreover, there's a cup of hot tea in prospect. My hands are so cold I can scarcely direct my pen into the usual scrawl. There is a bitter east wind abroad, that keeps people indoors. My reading proceeds irregularly, but quickly. Last night I stayed up to 1.30 a.m. to read Rosebery's *Pitt*.' Besides that I had read Trevelyan, Fournier's two heavy volumes on Napoleon, Flecker's Poems and was now embarked on all three volumes of Carlyle's *Letters and Speeches of Oliver Cromwell*. 'The further I go into the book, the higher is my opinion of it, and of the character of Cromwell. But it is a hard struggle not to be prejudiced by the manner of Cromwell's matter – all the phrases about the Lord's mercies, providences and dispensa-tions, "Truly God is loving unto Israel", and such.' Moreover, wasn't the whole tendency of this Puritan revolutionary, who had overthrown King and Church, conservative once he himself was on top? 'For the orders of men and ranks of men, did not that Levelling principle tend to the reducing of all to an equality? Did it think to do so; or did it practise towards that for property and interest?

What was the purport of it but to make the tenant as liberal a fortune as the landlord? Which, I think, if obtained would not have lasted long! The men of that principle, after they had served their own turns, would then have cried up property and interest fast enough!'

But wasn't that true of everyone? As my reading in history and political theory progressed I came to see that everybody's views – except those who were taken in – were but generalisations of their own interest. This thought possessed me more and more. Was there no disinterestedness to be found anywhere? Was there no objective truth in society, in political theory or economics? What was the relation between interest and value? What constituted value, over and above men's interest in giving it value? Was there any disinterested political speculation over and above men's party or group interests? If one were an adherent of the monarchy in the 17th century, one thought, with Filmer, that the Divine Right of Kings was true. If one were an opponent of the monarchy, like Locke, one believed that a contractual theory of sovereignty was true. Was there any objective truth in the matter? Did people even care about objective truth, or merely advancing their own interests, putting forward their preconceptions already arrived at on other grounds?

These questions bothered me more and more as I got further and deeper into my historical reading for Schools. I was genuinely perturbed – and there was no one to help. I don't think my history tutors knew that, under the surface of my not very satisfactory showing, I was heading for a genuine intellectual crisis. How to think my way out of this dilemma? Was there no objectivity, no disinterestedness, no truth? It was a genuine crisis of historical relativism: my thinking came to revolve around it more and more, especially in my third year, with the extra spurt one put on for Schools. I used to think it was partly a function of overwork, and exhibited some of the phenomena that might have led to a nervous breakdown; for it became an obsession, like the obsession that accompanied John Stuart Mill's breakdown, that one day all the possible combinations of musical notes would be exhausted. All the same the problems were genuine ones, and I did not come to terms with them until years later, when I did my best to think them out in the chapter on 'Historical Thinking' in *The Use of History*.

The vacation was given up almost entirely to reading, varied by walks. There was one with Len Tippett, in bright Easter sun and wind, across the cliffs from Charlestown to Crinnis. The clarity of the light brought out the copper, ochre and orange colours of those cliffs more sharply than I had seen them before, while the sea had a gem-like brilliance. The tide was out, and we could see fresh strips of uncovered sand gleaming at the base, while rocks and seaweed appeared distinct in every detail beneath translucent water. We were in the right mood for enjoyment of the sea, cliffs, the gorse at its brightest, butter-colour, and talk. That day a letter came from David Low, 'asking me for the fifth time to come and spend a few days in London. I very much want to do it, but am at this moment without a penny in the world even to go back to Oxford. I shall have to borrow from mother, and that's painful, for she has no money till M. sends some. The letter on several grounds disquiets me. And my little hour of content has already vanished.'

As usual when discouraged I sought consolation in poetry. There follows this little poem:

The Sea

When the night draws in to close
   The weary work,
And earth's a darkened rose
   Where shadows lurk;

The dust of the day now dim
   And far behind,
My thoughts sink under the rim
   Of my own mind;

And, tired as my eyes may be,
   They find at will
A shining peace on the sea,
   When earth is still.

Another little poem depicts the mood at the end of the day. 'Duty lay before me in the shape of Pollock and Maitland's *History of English Law*; but the evening has been too wonderful to keep me at the grindstone.' So –

Spring

All day the wind and rain
Have swept the land,
Laying upon the meadows
A heavy hand.

The trees within the garden
Are lank, forlorn;
The daffodils, a cluster
Of stars, are shorn.

And now the wonder opens:
The sky is riven,
In the strange light flickers
A luminous heaven.

Was history entirely winning over literature?

My last Sunday at home – 'another day of furious wind and driving rain' – I read Gibbon's *Autobiography*. I finished it just after midnight. 'Bed-time now. The wind is still howling about the doors and windows. Father has to get out at 4.30 a.m., which is really 3.30 a.m. It is hateful for a man of his years. I hope it will be milder tomorrow, and that he won't renew that nasty cold he had for so long.' The Diary brings home, what I had not recollected at all, the constant concern for my people: a nicer boy than the man, disillusioned about others and hardened by contacts with them, having taken 'the contagion of the world's slow stain'. I did not much care for Gibbon *then*: 'the whole book strikes me as vain and yet impassionate: it has a cold conceit. I don't see that Gibbon is particularly cynical; but his life suffered from its lack of love. A lonely creature he must have been at heart, for all his vain enjoyment of society.' And then – a moment of insight into the future: 'it's much the same path that I have engaged myself to tread.' I consoled myself with Gibbon's consolation: 'I was never less alone than when by myself.'

On my way back to Oxford I made a detour to stay at last with Low in London, since that was the cheapest way of availing myself of his invitation. It was only my second visit to the metropolis, my first having been on the never-to-be-forgotten occasion when I extracted a scholarship from the willing gentlemen of the Drapers' Company in Throgmorton Street. I well remember the kindness of David Low and his mother, and also the way David's fad about a-symmetry conflicted with my fixation on symmetry. David had dis-arranged the ornaments in my bedroom so that one candlestick was on the mantelpiece, the other on the dressing table, and so with everything else. This drove me frantic; I could not go to sleep until I had rearranged the poor candlesticks properly and everything else in symmetrical order. This led to no quarrel, for David always had an angelic disposition. He conducted me everywhere, by day to St Paul's and Southwark Cathedrals and the National Gallery, at night to Shaw's *Saint Joan* in its first sensational production with Sybil Thorndike, and to Rutland Boughton's *The Immortal Hour*, which was having an extraordinary popular success, swept me off my feet and filled my head with its Celtic nonsense and idiosyncratic harmonies.

A mysterious entry in my Engagements Book, 'Oracle, 11 Doyle Gardens, Kensal Rise, N.W. 10', I think refers to a programme which Harold Acton, with his flair for publicity, put across the early B.B.C. A troupe of us young Oxford poets were summoned by his masterly *bâton* to speak our poems into a wireless mouthpiece. There we all were – I can't remember anybody but the wizard Harold and Graham Greene with the marvellous china-blue eyes; I came at the tail-end of the more important poets (i.e. Harold) with a modest and fortunately short poem, for I felt the ridiculousness of the occasion and feared that I might giggle into the instrument. That was my first introduction to broadcasting – unpromising and unpropitious, and long, long ago.

Arrived back at Oxford, by the end of April I was 'somewhat more reconciled to it than at first. I didn't much want to leave home and return to the loneliness of this place. Home is the centre of my life and my longing.' I was overjoyed to come upon the new head-master of my old school, Barritt, and his wife, in the Broad. 'How happy I felt at seeing these people from home. They came round to my room, but would not stay to have some tea. I felt disappointed. But Thomas came and read; then Otis and Low arrived, full of the meeting at Ruskin where W. N. Ewer spoke. Quite a gay circle we made around the fire; and they have only just gone, leaving me with the embers.' My familiar worries about my people, and what would happen to them if I were to die, revived with my leaving home. And there was the worry about myself, whether I had not 'killed my affection for individual people: there is a price to pay for damming up one's natural inclinations in order to achieve an artificially increased strength'.

Other people had their troubles, too. Here is one who became a well-known Conservative politician, a kind-hearted, good man. 'I talked to —— last night for two hours in the J.C.R. I should never have suspected him of neurasthenia; but now that I see what is the matter with him I am repelled by the spectacle. It seemed to me dangerously near the borderland between sanity and insanity that he talked about.' What was wrong with him? – he was very rich and very nice. However, he came through all right; we were all young men afflicted with growing pains: time would show whether we could come through or go under. The touching thing is to reflect now how many of these young men went under, the wastage in the upper classes being so much higher than lower down in society: they expose themselves so much more, take more risks, move about the world more. Moreover, I do not suppose that it is a condition natural to man to have a more than average intelligence. It incurs strain.

The term's first meeting at the Labour Club strikes a new note.

The impromptu debate on the McKenna duties went quite well, for I (as usual) didn't speak. And yet, I am very tired of it all – all those people with their entirely academic points of view; the stock phrases with unmeaning professions of faith. What does it mean when people like de Gruchy and Woodward say, 'Now, *we*, as Socialists', in a politician's manner? It's sickening when they have little comprehension what their position is. But I have none at all; I am like a tired man, or perhaps a tired child. What is upon me I do not know. It may be physical lassitude.

It then dawned upon me, innocently, 'perhaps it is that the best of my energy goes into my work, with no very obvious results so far.' There follows an account of my reading in the last few days: Arthur Young's hefty *Travels in France*, a dull text-book on the

French Revolution, the reactionary Fortescue's *British Statesmen of the Great War* (i.e. the French Revolutionary war). To cheer myself up, I had read Wilde's *A Woman of No Importance*, some of Turgenev's *Dream-Tales* and Lytton Strachey's *Eminent Victorians*. Strachey's *Queen Victoria* I had had to read in 'Chaundy's little bookshop in the High, where a copy was on the shelves at 10s. 6d. The price was beyond me, and all the afternoon I stood turning over its leaves'. I was quite bowled over by the famous virtuoso passage at the end, suggesting the Queen's memories as she lay dying, going further and further back in her mind to rest at last with earliest childhood and 'the trees and the grass at Kensington'.

This was more rewarding to the spirit than electioneering, and marching up and down St Aldate's as a sandwich-man with a placard round my neck: I always felt a fool doing that sort of thing.

> There is an election campaign on in Oxford at the moment; Kenneth Lindsay is putting up as Labour candidate. But I haven't the least interest in the struggle; it seems to me much the same thing if a Tory gets in, as if a Labour man does. What difference does it make? It is just a sense of duty, or perhaps vanity, which kept me working (along with Wadleigh, Burn, Otis, Jones and Whitehead) till 2.30 a.m., and again this afternoon at pasting a card-index of the Oxford electorate for headquarters. A merry circle we were around that table, jabbering and pasting, snipping and swearing into the early hours of the morning. But to what purpose?

There was the oddity: fanatic and proselytiser outside, very far from fanatic, indeed a sceptic, within. It was, indeed, a lucky thing that, underneath all the pressures, I kept my writing going, never allowed it to die on me in deference to the external demands. But it wasn't luck or chance, for the inner thing was my real life, I see now: I was meant for a writer. But the dichotomy between my inner and my outer life, the life of reflection and the impulse towards action, lasted right through the 'thirties until it nearly ended my own life, with the desperate illness and operations just before the war. Taking some part in politics was unnaturally prolonged, as an elementary duty, by the crazy course of Appeasement the country was led into in the 'thirties. If it hadn't been for that, I should have had no valid intellectual reason for not being a Conservative – most of my instincts were conservative – and dropping politics. But – with Baldwin and Chamberlain leading a bemused country down the easy slopes to the gravest danger in our history, one simply couldn't. In agony, mental and physical, one dragged oneself on.

Would it have been a good thing if, in the 1920s, I had taken no interest in politics at all? I suppose one could hardly have helped oneself – as with Henry Adams, with whom also it led to nothing. In the long run it may have helped one's understanding of history, provided one with a practical experience of collective human foolery, which is the foundation of any understanding of history or politics. I suppose it was part of the process of one's education, the tensions – though towards the end, with the war coming nearer and nearer, they almost tore one apart – may have creatively enriched one's experience. Yet, how I regret the sheer time lost now, on other people's worthless affairs, or, to be more just, their affairs of little worth. Would it have been better if I had given myself up to the more educative delights of social life, like Cyril Connolly and Evelyn Waugh, gone to the châlet with Sligger Urquhart and the clever boys? Or taken more professionally to ecclesiastical archaeo-logy with the young Betjeman, and with a *petit beurre*

> Satisfying fleshly wants,
> Settled down to Norman fonts?

Or been introduced to the still more educative salon of dear Maurice (Bowra)?

I should certainly have received more backing, than by going my own independent, obstinate way. I am sorry now that I made things so difficult for myself. One's writing, instead of being a lamp under a bushel, would have come into the light of day along with the others, instead of having to wait on Baldwin and Chamberlain, Mussolini and Hitler, and then universal tragedy – until one hardly cared any more about anything. Shade of Henry Adams! – how well you, if only you, understand ...

At this point, there stare up at me from the Diary the words of one who paid a worse price for her involvement in politics, Madame

Roland's words written the night before she was guillotined: '*Dieu juste, reçois-moi. A trente-neuf ans.*'

In spite of the distractions of politics and working for Schools, I went to the Playhouse when I could: I find myself criticising the plays better than I could now – at any rate, I am surprised at the regular habit I had formed and the confidence. Here was Ibsen's *The Lady from the Sea:*

> a poor play, and worse acted. The idea is fine enough, but the manner incongruous with it. Moreover, it should have worked itself out to the only real end – the woman returning to the sea with whose spirit she is one, and where alone she will find her freedom. The introduction of the notion that freedom of choice will set her conscience at rest is unnecessary; as it is, it is also unconvincing. I can see how the play ought to have been written: like one of Yeats's, played throughout in a subdued atmosphere, full of mystery and silences. No trivialities such as the tutor's paying court to Boletta, or the sculptor and his life-work, should have come in. The theme of the woman's struggle for freedom and peace against the ties of duty and love should have had no accessories ... That is how my play is to go when I write it; for I have often thought of 'Joan o' the Moor' as a play. That lonely half-crazed woman who used to roam over the moor at Carn Grey in the evenings shall become a wild creature whose home is the moor, whose reason has gone amid the hardship and sorrow of her childless life. All the love she would have given her children, she has given to the moor.

And so on. This was a theme for a ballad or a story that haunted my mind when I remembered Carn Grey and the crazed woman I used to watch roaming in the distance over the moor in the evenings. I never did anything with it, not even a short poem: another of the sacrifices I made to the delights of politics and political meetings. Like Father D'Arcy's evocation of proselytising in Hyde Park: four persons under an umbrella in a downpour of rain, of whom three are already converted. On a more exalted plane, I note another sacrifice. On a Saturday in early May Harold Acton invited me to a session with Miss Sitwell at 4 p.m. There is nothing about it in the Diary –

though there is a good deal about it in his *Memoirs* – so I think I cannot have gone. I have a vague memory of going a little late, finding the room crowded and going away again. What a loss! much more fun than all the politicians, and I was really too modest.

My writing life went on more under the surface. Here I was working late into the night at my desk: 'I looked up just now, and could see a wonderfully clear picture of myself in the blackness of the window-pane. There was the red shade over the lamp, hanging like a flower in space; and beyond, behind me as well as before, the black masses of the doors that at any moment might open.' In the stillness of the reflected world watching, I made myself afraid. And indeed, I found a new subject for exploration and to turn into poems – the emotion of fear.

I suppose this may also have been partly a consequence of overwork, but I had always been susceptible to fear from my childhood. Going to bed held nameless terrors for me for years; I suppose I ought to be ashamed to confess it, but I am still liable to night-terrors – a primitive Celt. It wasn't a thing to cultivate beyond a certain point: one might easily push oneself over the edge. But I was very much interested. Here is a scene that might have come straight out of my forbears' life in the village at home. 'One night the electric lights went out, and four of us sat round the fireside in Wadleigh's room. In the flicker of the firelight I told them horror-stories, until they dared not move. I put a spell on Wadleigh that night. He scarcely dared go into his bedroom, he told me afterwards.'

This particular experience, myself in the reflected world, went straight into a poem, 'The Shadows in the Glass', which was published in *The Oxford Outlook* that June, and in *Poems of a Decade*, when I ultimately summoned up courage – not until the war – to publish a volume of poems at all. The poem had an authentic experience in it, the sensation of fear; and to express it, I had at length hit on a form that suited me – rhymed couplets, but disconnected, two by two. This gave the more extended sense of time that I wanted. I became much attached to writing poems in this form, with which I identified myself. I cannot say whether I had achieved a recognisable style of my own as yet – though David Cecil used to say that my poems had their own 'smell', their individual atmosphere – but here was a form that was more flexible and satisfactory than the sonnet, to which I had obstinately held. In the next numbers of *The Oxford Outlook* I find more poems in this form: 'The Immortal Hour', a less satisfactory one, 'Allegory', a better one; but these I did not re-publish.

Living the kind of life I did, unlike Acton and Quennell, I did not make the most of my acquaintance with the poets – indeed I made nothing of it at all. (However, Harold and P.Q. were not under the necessity of working for Schools. They could give their time to the poets, and other little things.) The week after I had been so silly as to miss Edith Sitwell, I was meeting Robert Graves. He was coming to give a paper at the Ordinary, which I helped to run. Among my immense *Archiv* I find a pleasant letter from the World's End at Islip, where he was then living with his wife, who, by way of being emancipated, wouldn't take his name but insisted on being called Mrs Nancy Nicholson. I asked him to dinner. The poet replied:

> Many thanks. I make it a rule not to dine in Halls unless I can do so without wearing a dinner-jacket: giving this paper involves 14 miles pushbiking, perhaps in the rain. Kindly reassure me by postcard and I'll call for you 7.15. If you can't, expect me in Curtis' Rooms at 8.15. I have a fairly decent address ready. Yours ever, ROBERT GRAVES.

The poet duly turned up: I remember him on my staircase, a big dark fellow in breeches with a knapsack, gipsy complexion, fine head, rugged, uneven features, black curly hair, half-Irish, half-Greek in appearance, at any rate Mediterranean in type. Rather god-like to me, since he was a survivor from the war-generation I idolised, a name to me along with Siegfried Sassoon, Robert Nichols, Richard Hughes, most of whom had come back to Oxford after the war and only just gone down – or, rather, up to Boar's Hill to join Robert Bridges and Masefield, 'a nest of singing birds' as Dr Johnson said of Pembroke College in his time. Here was one of them in the flesh. Sad to say, I can't remember a word of what he said, merely an idiotic remark I made to console him, complaining of a large family of children: 'Happy is the man that hath his quiver full of them.' (I did not really mean it.) To which the poet replied, rather disconsolately, pointing out that the Jewish quiver held only two or three arrows: he already had five children. I got the impression that this kept him pretty poor.

This was the time, too, of my first acquaintance with Lord David Cecil. He suddenly arrived in my rooms one day, unannounced, unintroduced, to talk literature with me. I rather think it was Masterman who suggested he should look me up. This strange apparition, with the very rapid, highly Cecilian manner of speech that must be familiar now to thousands of television-viewers, somewhat electrified me: I made out only two out of every three words he uttered. But there was a common interest in our passion for literature, and subjects, themes, literary topics were what we talked about – later on, adding history and politics.

Two years my senior, he was then living out of college in rooms in Beaumont Street – in the days when those fine Georgian houses were still lived in and were not mere offices or institutions. He asked me along to lunch: it would have been kinder to ask me to tea, for I foresaw that some fearful social obstacle would rear its ugly head. It did – in the form of asparagus – and I was inwardly vexed. How did one eat it? It was the same conundrum that was raised in an aristocratic Officers' Club under the Nazis: how did the Führer eat his asparagus? I could not bring myself to plunge my fingers into the mess, as my host did without ado; so I proudly left it on the side of my plate. I was very pleased at being asked by him, 'but he seemed a strange creature at first, almost a product of another civilisation. However, I like him, and I got to appreciate his opinions after the ordeal of lunch was over, and we got out for a walk around the park at Magdalen.' This was the prelude to a friendship that became much closer when he was established as a Fellow at Wadham and I at All Souls.

As for my work, I was far from satisfied with myself: 'of all the reading I do, I don't see much in the way of result.' The plain fact was that, as yet, I couldn't see the wood for the trees. I was reading hard enough, but not always what was required of me or at the time my tutors expected it. I could only hope that it would all tell in the end, come in useful somewhere, add up. 'I have always had an antipathy to keeping to one plot alone – English Constitutional history, or economic history, or the French Revolution. And this disappoints my tutors, whom I would do anything to please, *if only it were not opposed to my inclinations.' O sancta simplicitas:* I have put that saving clause into italics – it is such a clue to so much in my life: ready to do anything to please, provided it does not conflict with what I please! But there is a more important clue to the ambivalence of my interests as they subsequently developed: the poet who wrote history, the historian who was equally devoted to literature, regarded history as an important part of literature. I favour ambivalence in every respect: a more fertilising frame of mind. I have enjoyed the advantages and reaped the rewards, as well as the incomprehension of the one-track minds, the obtuse and the dull.

The result of my reading all over the place and as the spirit moved me, rather than as my tutors required, meant that I never won any of the Collections prizes, which I could well have done with, but which were apt to go to dull people who haven't been much heard of since. And I really think my tutors were disappointed – Masterman said as much once – until they received a surprise in the end. I myself thought I was stale:

> I have not had a real holiday that I can remember – except in hospital over my operation. Even then I read Tout within a fortnight of the operation, which couldn't have done any good. Now my eyes are being over-taxed: I can't recognise anybody across the quad, which causes a good deal of annoyance, as I cut my friends. I intend to get glasses; but the County Authority has not yet come up with its grant, so that at the moment I am overdrawn at the bank. However, one item of good news: the Drapers' Company has renewed my scholarship for a third year.

There is little enough in the Diary about my work for Schools: I took that for granted and did not waste time on criticising it. Not that my attitude was uncritical: I was so disappointed with Godfrey Elton's *The Revolutionary Idea in France*, that I exploded *par exception* into my Engagements Book: 'A thoroughly bad book.' And in my Diary: 'again and again I have felt like cursing G. Elton for his perversities of style; I have discovered myself halting in the middle of a chapter to reconstruct sentences. Young Godfrey ought to have been spanked.' It might have done him some good at that period. A survivor from the war – after a romantic, indeed heroic, episode at Kut-el-Amara – he was rather spoiled by post-war Oxford. We all crowded the hall at Queen's to hear his lectures: it was the thing to go. There was the romantic, Byronic appearance, a mass of black, curly hair, the author of *The Testament of Dominic Burleigh*; in lecturing, also, his sentences would tie themselves in knots. We didn't suspect that he did not really know much about the subject.

More rewarding reading were a book of Santayana's, 'which I admired immensely, though there is little that is either original or constructive in it', and Russell's *Our Knowledge of the External World*. 'I think I agree with Russell more than with anybody else; I hope to find in him some sort of philosophic ground upon which to get a permanent footing.' This was partly by way of keeping up with Wadleigh's philosophical pretensions; but, in fact, in the severe stoicism of Russell's famous essay, 'A Free Man's Worship', in *Mysticism and Logic*, I found something like my own formulation of religion without belief. I copied out whole pages of Russell in my Diary.

> The life of Man is a long march through the Night, surrounded by invisible foes, tortured by weariness and pain, towards a goal that few can hope to reach, and where none may tarry long. One by one as they march, our comrades vanish from our sight, seized by the silent orders of omnipotent Death. Very brief is the time in which we can help them, in which their happiness or misery is decided. Be it ours to shed sunshine on their path, to lighten their sorrows by the balm of sympathy, to give them the pure joy of a never-tiring affection ... Be it ours to feel that, where they suffered, where they failed, no deed of ours was the cause ...

It would be cheap to say that his numerous marriages hardly exemplified 'the pure joy of a never-tiring affection', and that 'where they failed' ... One perceives now that all this was rather cheap rhetoric, with a strong dose of sentiment. Nevertheless, I am grateful to Russell: he was a great stimulus to one's own developing mind and helped to clear it of a lot of nonsense.

Where was Wadleigh in all this? – Going out of college, into digs with the man I thought of as the long-nosed, snivelling Quaker from Queen's. (He had, quite young, a perpetual dewdrop.)

> I have not made a sign to show whether I want to keep him in college or no. I want him to be near me really; but somehow I should never say so. In fact, when he made his decision to go away, I said I thought it was the right thing for him to do. [Just what I should do today – with pride inveterate and un-breached.] I don't want the responsibility for having kept him against his inclinations, though he would have stayed if I had determined he should.

No doubt they made a more equal partnership, and went on to get their Seconds together.

I had not lost touch with my old friends from home. Before the end of term Len Tippett came to spend the week-end with me, accompanied by the devoted girl-friend with whom I had acted in *Twelfth Night*, now at the University of Reading. Jimmy Crowther came another week-end and addressed the Symposium I ran, on 'The Genius of Youth is Sincerity'. 'And a very odd performance it was. He had no consistent speech to make, but merely a succession of disjointed points. A disappointing evening, though the discussion went on in a lively enough fashion.' He was contemplating marriage; this was, as usual, disapproved of by me, nor did it work out well. When my friends contracted other ties, I decided, 'then they can be my friends no longer. Still, what else is to be expected? They never have my complete confidence, and it is perhaps better that I live my own life apart, in essential isolation.'

This constant emphasis is rather curious, considering the apparent gregariousness. For the last week-end my old churchy friend, Booth, arrived and we sallied forth on the kind of round *he* liked: 'Saturday, 5 p.m.: evensong at the Cathedral; 6 p.m.: evensong at Magdalen. 8.15: *Love's Labour's Lost* in Wadham Gardens. Sunday, 11 a.m.: High Mass at St Barnabas; afternoon: Blenheim; evensong at New College; at night, the Elizabethan Singers at the Playhouse.' Next day I went home to Cornwall, and to read *Love's Labour's Lost*.

V

Summer Vacation in Cornwall

ONE problem in going down for the long vacation of nearly four months – if one wasn't going anywhere for a holiday and there was nothing else to do but work – was to get together enough books, enough history books for Schools, to last one. I used to borrow the maximum number from the undergraduates' Reading Room, as many as one was allowed from the college Library, and the maximum number from the Union. It was rather a problem to get enough, for other undergraduates were also after some of the books one needed. So I started a scheme by which my group of friends exchanged among ourselves the books we had borrowed, by post during the vacation. It worked quite well, and meant a considerable accession to our resources.

Here I was, settled down not uncomfortably in the cosy, cramped quarters of 24 Robartes Place, a new council-housing site only a couple of fields down from the old village of Tregonissey where my father's people had always lived. – All now ruined and built over, of course: no doubt a disappointment to persons who have been seen, years later, exploring the village with *A Cornish Childhood* in hand. Like all the best experiences, it is now almost wholly a village of the mind.

Ours was the middle road of those council houses, a quiet, respectable road inhabited mostly by quiet, respectable, middle-aged working-class folk, with most of whom I was on friendly terms – indeed rather more hailing terms than my people were, especially my mother, who kept very much to herself. My Aunt Bessy lived next door, with her husband, a Naval pensioner, and that increased the sense of having the place to ourselves. Though in my youth I hadn't much sense, I had enough not to be stand-offish with people just because I was going to Oxford, and indeed it would have been contrary to my nature. I have the impression that people were distinctly friendly, even the absurd Mileses who regarded me more with sorrow than with anger. There was one woman in the upper row of houses, who rejoiced in the name of Organ, who was jealous on behalf of her offspring and considered her boy could do as well: he graduated to the ranks of the county constabulary.

I had the front of the house largely to myself, for working people in those days lived mostly in the kitchen. Most of the day I spent upstairs in my bedroom reading, to keep away from any noise in the house – concentration is intensely important for any excellence in intellectual work, as Americans never realise, with their doors for ever open and people constantly dropping in to interrupt. (How can people expect to write well in such conditions?) I came down for meals, but, preferring to read during my meal, got into the habit of carrying my meal off to the front room to eat by myself; I didn't like kitchen life and only came into the kitchen for tea, or occasionally supper. So life was essentially lived to myself, for all my 'hail-fellow-well-met' attitude to the neighbours. It wasn't possible really to talk to any of them: we didn't live in the same realm of discourse. I saw them from the upper window where I sat unmoving for hours in the narrow chair; I observed them and their routine doings out of the corner of my eye; they held no mystery for me – except the greatest mystery of all: the want of intelligence in humans. Now that *is* mysterious. For the rest, I could have said, with Tante Eulalie in *A l'Ombre des Jeunes Filles en Fleur*, who also lived upstairs: 'Comme si je ne connais pas le chien de Madame X!'

Thus settled, I spent the next three and a half months mainly in reading and writing, walking and thinking. It was the habit at Christ Church to leave us to tackle Political Theory and our special subject for Schools on our own – not a good idea, so far as the former was concerned: it needed teaching more than any other part of the syllabus. Later, as a tutor, I came to teach that subject, with conviction, more frequently than any other paper, except possibly the Tudor period. For special subject I had chosen 'The Concert of Europe, 1813–1822' – goodness knows why, for it was exceedingly dull and I had, and have, no liking for the dry dust of diplomatic history. I should have chosen the Italian Renaissance, learned Italian and gone to Florence, where the Actons owned their superb villa on the slopes of Montughi Hill. What hope was there of that? However, I read French with ease, so I settled down to the thick mass of the Memoirs of Metternich, whom I found conceited but interesting, of Talleyrand, whom I rather enjoyed (the lying old cynic), of Gentz, a reactionary whom I nevertheless respected; along with volumes of documents and treaties – only of use if one were going into the Foreign Office – and those inspissated Cambridge diplomatic historians, Temperley and Webster. They were not my idea of bliss; Trevelyan was.

I read for five, six and seven hours a day at my history, sometimes getting up to nine or even ten; in August, when I relaxed a little, sinking to three or four hours. For 24 July, I find inscribed: 'Damned day wasted.' This kept me up to the mark: it happened very rarely. At seven hours a day I quickly finished Grant Robertson's *Bismarck*. 'The only halts were when I felt compelled to remark on the worst journalistic passages in the margin: they were fairly frequent. Fancy a respectable historian writing in this vein: "The personal relations of these two, William and Bismarck, so *momentous* in their consequences on two generations of *civilised* Europe, are an *intensely* and *infinitely* human background to the *grandeur* and *pettinesses* of the *drama* in which they are the leading figures." ' There were other passages I objected to: I was becoming more critical, the process of self-education was advancing. I came to be very fond of Robertson as a person later on at All Souls, and to admire him much; all the same, he was a past master of historical jargon. This arises from defective sensibility, a narrowness of aesthetic horizons. And indeed, one of the most discouraging things for a person of literary sensibility in reading modern historians – this does not apply to the great historians – is the sheer inferiority of the writing. This is far, far worse in America: American academics seem to have no idea how to handle the language. It is anguish to those who can, to have to read them.

Without savour or taste, colourless and humourless, written in empty abstractions often without meaning or significance, weighed down with double adjectives and adverbialities, where do American academics get this rubbishy verbiage from? From Germany, I suspect. Yet they have excellent models in their own tradition. Why don't they write like Parkman or Prescott, Henry Adams or Samuel Eliot Morison? Only the other day I saw one professor in the *American Historical Review* praising another professor's book as 'brilliant', twice over. He obviously did not know the meaning of the word 'brilliant': it means shining. The book, of course, was like lead. An Irish writer who well knows what the situation is with so much American writing, herself a really brilliant writer, writes me: 'You are, I fear, only too right about the critical sense of the Americans, and more unnerving still than the portentous banality of their ideas is the language in which they express them; that elephantine packaging that robs English of all sinew, largely I suspect because the users are ignorant of the roots and provenances of the language itself.'

There is something in that; but it is more specifically an academic disease, for the Americans have excellent *literary* writers of the language – Hemingway or Edmund Wilson, Eudora Welty or Carson McCullers, fine poets like Eliot or Pound, Robert Lowell or John Berryman, even Tennessee Williams (but certainly *not* J. D. Salinger, the idiotic over-estimation of whom is one of the most obvious evidences of the American lack of critical sense). Why can't the academics, then, follow good models? It is partly because they have false standards: they really do not know what is good writing and what is not. They do not know, for example, what an excellent writer Samuel Eliot Morison is; I have frequently come across American academic historians who just couldn't see it. The reason was that they were without the faculty of perception and had been brought up on false standards: they think this portentousness and pretentiousness impressive. But it only impresses the third-rate. I happened to say once to Garrett Mattingly, one of the few among their academic historians to write like a cultivated man: 'They do not know *how* to write.' Mattingly replied: 'But they *do*; only they know it *all wrong!*'

Why don't they write like their own Nathaniel Hawthorne? – They couldn't do better. Or at least read him, and take note how to do it? Here I was in July 1924:

have bought Hawthorne's *Twice-Told Tales*, and last night I read several in bed before going to sleep. 'Legends of Old Province House' are wonderful pieces. I went to sleep thinking of the things like them I want to write about Duporth and Tregrehan House, and other old mansions gay and busy in father's day, now empty and unkempt. After supper we talked of the departed glory of Heligan, big house of the Tremaynes of Menabilly which Dr Rashleigh hardly ever inhabits, of Prideaux, neglected by Sir Colman Rashleigh for a bungalow on Par beach. I talked with a man in Luxulyan Valley a few nights ago about the same thing – the old gentry selling off lands and farms, cutting down woods and trees. [Sir Colman had sold off the fine carved Tudor chimney-piece of Methrose to America. Where is it now?] Father is frankly in favour of former days, when the big houses buzzed like a hive with various activities: they were the framework of the old rural society. I have a sneaking regard for their past greatness, and there's a good deal of hard sense as well as sentiment on their side.

Here was the conservative countryman under the exterior of the Radical intellectual.

I finished Grant Robertson's book with some satisfaction, even 'with enjoyment and a certain amount of approval'. It was mainly the style that had disagreed with me. I preferred the general plan of the book to a pure biography, with too much of Bismarck's family life in it and not enough history; but 'more and more I realise how much the orthodox historian loses of the significance of events by neglecting the economic interests behind them.' Here was a sign of the growing grip of the economic interpretation of history over me: I was soon to become a monomaniac on the subject – yet another long tunnel one had to go through, in the course of one's education, before one emerged into the clear light of common sense. Grant Robertson was, of course, a better judge of the odious Bismarck, with his lying and trickery, his bullying and his appeal to force, his sinister influence in putting the clock back by a century in Europe, than I was: as to content, his biography remains far the best among English historians of the deplorable subject of modern Germany.

As usual, mitigating history with literature, I was reading Byron, the whole of *Don Juan*. I went for an evening walk to Carn Grey and Tregrehan,

> to think hard about Byron, for the Newdigate next year. Several ideas came into my mind, and I got quite excited at discovering that a long poem might not be impossible of achievement. I disbelieve in long poems, and so have never felt capable of writing one. But I certainly must try this time, even though the subject is more unfavourable than the preceding ones. I now have a good beginning and a good ending in mind. I shall begin with a passage about storm over the moors – a metaphor really: Byron's is the voice of the wind in storm,
>
> > Moaning in desolate gullies of the moor.
>
> (The line came to mind as I passed the gullies left by the old tin-streaming in Garker Valley.) The overcast skies and lowering clouds are the time, the background of his life. The last scene at Missolonghi should make a fine storm scene, day sinking to a quiet glow at evening when he died. I must make something of his speeches in favour of the Luddites and his general sympathy with the oppressed. But I am still very dubious, having never tried a long peom before. I should be much happier at a sonnet-sequence; but the innovation would be too much for the Newdigate. Still, if this evening's excitement remains, I am hopeful.

There were too many things at which, utterly unsophisticated, I had yet to have a first experience. There had been an odd happening just before leaving Oxford.

> At the beginning of the Symposium, a porter came up to say somebody wanted to speak to me over the telephone. It was the first time I had ever used the telephone; and then, quite unaccountably, we couldn't get through to the man who had rung me up in London. I was in an agony of suspense. I never get a telegram but I think of home, and fear lest something has happened to father or mother. Last night I was completely un-

nerved: I really believed something had happened to them. Only when the meeting was half-over did it occur to me that it was probably Wah ringing me up to explain his absence from the meeting. As it was, the early part of the meeting was nearly wrecked; I never remember being so completely at a loss and so unnerved.

I still, years later, do not encourage people to ring me up; I avoid using the telephone whenever I can. In America, where people have the habit of leaving a message for one to call back, I never do – such a saving of time. Nor do I much appreciate being the recipient of telegrams, especially when they follow one all round the country, with the charges mounting up. Bernard Shaw found a postcard simpler and more expeditious; so do I. I haven't the time to waste, waiting at the end of telephone-lines for other people.

I went on – a suitable transition – with my Byron campaign, reading *Manfred* out on our little patch of front lawn. This much impressed me, self-portrait of Byron as it was – like everything he wrote. 'I was surprised by its grandeur and the almost complete absence of prosy passages and blemishes in workmanship. I want to read "Prometheus Unbound" now, in order to compare. My opinion of Byron has gone up by reading him. Does that happen to everybody, I wonder? I read "The Siege of Corinth" and "Mazeppo" during the week: the latter while waiting half an hour before a concert in the Public Rooms.' This may have been a performance of Handel's *Judas Maccabaeus* I heard there some time that year. Hitherto I had been brought up, or, rather, brought myself up, under the wing of Keats and Shelley; the quality of Byron in bulk was something of a discovery, and that it appealed to one who was incurably a Romantic was a sign of developing taste. I duly read Shelley's 'Prometheus Unbound' and 'The Mask of Anarchy'; no comment: it was a very different view of Castlereagh from that which emerged from the historians and the documents, and did not say much for Shelley's justice of mind.

Occasionally I varied work with a spell at the piano.

2 July: This morning, having achieved an early rising, I sat down to the piano, found a Mendelssohn Song without Words (the

only music I've got) which I hadn't yet learned after a fashion. There are about half a dozen of them that I can't play; this was one of the most beautiful and most impossible. I kept at the damned thing all the morning, and yet couldn't get the cross-rhythm working properly. The end was an unhappy temper, and a morning wasted. I couldn't leave off somehow: I could have eaten my heart with vexation at not being able to play that piece.

I had, of course, never had any lessons; those had been wasted on my sister, in accordance with the working-class view that the piano was an accomplishment for girls.

I consoled myself with a rare bout of gossip with the piano-tuner, rather a dear little man, with up-turned, waved moustaches, bright bird-like eyes, a slightly lisping manner of speech, which recalled his great days in London and rubbing shoulders with celebrities. He had been piano-tuner to some well-known pianist – I think Adela Verne – of a previous generation. From him I heard the gossip of county society, and life at Truro, our cathedral city. 'He used to tune at Lis Escop [which means, Bishop's Court] when Warman was there; but doesn't think the new bishop has a piano. Criddle and Smith, who shifted "what furniture he had" didn't shift one.' This was Walter Frere, of the Community of the Resurrection, newly appointed Bishop of Truro, to whom I was to become devoted. In fact, among his many gifts – historian, linguist, liturgiologist, saint – Frere was a distinguished musician; later on, there was a piano at Lis Escop and regular sessions of music at which the Bishop would take his part with men from the Cathedral choir. But, as a monk, he had not many possessions of his own: only what the rules of the Community, which he observed, permitted him.

The talk in Truro was of Canon Trevor Lewis, an Evangelical after Warman's own heart, not much relishing the new dispensation, and thinking of leaving. Warman, an Evangelical, very popular. I countered with finding him rather episcopal at Chavasse's, noticeably on his dignity. Nor did I like Vernon Shaw, the boy-scouting curate at St Austell, of whom the piano-tuner, a Nonconformist, approved: I was glad I had taken the opportunity of falling out with him, a hard-voiced, unsympathetic man. We approved of gifted Mr Middleton from Cambridge, the Cathedral organist: he was getting an Erard Grand from Criddle and Smith. Mademoiselle Lenglen was decidedly not a sport; I didn't care about this. Much more interesting to me, Canon Raffles Flint had had an operation: what a handsome man! I had never seen him. The road at Ruan Lanihorne was impassable, what with high tides and the rain. And so on, round the clergy of Truro, and Dr Panting, my surgeon: the world seen through the eyes of a piano-tuner.

In a way [I reflected], his life must be pretty various. I should love to be getting the glimpses he has into all sorts and conditions of homes. What an equipment for a novelist! Besides, he goes to all the out of the way spots in Cornwall. He talked of Godolphin, and the old mansion there, now in the hands of a farmer who blocks up the granite colonnade with waggons and carts. How it brings back that famous family and the days of their greatness! I have been thinking again, as I walked the moors tonight, what a book I would write of the Civil War in Cornwall. What will Miss Coate make of it, I wonder? Last night I couldn't sleep for thinking of other subjects for books I might write ... According to mother, I talked in my sleep a good deal of last night; so I had better stop here, before becoming too excited.

It was just as well that one had such an exciting intellectual life all on one's own, for there was little enough in the environment. It seems that I made something, if not the most, of what there was. I was for ever collecting scraps of Cornish phrases and folk-lore from my parents – one form of what the Americans would call 'meaningful' (odious word) communication. My mother would apply to me, in inverted commas – a kind of substitute for humour – the phrase, 'Ole live-upstairs, 'n pay no rent.' When I walked up the steep hill to Carn Grey, the sharp granite declivities all round me, the phrase that was frequently on my mother's lips was as frequently in my mind:

> When ever I hear the old folk say,
> 'Old as the hills', yes – old as they ...

I was telling mother all about the poem I have been thinking of writing around those words, and this brought an old song into mother's head:

> Jack had a wife, and her name was Grace:
> Two black eyes and a rosy face ...
>
> Rise up soldiers, and take your pay,
> And Monday morning march away.
> Over the hills and back to France ...

But are these fragments from the same song, and is it really an old folk-song, or just of the music-hall variety from the last century? I'm not likely to be so lucky as to get any really good catches such as Cecil Sharp did, though I've been at it for more than two years now, collecting phrases and scraps of songs. This little scrap, which was one of the first I got, has already been appropriated by Q:

> Old 'oman Widdle-waddle jumped out o' bed
> And out of the window she popped her head,
> Saying 'Run John, run John,
> The grey goose is gone,
> And the fox is run out of the town-O.'

Lennie [my little half-nephew, whom I took for cousin] is shouting over the stairs to say he knows all the rest of that old song; so I suppose the whole thing has been brought to light somehow and somewhere.

Last night the moon was so bright that it seemed a shame to sleep the moonlight away in bed. So I sat up thinking over another poem the idea of which has been with me for some time: the record of a walk under the moon in a strange land, as if a ghost were wandering in the lanes his body loved before. The houses all unchanged are still, as if empty; at a corner the curious face of the moon peers in recognition over the humped shoulder of a house. Nothing stirs there now. It came to me as I walked homeward through Bethel and passed Lennie's home, where Will and M. lived, and Will died. I remember calling there a few times, and what it was to feel that a young married fellow was coughing out his life in the last months of miner's phthisis.

He had been a gold-miner in South Africa: a story characteristic more of the generation before, it concerned our family more nearly than I knew or sought to inquire.

I began the poem:

> The silent land I wandered strangely through,
> As one who should return from the dead to view
>
> The place he looked on when his eyes were bright.
> Through the dim lanes under the moon's light
>
> I passed, nor paused beneath the moth-hung skies
> For all of night the lonely mind may prize ...

Why did I not go on with it? The answer is given, I now realise, on the opposite page of the Diary.

> On these walks that I take in the evenings, after a day's work at history, my head brims with ideas and phrases for poems. Tonight, after coming home, I jotted down these lines without much of the usual effort. And I have one or two far more important ideas to work upon at the moment, besides my everlasting thoughts about other projected Cornish books, and the (rather sterile) attempts at a scheme for a poem on Byron. With all these things fermenting, it seems a waste of precious time to be poring over Sorel and the other interesting, but not vitalising, historians. I must have read about 6½ hours today, 7 yesterday, and 8 on Monday.

There was the answer why I did not finish poems I had begun, write more or carry out the ideas that besieged my head. History was winning; at any rate, history was 'work', and I was making myself work. If I had been a slacker, I might have written more poems and my life taken a more literary turn: I might have ended up on a paper, writing reviews. As it was, I tended to keep poetry more and more in an inner recess of the mind, something to turn to for consolation, and in the end I could hardly bear the idea of bringing out a volume of poems, I had formed such a complex against it. Only the excitement and inspiration, the recklessness, of war-time made me belatedly bring out *Poems of a Decade, 1931–1941*.

How strange my attitude seems to me now: I can hardly understand it. I suppose it may have been due to personal sensibility: 'one skin too few' as a reviewer diagnosed, not unkindly – indeed he proved one of the most generous of the reviewers: Raymond Mortimer. Making poetry take second place – though, of course, I estimated it as of greater value and more precious than history – driving it into the inner recesses of my mind to express only the most intimate impulses was a sacrifice that I made to the necessities of my life. On the other hand, it was not without an ultimate advantage: it kept the impulse pure, and I have never professionalised it. Amidst all my reviewing, for example, I have never reviewed poetry: I think far too highly of it. And this attitude, though it too involved sacrifices, has had its rewards: writing poetry has never dried up in me, as it has with many more professional poets, my contemporaries.

I realise quite well that the upshot has been that my poetry has received very little recognition, particularly from the critics. (The ordinary reader, unhampered by prejudice, responds more easily, is often quite appreciative, given the chance.) Because a man is well known as an historian, his poetry is totally neglected, unheard. There is this much justification for them, that no historian (except Macaulay) seems to have been a poet as well. But that consideration is precisely what is unusual and should alert their intelligence, or at least give them some pause.

It was obvious that I was becoming more engaged by history. At this moment I was reading Max Beer's two-volumed *History of British Socialism*, and Sorel's immense *L'Europe et la Révolution Française*. The Diary has a sensible judgment on the latter work.

A magnificent work Sorel's history must be, to judge from the first and last volumes, all that I have read of it. Still, for all thè emotion with which I read its close and the sympathy I have with Sorel's outlook on Napoleon, the book appears to me a lesser work than it might have been. Sometimes the veiled

justification of Napoleon's policy and diplomacy wears so thin
that one revolts. Perhaps Sorel shows more sense of fairness in
the other volumes, where he has an opportunity to observe
Napoleon sacrificing all other interests to his own, just as later,
when the tables were turned, the Powers meted out the same
treatment to him.

The entry goes on to reveal the growing perplexity of mind that
over-reading myself into historical relativism was inducing.

> I seem to have lost any clearness of perception I may have had,
> and am now groping blindly in the dark. One thing seems to be
> as good as another. Why bother to resist temptations, for in-
> stance? – It's all the same thing in the long run. Why become
> enthusiastic about any political party or its aims? – The world
> goes on unchanged, or, if it does change, it does so independently
> of any efforts we may put forth. The purpose of everything has
> become so questionable. I hope this is only a phase, for it cuts
> away the ground from all action. However, Sorel is finished.
> Perhaps all this pother is due to over-work?

That suspicion may have been justified. But the symptoms of this
state of mind went on for years: *was* there any objectivity, any disinterestedness, apart from the pulls of people's interests, overt or
occult, economic or political, intellectual or psychological? Was
there any truth to be found? Was there anyone to be believed?
Could anyone ever be trusted to state things exactly right, without
parti pris? Was truth attainable? Was there any justice of mind
among human beings? What constituted value, the value one set on
things? How much of it was interest? One's mind went round and
round in this groove, and there was never anyone to help. For these
were serious intellectual worries to me; the life of the mind was all
in all, and these thoughts troubled me for years.

When, years later, I read Pareto I recognised a kindred spirit –
someone with a very acute nose for human interestedness, hypoc-
risy and humbug, who recognised the constant habit humans have
of dressing up their own interests or prejudices as objective generalisations, when they are really mere rationalisations of their own

6

interests. Who is taken in by it? Certainly not Pareto, nor, I may say, A.L.R. So I got in the habit, when I came across particularly flagrant examples of this tendency, of sign-pointing it in the margins of my books – 'Pareto – A.L.R.' Sometimes adding, Q.E.D., for there really is very little of human thought that passes the test, and thereby deserves attention on its merits. This means an immense saving of time: one really does not need to pay much serious attention to what humans suppose themselves to think; more important is to observe what makes them think as they do.

My mother sometimes stood in the way of the overflow from this mood. And though I doubt if any intellectual consideration ever entered her mind of its own accord, her verdict on this one was not without point and may serve as an epigraph on the whole issue: 'If that's the case, then there's no difference in anything!' Though that summing up is a little drastic – and indeed hers was a ruthless, un-compromising and honest character – there has always remained this core of historical relativism, a real intellectual scepticism under-neath the downrightness and straightforwardness of my political views. Perhaps people may be forgiven for failing to understand – but they might at least have tried: a little intellectual effort would do *them* good.

There remains always the absoluteness of art. What I liked best in Sorel was the conclusion: 'Et il signa l'abdication, le 22 juin 1815, pour la seconde fois. Puis il partit pour Malmaison, où Joséphine était morte, Malmaison toute enchantée encore de verdure et de fleurs, respirer une dernière fois l'air de son printemps, avant de partir pour l'exil dont il sentait bien qu'il ne reviendrait plus.' It was to be many years before I came to the source whence this accent was learned, a far closer and more congenial spirit, my fellow-Celt: Chateaubriand.

A few more phrases from my mother are jotted down:

> Rain, Rain, go away;
> Come again another day:
> When I brew, when I bake,
> You shall have some saffron cake.

The reference to saffron cake shows that this must be a Cornish version, for only the Cornish really like saffron cake.

With all the interests going round and round in my head I didn't mind my loneliness; indeed I much preferred it to society without significance or savour. On a July day at Porthpean I ran into Jean and her friend Elsie, and also my old companion Bacon. I preferred the company of their dog,

whom I took out on the rocks at low tide, and then on to Trenarren, never once offering to take them or even walk home with them. Coming through the lanes, however, I was happy over the honeysuckle, the briar-roses and trailing vetch, which I gathered into a big bunch. Gyp, who was left on my hands, kept getting lost down side lanes and through gateways; but just as I was getting anxious over his doings in the fields (he might have been killing Sir Somebody Sawle's game, or worrying his sheep), Gyp would turn up at the end of the lane waiting for me. Since then I have had supper, been arranging flowers and writing. *O fortunatos nimium:* I wish I knew Bridges' poem by heart.

Any social entanglement was a derogation from solitude. My mother decided me into going to the School Swimming Sports at Porthpean,

and since I haven't ceased to regret it. Began inauspiciously by meeting W., then ran into the art-mistress's circle. Took them to tea at Brenton's, which ran away with all the money I earned so laboriously from Bacon. Worst of all, I found myself saddled with W. at the end of the day, and became a martyr by offering myself for a walk along the cliffs to Charlestown and Crinnis. God! Never have I spent such an uninspiring day.

A relation of my mother's at Fowey had a daughter to dispose of; and as the daughter was going to college and so was a niece who was staying there, the mother thought what a good thing it would be to get me to come over. Great pressure was put upon me, and after one awkward refusal I promised to come. A second importunate invitation gave me much disturbance of mind, which wasted part of a morning. 'This being the second refusal, it may discourage any more importunities.' It satisfactorily did, though it made an open breach. I fear I was rather a hopeless proposition for any designing mother – or her daughter, for that matter – to entertain.

Even kind Miss C., who brought me news of her Cambridge friends, was hardly welcome at this juncture. '11 August 1924: Heavens! only two months' vac. left. It's enough to make one frantic. Interruptions in my work still continue. Miss C. is staying here, and yesterday I dutifully took her to Luxulyan Valley ... A fine and exhilarating talk. But I'm not sure that I shouldn't have preferred as usual to be alone.'

An exception was made for my old school-friend Marion Yelland, who had interesting news of *her* young friend, Violet le Maistre, who had just married Middleton Murry after Katherine Mansfield's death.

> Marion let me read her letter: all about how happy she is with Jock, and how they seem to have been made for each other from the beginning, and the wonderful night after 'The Immortal Hour', when he proposed to her: how he came over to her, and that was all. I wonder if she'll feel always like that? Still more, I wonder if Middleton Murry felt like that about it – after such protestations of devotion to Katherine Mansfield's memory. He'll probably consider himself a martyr to his own idealism before long – taking a young thing like that under his wing, to watch its mind grow and mould its development. I set out by liking the *Adelphi* much more than I disliked it; now the proportions are almost exactly reversed. Sentimentalism, sickly and trashy ... Well, I'm unfair about what is none of my business. I ought to know Murry really, and then see if his outlook is so very different from my own. Bacon always says it is very like.

Actually I did come to know Middleton Murry in the 'thirties, though our relations were never close and they were deliberately ended by my volition. He published two or three pieces of mine, though I was not in sympathy with the *Adelphi's* line. He came to stay with me once at All Souls, when his mind was turning towards politics and I wanted to recruit him to the Labour Party. But, so like the asses that nearly all intellectuals are about politics, he insisted on joining the I.L.P., which was in its last death-throes. What a fool! However, he told me a great deal that was interesting about his relations with D. H. Lawrence, which can be corroborated from other sources. When young, Murry had been exceedingly handsome: a mass of raven black hair, grey-blue eyes, an incandescent pallor of complexion, a regular profile that could have gone on a Greek coin. Lawrence was, of course, in love with him. In *Women in Love* Lawrence is Birkin and Murry is Morel: the significance of all that wrestling they go in for on the floor should be obvious even to the uninitiated. Murry told me that when Lawrence revealed to him that he was Morel in the book, 'you could have knocked me down with a feather: I was never more surprised.' I can only say that this, if true, was extremely obtuse of him; but then, Murry was entirely masculine. Lawrence used to say, 'The trouble with you, Murry, is that you're so dead, essentially dead.' Murry to me: 'And I know what Lawrence meant. In a sense he was right.' I, too, know what Lawrence meant: he meant that Murry was uncreative, merely a critic. This self-abasement, with an overtone of propitiation, I found repellent.

It wasn't that, however, that put me off Murry; it was an unexpected encounter with his wife, his third. He had asked me to look in on him at Harling if ever I should be in Norfolk; and once I did so, to find him away from home on one of his religious-communal week-ends, and to receive such a shower of complaints from his wife about his behaviour, his cruelties and neglect that I felt as if dragged through mud. Not for me these matrimonial amenities; I was appalled by the squalor of it all and, when Murry wrote me again, did not reply. Nevertheless, years later, after the war when he produced a surprisingly good book about Swift, I wrote him an appreciative fan-letter, which much pleased him: 'Fancy hearing from you, of all people,' etc.

What I gathered about his second marriage was that he placed the ingenuous girl-friend of my friend straight into Katherine Mansfield's mould, into her room and habits, surrounded her with K.M.'s things, and that she, too, developed tuberculosis and shortly died. So many things about Murry were highly unattractive, most of all, his shaming heart-searchings after God; and yet, as a pure literary critic, he was one of the best of his time.

My own pleasures were simple enough: needs must. The articles I wrote regularly for the *Local Leader* brought me in, irregularly, a guinea or two. (I had never thought of them from that day to this: it would be amusing to look them up, if they have not totally disappeared.) '22 July: I got two guineas today for my work, and very welcome it was. I don't know how to get on on the £4 or so which remain at the Bank for me till October. I want to see an oculist about my sight, and then glasses of course. I must have some teeth filled, I need a new suit and some more underclothes. What a problem it is merely to exist, much less to exist well.' I concluded, with conviction: 'I am burning the candle at both ends.'

In these circumstances it was a major operation for the family to invest in a new bookcase, to put away the books that encumbered tables, chairs, shelves. Later on, in the 'forties, when I had more money to spend on books, I hit on the ingenious idea of bringing the staircase into play at Polmear Mine: if you placed ten or a dozen books on the top stair, you could double the number on the next down, treble the number on the third, and so on. In the end the accumulation of books drove me to take on a country house, if a small one, at Trenarren: never before had I lived in a house that could contain all my books. Even there, now, with twenty thousand ...

In the Market House there lurked a shambling character, an old sailor, beery and blowsy, with a loud, hoarse voice, gruff ways, but not without a gruff kindness. He knew me as a prowler among his books, and occasionally I got something cheap but worth reading from him. At last negotiations with old Dungey were brought to a head:

for a long time we have hesitated: his price of 25s. seemed too high. At last, armed with the two guineas which I earned by my articles, I have made the plunge. Father was there in the Market House, and Bacon was there to advise. His advice, in the midst of the bargaining was that, considering the price of wood, the bookcase was cheap! So Dungey wouldn't lessen by half a crown or five shillings. However, I'm quite excited by the pleasant prospect of at length getting straight – to think of the joy of arranging whole shelves of books and putting them in proper order.

Here was a simple, unsophisticated pleasure, inexpensive enough. One that was still more so, and yielded a more intense pleasure, was my solitary evening walks after the day's work was over. Monday, 28 July, after six and a half hours at Sorel and finishing him, I set out at seven for Luxulyan and home by way of Prideaux, some ten miles in two and a half hours –

and I don't feel so very tired now. A wonderful evening, of a rare sort for walking in. When I set out, heavy clouds were breaking into rain right across the bay, from the dark pine-woods of Crinnis to the flat clump of wind-shorn pines at Trenarren. The road to Luxulyan seemed clear, and I tramped across the moor with blue sky before me. But the clouds were coming up behind, and on the right was a splendid rainbow spanning the woods and fields. I had it on my right from Trethurgy onwards for almost a mile.

O rainbow of 1924, roads and granite hedges where every twist and turn were once so familiar to me, and I a dark-haired boy marching along as familiar a figure to the passer-by, roads that I have so long deserted, where I am no more to be seen as in those years when my friends and I were young and all the world seemed opening before us, like the view as we breasted the hill and there was the open moor stretching away across all those scented miles to ancient Brown Willy and Rowtor on the horizon – if we could have known what the years held in store, from those days while mother and father were alive, the home held, the world seemed secure around us and all would yet be well; if we could have known what anguish and tribulation the years held in store, death for some, dropping by the wayside, irreparable injuries and heart-ache for others, the mingled sadness and wonder of life, like the contingent, passing beauty of that rainbow of 1924, emblem of what, promise of what, signalling transfiguration and joy inexpressible, some unspoken message to which one has yet held faithful through all the sullied years!

The fields that the pathway crosses looked spring-like after the rain; one of them, the last before Luxulyan, was bright with marigolds among the corn. At Luxulyan itself I spent a few minutes in the church; the parson's dogs were waiting at the porch, but the parson himself not to be seen. I hesitated before going down the hill, past the holy well, into the Valley, because the thunderclouds were threatening. It was quite eerie going down all alone under the trees; the granite viaduct lowered gloomy and forbidding, above it a black ribbon of thunder-cloud; just here the stream rushes down with a roar of waters; the trees become thicker and higher, the pathway darker. Through the leaves I felt the raindrops pattering. Where, in case of a thunder-storm, could one shelter?

Across the bed of the Valley and up to Prideaux, a fearful hill to climb, I hastened, deciding to go round the back of the park and back to Trethurgy. At the edge of the park under the trees it got blacker and more ominous than ever. Tiny pools in the road looked like eyes gleaming in the darkness, and the ruts like mirrors. Coming down through the Valley I thought what an occupation it would be to gather the various properties in the Valley into one large estate; to replant the slopes with trees, make pathways through and across the woods. Then, in some select spot build a great house, which should serve as a house of learning, a sanctuary to save the Valley from being des-poiled, preserve it from the quarries and clay-works which are beginning to blight its beauty.

Whether it should serve as a college or a library I had not decided; this dream does not now appeal to me: the world has too many of both. If I had a dream at all today, it would be to fence the Valley off from the world and leave it to itself, wild and free. But I no longer hope.

A much longer walk, full of irritation and delight, was due to mismanagement on my part or, rather, to my extraordinary in-experience. With no means of transport, except as far as Neddy could take one in the jingle, I knew very few places, even in my own neighbourhood, beyond walking distance. One August day I received a telegram from Bainbridge, who was staying at Polperro, telling me to meet him and Geoffrey Grigson at Couch's Mill. I had never met Grigson, who was growing up at this time in the parsonage house at Pelynt – with not much more money than I had, to judge from his delightful book, *Freedom of the Parish*, and so he spent as much time on the roads as I did: with even more profit, for thus he developed his enviable knowledge of wild flowers and birds, fishing the streams and talking to the farm-folk. He was the youngest of seven sons of the Rector, every one of whom, except Geoffrey, was killed in one or other of the two German wars that have ruined our time. Though I never knew them, I am always affected by the memorial to them all in Pelynt church: 'They were baptized in this church and were lovers of this parish.' There is a small piece of the history of our age.

But where on earth was Couch's Mill? – of course, I didn't possess a map. I had originally arranged to meet Bainbridge at Fowey, so I judged it must be somewhere in the vicinity. I rushed off to Mount Charles – to find there were no buses to Par or Fowey in time. I set out to walk it: heat, flies, face and neck scalding in the sun, a mackintosh to carry, across Par Moor and up the interminable, steep Polmear Hill. At the very top an old man on a black donkey told me where Couch's Mill was – four miles the other side of the River Fowey, which I was still a couple of miles from and quite out of the road. Impossible to meet Bainbridge there at 12.30, I trudged on to Fowey.

'At Fowey it was Regatta Day, and the first thing I saw as I came down the hill into Lostwithiel Street was the beautiful *Cutty Sark* with her masts dressed rainbow-fashion. Lunch in a poky little place packed with men, women and children. Afterwards an abortive attempt to look into the church' – that fine church, foreign in style for it has a clerestory, unlike Cornish churches, full of interesting monuments, but the interior demeaned by three generations of bad taste. What would a Comper not have made of it! – something to remember wherever one might be. The same applies to the grandest lost opportunity of all – the interior of the finest of

Victorian churches, Truro Cathedral, which was being completed and furnished during the lifetime of this genius among modern ecclesiastical architects. Not once was Comper called in by the tasteless people in charge. The only church Comper decorated in Cornwall is the tiny church of Little Petherick, and very rich and satisfying it is. But that was arranged for by a man of taste, Athelstan Riley. Is it any wonder that I detest Philistines?

At W. H. Smith's bookshop, which was rather high-brow in those days and used to have a good show of Q's books, I bought Robert Louis Stevenson's *Poems*:

never have I been so thankful to have such a book in my pocket. A short stay on the Town Quay, where the cheap-jacks, fruiterers and loiterers were assembling, a darkie resplendent among them in top-hat, morning coat and spats. At Whitehouse Ferry I suddenly made up my mind to cross to Polruan and go on to Polperro. Once started on the long stony road across the coast, lugging my mackintosh and with no shade from inland trees, I looked longingly down a few hundred feet from the high plateau to the little coves where the sand was cool and wet, the sea clear and inviting. Halfway to Polperro a farmer was talking to a handsome dark man in a trap. I said, 'How much farther to Polperro?', thinking myself a mile away. He said, 'About three miles.' The dark man asked me to ride to the top of the hill, and was surprised that I had walked all the way from St Austell. I was much taken with his looks, dark skin and beautiful black eyes. No wonder people think we have Spanish blood in us: a pure Iberian type, and an out-of-the-way district like this, without main roads and railways, best preserves its original character.

Nearer Polperro a farm lad, who was ploughing a field, hailed me and asked if I wanted a young hare for supper. He had a little furry rabbit in his hands. I couldn't see very well, and was afraid to see too much. After all, playing the Good Samaritan to the poor creature would have made an awful addition to getting to Polperro. Quite unconcernedly the farm-boy said, 'The gulls have carried off a lot of 'em.' I looked over and a cloud of gulls rose from the field. He took the rabbit by the ears and threw it over the hedge to me, among the long grass and vetch. I passed by like the priest on the other side.

I was quite upset by the episode, as I always have been by the heartlessness of Nature towards helpless wild things – I thought of the tiny creature starving away from its burrow, paralysed with fear by snake or weasel. As a child I had been tormented by the thought: couldn't God look after His own? What about the assurance in the Bible about the fall of the sparrow? I found it strange that I felt much the same shock when brought up against the cruelty of existence 'when I no longer have any use for thought about God'.

At Polperro I was restored by a cup of tea, though I was vexed to find no one at home at Chapel Rock. When I rested on the cliff for a while, there was a fat vulgar woman with a Cockney accent that could be heard all over the place, who had attached to herself a diminutive ginger man with yellow spectacles. What a couple! She kept screaming that there was a thing on the grass which upset her peace of mind – I suppose to attract attention to her beautiful self. The poor little man said it was merely an earwig. She thought it might be a flea, and fled to the rocks, where he joined her and they ensconced themselves for life's usual purposes. I suppose it does take all sorts to make a world, as mother is always telling me against my intolerant views.

I was happier walking back to Fowey by way of Bodinnick in the cool of the evening. The miles slipped by as I read poem after poem out of R.L.S.'s book; I passed a signpost with the unknown names of Tregavithick and Trenewan.

I still remember that walk, the poems, the lines and rhythms dancing in my head, the cool tiredness without feeling jaded, the long grasses swishing by as I walked mile after mile: one couldn't do that today with the motor-cars swishing by instead. When I arrived at Fowey, there was the town 'all gaily dressed and in the streets. I thought of Q's gentle irony at the expense of Trojan festivities.

Two pears which I bought I ate as I sat reading on the bench between his garden and the sea. O, Q, too fortunate in some ways: perhaps if you had had a little less good fortune, you would have been a greater writer. Still, I should have liked to hear his voice; but I listened in vain.'

*   *   *

That memorable walk to Polperro might be described as a kind of 'Waiting for Grigson'. But now my friend, Len Tippett, was down on vacation and I had company. We walked to Trenarren, where in those days one could get tea at a cottage, and sat on the cliff at Hallane, that V-shaped mouth of the emerald-green valley scooped out by the stream that flows under thick brambles, sloes and honey-suckle, to tumble down upon the beach under the towering mass of the Vans.

> We discussed the disillusionments of this after-the-war world. Len is very sceptical whether any perceptible progress is the result of political action. And I am as sceptical of the intelligence from which alone political action can result. I have long felt this reaction from the futile bustle of politics, and I have been turning again to my old musings, which give a deeper satisfaction. And, perhaps, it is my dreams that may turn out more good than any direct mingling in active affairs.

That, after many efforts to make a direct contribution – all of them frustrated – seems to me now prophetic: I have come back to it, after years, and no longer have any desire, or intention, to make any contribution whatever.

My estimate of the situation was without any illusions even then. 'My poems aren't really much yet: the best I have written was sent back from the *Adelphi* only this week.' I suppose that, going my own lonely way, not knowing anybody in the literary world – unlike my contemporaries, Acton and Quennell, Connolly and Evelyn Waugh – it was only natural that the way should have been much harder and longer (like the road to Couch's Mill, which I never reached). But the fact was that I never did receive any encouragement, let alone backing, until much later in the 'thirties from Eliot, so that it is no wonder that they should all have become so much better known, been so much more successful, so soon.

All the same,

> when I am writing my poems, I feel that my whole soul is in them in a way that is not so with political articles I write or even my historical essays for my tutor. My Diary, my poems and my ideas for things to be written in the future absorb the intensest of my energies. The rest I have an active interest in, but it does not stir me in the same way. Len must be a happier individual than I, his capacities being more suited to his aims: he is satisfied with being a scientist, and he is determined to be a competent one. He has a solid and reliable foundation of industry, whereas I ... ! Feiling is rather mistrustful of my capacity for work. Perhaps he thinks what another Christ Church tutor said of another volatile Celt: 'Very intelligent; but lives on his wits.'

(Now I wonder of whom that could have been said? Could it have been applied to the author of another Christ Church autobiography, of whom I did not at this time approve, careering on towards a catastrophe over his Schools?)

For myself, however hard I worked I did not feel satisfied. '11 August: Heavens! only two months' vac. left. It's enough to make one frantic.' And this, after a week averaging seven hours a day at Metternich, Sir Henry Maine and the dreary Webster, apart from reading Anatole France for my own pleasure. Next day I was better pleased, 'after a day of great effort and satisfactory results. The article I wrote for Mrs Streeten's paper is much the best of the little series on "Science and Civilisation". Besides that, a certain amount of time at Canning's foreign policy, and a half of *Penguin Island*. Today about five hours at work, and then have finished Anatole France. Quite good, considering the indigestion that doesn't desert me whatever I eat and however carefully I treat my stomach.' There follows a frightened entry: 'An awful thought has been ever-present with me of late.' I think this refers to fear of cancer which from time to time cropped up when I wondered what was gnawing my vitals. (It occurs to me that Kipling was obsessed by the same thought in his last years, though his ulcer was quite enough to do him in. To what splendid use he turned his fears in the philosophic late story, 'The Sign of the Zodiac'.)

An intermission from work to attend a couple of Labour meetings hardly yielded pleasure.

19 August: Tonight to a Labour meeting at Mevagissey, as last night at Carthew. It was mainly Len Tippett's sense of duty that induced me to go. Left to my own devices I should have read another fifty pages of Metternich (who is quite interesting when he is off the point) and borne a few more hours of indigestion without moving from my chair. Instead of that fate Len and I walked by the coast roads to Mevagissey, six miles or so. The meeting had been on for half an hour when we arrived on the quay. A motley crowd of fishermen had assembled along the two arms of the quay, with the speaker at the strategic point of contact. And what use he made of it! What a speech the man gave us! – pure, tub-thumping mob-oratory such as had disgusted Len the night before. Moreover, he was completely out of touch with his audience, never at any point came to grips with it or got across to them. When it came to questions he was worse than helpless: a mind so obtuse I have never come across. He simply couldn't answer a question straight, or even get the drift of it. The result was that he got himself into an impossible position and created an atmosphere of hostility that didn't exist before. At the end of his speech, T. J. Bennetto beckoned to me to take up the collection in a hat; summoning up my courage I went through the crowd.

It was a shaming experience, for the men were by this time openly derisive and, if they had not been good-tempered, might have tipped us over the quay into the harbour. This fool of a Welshman, trained at the Central Labour College on a Marxist diet as exemplified by *Plebs*, its intellectual organ, had been sent down to us from Labour headquarters. Without any spark of humour or sense of reality, living in a world of *Plebs* jargon, he did far more harm than good. For, of course, he corroborated the Mevagissey fishermen in their

Nonconformist Liberalism. Tom Bennetto was an angelic old elementary-school headmaster, of the sweetest disposition; many of the fishermen had been his schoolboys, and but for him they would never have given a hearing to such trash. We could have done a much better job ourselves. For me it was a particularly bitter pill, because my friends Crowther and Ralph Fox regularly handed out to me a diet of *Plebs*, which, though I could not quite comprehend it, I respected for its veneer of intellectuality.

The height of our humiliation came when, having missed the bus through *Plebs* long-windedness, we were given a lift back by our leading opponent, Howard Dunn, the genial fish-merchant, County Councillor and what not, who held the fishermen in the hollow of his hand. I was still more irritated when that fatuous Labour College man, 'arrived at the bottom of Menacuddle Street, offered to walk up the hill with us.' I was surprised to find that he had no idea of the damage he had done to the cause: he had an impermeable conceit. However, I found the unaccustomed experience of a car-ride exciting, 'though somewhat cold in the rushing air. The new road to Mevagissey has some splendid outlooks down gullies to little coves and the sea.' *There* was something more rewarding to the spirit.

Another Marxist periodical which I faithfully read at the behest of my Left-Wing mentors was *The Labour Monthly*. In this Palme-Dutt held forth for years with self-confidence and a sort of geometrical precision, but one could never recognise what he was talking about as the real world one lived in. In short, he lived in a world of Marxist jargon, as sociologists are apt to inhabit their world of jargon, and educationists increasingly theirs. He spun it all out from his insides. It wasn't until years later that I got a clue. Palme-Dutt was Swedish on one side, Indian on the other; perhaps the world he wrote with such facility and verbosity about was Swedish-India, the realm of the non-existent. It reads like theology: it is about nothing, or nothing tangible or visible, sensible or recognisable as real.

These people mixed me up a good deal when I was young; but, having a mind of my own, I did not swallow what they said. I thought my own way through the verbiage. Here is a specimen, at the age of twenty. I offer it not for the merits of the case, but to the social historian as an example of the way we in the 1920s were affected by the early Marxist propaganda emanating from the Russian Revolution.

30 August: I have just finished the August number of the *Labour Monthly*, which is as disquieting and upsetting as ever ... Things appear to be simple enough for Palme-Dutt in this intricate world – a damned sight too simple. I wish I could persuade myself that the Right and the Wrong are so clearly defined; or rather that a certain inevitable (ought I to say?) process would not necessitate more suffering than the drifting tendencies of the moment. By throwing in one's lot with the whole-hoggers and making one's objective the overthrow of capitalist leadership, is it certain that much improvement in the world will be effected? I am not convinced that the alternative would be much of an advance, still less that that advance would be worth the effort and the sacrifices of the struggle to obtain it. Although it is evident that these revolutionary processes are carried forward by the fanatical type, it seems true also that movements of which this type are the instruments are more ruthless and sanguinary than if the world merely ambled along under the influence of the sceptical minds. Is Russia at present so very different from capitalist America? Crowther told me that much the same go-ahead spirit as in big business was in evidence. It was a shock to hear that. The experience of the past and what we know of men's characters are too disillusioning to allow us to expect much of human nature.

Palme-Dutt, for all his despairing view of the external situation, has the sanguine expectation of the fanatic of one idea. He is always talking of the necessity for us to work out the great historic process of the British working class. But it is none the less vain to flatter ourselves that we stand in a key-position in regard to the working-class movement of the world. And isn't it a still worse kind of vanity that leads him to harp ceaselessly on the futility of the present leadership, and the new force that must be created to fill its place? I don't know ... I want to read and know from experience more of actual conditions and tendencies in the working class than I do at present. Up till this I have been a recluse, and a willing recluse. It is a duty to step beyond the bounds of one's own inner life; but is it worth it?

In short, underneath the activity of my inner life, so much concerned with poetry and writing, there was an indefeasible, working-class, common sense. I *was* working-class; Palme-Dutt and Page Arnot, G. D. H. Cole and William Mellors were not. (I had a curious experience with former Communist Bill Mellors even as an undergraduate: the big bully of a fellow collapsed on me when tackled, and said he wasn't feeling well. Inside, he was all soft: I felt sorry for him, warmed to him and nursed him round. All the same, I was astonished at anyone caving in like that.)

The above long excerpt from my Diary may not have expressed the issue very well: I had difficulty in thinking out what I thought about it all. But it doesn't seem to me even now far out, after the sinister way things went in the years between, the deformation of the idealistic hopes of the Revolution, the mountainous losses of lives, the wrongs done to the human spirit. *Was* it all worth it, to achieve even a recognisable improvement in the standard of living? The millions of the dead who were being superfluously sacrificed can hardly have agreed. While the standard of living would certainly have improved with the extension of industrialism under capitalism in Russia – and much more efficiently. As for agriculture – look at the contrast between America and Russia: the vast production of foodstuffs given away in the one, the inability to increase production significantly, in spite of a much larger area, in the other!

The arguments that so much bothered my mind in the abstract when young, before we knew the way things were going to go, have been settled now by the way things have gone. We know now what was what: pity it should have involved so much human suffering. There was no strict necessity for it in the nature of things.

* * *

At the beginning of September I had two days' intermission from my incessant labours, which shook me all the more emotionally. Two or three years previously an architect and his family came to stay at Tregonissey, before we left the village and I went to Oxford; the wife took to me, was kind to me, and admitted me into the bosom of the family – there were two sons, one slightly older, the other younger, than I. They were a happy family, with interests of mind; I had never known such a family before or what such a family life could be: I could not but respond to their kindness with affection. They had a tiny bungalow on the brackeny slopes of one of the loveliest of Cornish beaches, Pendower, then quite unspoiled. It occurred to this good angel, Mrs T., to give me this respite within sight and sound and smell of the sea, the noble wrinkled dinosaur of the Nare Head dominating the bay.

Friday, 5 September: For the space of twenty-four hours or more I have been living in Eden. And I have only just come out of it, trying mainly through all interruptions to keep myself within its fast-retreating atmosphere. This evening for two hours I was jolted back in G.W.R. buses from Eden to St Austell. I felt so sullen after coming back again, just as I remember feeling when a child coming home from a rare holiday at Falmouth. Coming home, I tried hard to keep my mind in the little gully that runs down to the sea, now further and further away. But there were interruptions to the dream: a strange character in the Portscatho bus who had been to Jesus College, Cambridge and University College, London, and was now a peddler of patent medicines: his principle of life was just to be happy, he carried his soul on his face, and his face was a continual smile. While the dream continued through tea-time, W. came! Usually subdued, tonight she was quite alert and almost vivacious. We consumed two hours, and I walked down the road to Polkyth with her. But my mind was all the while with L., and shaggy faithful Spud, as we climbed up cliffs and hills and brakes; and the dream was fading.

Not that I wanted to go at first; one day I had had off already: I did not want to go away from my books, in which lay my whole existence for the past two months. I came back with a distaste for my work, and a feeling of dissatisfaction with my way of life. Plodding at wearisome books all day; poring over interminable memoirs of boastful, egotistical old diplomats. (Both Talleyrand and Metternich are vain; much-abused Friedrich Gentz is a more likeable creature.) Well, there it is: a dream now. I shall fold it up and put it away in my mind, to return to when I have need.

However, the dream would not let me rest. It brought back the memory of the older son of the family, with whom I used to walk to Carn Grey and Luxulyan and towards whom my feelings had been something like Lawrence's towards the eldest son at Haggs farm, as described in his first, lyrical novel and again in *Sons and Lovers*. I had selfishly forgotten my earlier companion, overlaid by so many new experiences, Oxford, and the pressure of work. Now it came flooding back with the release for a couple of days' company at Pendower from the strain I put upon myself. I thought to exorcise my unhappiness by analysing it: I considered it 'mainly an instinct for friendship revenging itself upon a life of too selfish abstraction'. I recalled the misery I felt when my first school-friend, John Clark, died in London, and the nights I used to mope around the school-corridors and out in the grounds thinking of him. We were very young then: no one remembered him more faithfully.

Thinking of these idyllic days at Pendower, and how before going to bed we watched the moon set on our right, while on the bay there was a faint beam reflected from Mars, to the left the up-heaved mass of Nare Head in the darkness, brought back the memory of C., who had gone completely out of my life.

Now he has come completely back again: for two days and a night he has been in my thoughts all the time ... Isn't it a strange condition? No abiding affection for anybody, and what affection there is being throttled, until at times it springs back with a rush at me. That is how I concentrate on my work; but it is the way a life is withered and all that is best stifled. I can't stop in the way I am going: I must go on. My work lies straight ahead and must be mastered before I can get a breathing space.

Well, it's insane, what I have written; but it's a relief – especially after a whole evening spent in summarising Wellington's Dispatches from the Congress of Verona, while my thoughts were elsewhere, miles away.

I see now that these outpourings were a perfectly natural reaction to the severe control clamped down upon a passionate temperament with a real *engoûment* for life denied it – by necessity and my own strong will. However, I did not succeed in exorcising the experience, or rather coming to terms with it, until I wrote those memories into a poem. Here was another of the functions writing poetry performed for me – as a catalyst of the emotions. Here was the poem, never published, for it did not satisfy me; but at least it was part of the process of learning to write.

> Alone I turn over the leaves of memory,
>   Stirring the fragrance of forgotten days,
> Until I come to that remembered time
>   We were together and trod the moorland ways.
>
> It all comes back to me now: our eager youth
>   That drank the green and summer hours,
> And breathed the scented air upon the moor,
>   Brimmed with the murmur of bees and flowers.
>
> Under the hill, a cloud of butterflies
>   With all the rainbow-colours on their wings,
> Fluttered their brief life in the path of the sun:
>   You lingered there amid their flutterings.
>
> At the bend of the road beneath a quiet shade
>   Deep in the grass we dreamed the moments through;
> While from the tawny mirror of the pool
>   Gleamed the washed spaces of the cloudless blue.
>
> Through what gaunt villages the white road led,
>   Old Carn, Trethurgy and Luxulyan grey;
> Beyond, we came upon Lanlivery tower
>   Suddenly, at the closing of the day.

> At last, we saw the lights of the distant town
>   Reflecting a glow upon the sky behind,
> A field of stars in the hollow at our feet:
>   How rare a radiance in the remembering mind!

Another overflow from this upset to the emotions was a little poem about Carn Grey:

> That night we were together on the moor –
> Do you remember? –
> That night when all the wine-red hues of late September
> Sank into a violet haze,
> And all the day's
> Innumerable sounds had sunk to silence
> So deep it seemed the night had ears,
> As, breaking from her anchorage of cloud
> The moon swam into a heaven serene
> And all the moor became a moon-washed sea.

I rather think this was jotted down impromptu, and intended to be turned into the formality of a sonnet.

After this outlet for the emotions I found myself in a better condition for pushing forward once more.

> A strenuous and profitable day: I must have spent over eleven hours at hard mental work of various sorts. All the morning and afternoon at Gentz; then two hours at reducing Hobbes to notes. Two more hours at an article on Feiling's book, at the end of which I had produced exactly one page of manuscript. Then a walk to Porthpean and along the coast to Charlestown. The sea as quiet as an inland pool, and of a soft dove-grey colour. Called at Will Rowse's, where their Granny was sitting by the fire: very old and frail she looked. She will have gone before the year's out. Came home to supper, another hour at Feiling; till midnight sat up in bed writing this first draft of a poem.

I thought well enough of this, 'An Old Cornishwoman by the Fire', to include it among the Early Poems in *Poems of a Decade*.

Perhaps it might have been distracting if any of these Juvenilia had been published, or if I had received encouragement on this side; but I should have been glad of it, even more than of the money, though that would have been helpful too. For want of it I had to be so careful. One day at Truro

> my conscience troubled me all the afternoon, as in the morning I bought a book which I didn't want, for lack of a book which I did. I tramped the streets disconsolate, until finally the struggle was resolved (after a vain attempt to change the book at another shop for *Poems of Today* plus 1s. 6d.) by buying the latter for 3s. 6d. Q's *The Delectable Duchy*, which I must have read more than four times – my usual limit with great favourites, for example, *Jane Eyre* and *Martin Chuzzlewit* – I kept after all. *Troy Town* in the same edition I regret ever having given away. Several poems and most of the little biographies I read as I sat on a bench under the trees of the Malpas Road—

that curiously Continental quayside, like something in Brittany, with the triple-spired cathedral up-river, and below, Malpas where Tristram crossed the river to Iseult waiting for him on the other bank.

But there was no encouragement for me – perhaps inevitably with the loneliness, the independence and seclusion of my life. When I turned to the *Adelphi*, 'a poem called "Ghost Hunters" by Marion Yelland's friend, Violet le Maistre, I liked in spite of myself: it is so much in my own vein and so well done that I am a little jealous, as the *Adelphi* won't publish a thing of mine.' (It did some years later.)

> With much in both Murry's and Lawrence's articles I am in sympathy; but the manner is not to be trusted. Middleton Murry is glib and sentimental; D. H. Lawrence is hysterical and rather mad. But there's no doubt that their message (or messages, for consistency isn't a virtue with them) answers to something in the reactions and developments of the post-war mentality. Murry's distrust of 'formulation' is the thing that I have talked about with Bacon and Len Tippett on occasion.

It is just that I have felt how impossible it is to get at all deeply into the nature of things by the usual process of differentiation. I feel how superficial are the opposites and antitheses we make of our concepts, how futile it is to take up any definite line of thought, since the other is equally true. It is this feeling that has withered up my political enthusiasms for the time (I always insist it is only 'for the time'); what is the difference between a conservative and a socialist outlook?

I suppose this may be taken as intellectual growing pains. 'When in doubt turn to Carlyle' seems to have been my motto. To steady myself I twice quoted the passage: 'Manhood begins when we have in any way made truce with Necessity; begins even when we have surrendered to Necessity, as the most part only do; but begins joyfully and hopefully only when we have reconciled ourselves to Necessity; and thus in reality triumphed over Necessity, and felt that in Necessity we are free.' I went on, 'the truth is that it has been bred into my bone to jib at the acceptance of things – whether material circumstances (since I am poor), or friendship (because I am lonely), or death (because I have not yet experienced what there is in life)'.

*   *   *

Meanwhile, how were my Oxford friends spending their vacations this summer of 1924? This was the year of the big Wembley Exhibition, and Lawrenson had stayed with David Low to visit it. The Londoner took our Geordie friend

on the giant switchback and Thomas didn't like it at all. Apart from some of the beautiful fabrics and glass in the Hall of Industries, I think the switchback is the only sensation worth having in the Exhibition. And my nerves being now jaded, I just admire the concrete masses from a hill up the road. Here I have had generally a nice homely time – if there is such a thing in London. Worked spasmodically – read a fair amount outside my subject – gone to most of the good plays in London – seen almost all the private exhibitions, 'Brangwyn', 'Collings', 'Gauguin' etc. – heard the opera and now about to go to the Promenade concerts in the Queen's Hall. Then I have paid a few visits – among them one to Streeten at Tonbridge – and I went for a week to the Fabian Summer School on the South Coast.

As a period-piece with its period-characters I append David's description of this educative entertainment.

In the mornings we had Sisley Huddlestone, Mrs Swanwick, Austin Harrison, Haden Guest, S. K. Ratcliffe ... It was all very general and more interesting than informative. Austin Harrison was especially wild in his prophecy of continual bickerings and weary treaties and animosities. The Fabians did not like it at all – became heated themselves and we had a very topsy-turvy discussion which was finally side-tracked on to the Jews. Here the meeting became rude and the lunch bell went after a most illuminating morning. Haden Guest was directing the School my week and he certainly has very clear ideas on his interests, i.e. his profession, Russia and the Commonwealth. We had vegetarians – psycho-analysts – 8 nationalities – Jews – schoolmistresses – anti-vivisectionists – ex-colonels – some charming American girls – a married man who wasn't living with his wife – G. B. Shaw's secretary – a clergyman from the East End – an official from the House of Commons – one Christian mother with a daughter who would talk about the will of the Lord – the single woman who unceasingly attempted to dominate her table with Divorce Law Reform – some Irish girls who were not capable of following or understanding politics and made rude comments on the front benches.

It seems a fair summing-up of one of those Fabian jamborees. After this orgy David was proposing to top it up with a caravan-tour, then something new and original, from Winchester to Salisbury and then across the Plain to Shaftesbury, Dorchester and the Hardy country. David asked if I had any news of Wadleigh; of course I had not, nor had I written him.

From Cheltenham A. H. M. Jones, who, as Secretary of the Labour Club, was making the fixtures for next term when I was to be

Chairman, wrote: 'I will pass over all my woes – how one was ill, another abroad, another overworked, another writing a book etc., etc., but will recount only my triumphs.' He had secured Page Arnot, a Communist all too available, Andrew MacLaren, E. F. Wise and Purcell. But

the respectable Trade Unionists, viz. Cole, Laski [sic] and Margaret Bondfield have all failed. Can you suggest anyone else? Rakovski and A. W. Haycock are both at large in foreign affairs, though I have received a polite note from the Russian Embassy saying that Rakovski will soon get my invitation ... I have suggested Foreign Affairs to Haycock and Russia to Rakovski. Could they not both stand, *if* they both accept, and could not the intellectual Trade Unionist slide? Give me some more names, however, in case they don't. That, I think, ends official business. I spent three weeks in your delightful county (and it rained only five complete days) at Porthcothan Bay between Newquay and Padstow. But the rugged coast, charming moors (this, I understand, means a marshy river-bottom in your part of the country), bleak and romantic downs with their cromlechs, menhirs and barrows are, I presume, familiar to you. P.S. Wadleigh has not yet sent me the Minute-Book!! What are his initials and, if possible, home address?

From David Cecil, from the Salisbury house in Arlington Street, came a characteristic letter.

This is just a line to tell you how much I enjoyed your poem in the last *Outlook* which I have just read. It has real atmosphere. Do let me know if you print or have printed anything else as I should so like to read it. I am afraid you must have thought me very rude never to have come to see you. I felt very guilty towards you. But from when I saw you on till Schools, I had absolutely not a minute. I went away for the last fortnight and again from last Wednesday after Schools till Friday night. But I did want to come so very much. I hope you will forgive me if I looked rude. We shall meet anyhow next term. Excuse bad writing.

The curious thing about that idiosyncratic, spidery, scratchy writing is that it is very like the hand of his famous ancestor, Lord Burghley, which was to become so familiar at the Public Record Office in later years of research.

Here was another crabbed hand, from Mark Thomson, who became a well-known professor of history, an authority on the eighteenth century. He was the son of a parson at Devonport, and was half French. This contributed to a remarkable personality with a still more remarkable voice: half of it was normal enough, though distinctly clerical, the rest would go off into a high falsetto. This added to the eccentric effect, and the amusement his speeches gave, at the Union. A tall big fellow, with a fine broad forehead, an amused expression playing around his eyes, he already fancied himself as a *gourmet* and on his taste in wine; and he had the advantage of being bilingual. He became an excellent, if somewhat constipated, historical scholar; he did not leave much on record in the way of books, of all that he knew, when he died – poor fellow – in his fifties, his work unfulfilled. He wrote me from Devonport:

I hope you are enjoying Cornwall as much as I have enjoyed Dartmoor. I say 'have' because after spending three delightful weeks at Bridestowe in the country, I have returned to this vile place, which, whatever it may have been in the days when Drake played his famous game on the Hoe, is now the stronghold of all that is dull and stupid ... While I was in the country I gave the Classics a rest and read nothing but English poetry, for which I have had very little time during the last two years. For the first time I dived into the 17th century and read those two anthologies I showed you in the train. I quite agree with you in admiring the period, though I still have an affection for the next century. [This became his life's work.] We must look forward to a row in the political world. Ireland again is going to be the storm-centre. If Ramsay tries to coerce Ulster it will mean civil war. However, an election would probably go against him, which you, I take it, would deplore. After our successes at recent by-elections I believe we will carry the country. In any case a few weeks will see a change one way or the other.

Mark, as a son of the Church in those days, was naturally a Conservative. Hadn't Disraeli observed that the Church of England was the Conservative party at prayer?

So much for a sample of the activities and interests of the serious-minded young men of my acquaintance in the 1920s.

*   *   *

I finished the vacation in a more contented frame of mind. '19 September: I must have read ten hours today at Max Beer's *History of British Socialism* and Aristotle's *Politics*. And at last I have come to the end of them both. For all that, the poem that I wrote two days ago is a greater cause for happiness. When I can get further away from it, perhaps there are phrases that I shall be able to improve.' I returned to my old resource, Carlyle, to vary my diet and was much impressed by the biographical essays on Burns and Boswell. I appreciated already how much more perceptive he was on these two controversial characters, much mis-estimated by conventional opinion that had got them both wrong. Carlyle was the first to perceive that the author of the Life of Johnson must have been a remarkable man in his own right – as against Macaulay and all the conventionals.

> In several places where Carlyle must have had nothing to go on in contemporary criticism, his own pioneer estimates have remained unchallenged. Last night before going to bed I read his 'Chartism', as the night before I read 'Corn Law Rhymes'. There is nothing in either to equal the 'Burns' or the 'Johnson'. I felt about his social criticism that it was all from the standpoint of the individual, and hence incapable of dealing with mass-movements. The temperament of the artist runs away with him even when he is diagnosing general evils. It is this contradiction, I suppose, that accounts for the unsteadiness, the hysteria, of his thoughts on the Condition of England.

Looking back on the undergraduate of forty years ago as if he were my pupil, I observe the judgments improving, indeed the capacity to judge was forming – but by the hard way, a very long way round. I derived encouragement for my sort of poetry, as against the exoticism of that of the Oxford aesthetes, from this pronouncement of Carlyle's: 'The poet, we imagine, can never have far to seek for a subject: the elements of his art are in him, and around him on every hand; for him the ideal world is not remote from the actual, but under it and within it: nay, he is a poet precisely because he can discern it there.'

My walks resumed their solitariness, and were not the less satisfying for that. 'To Carn Grey in a more resigned frame of mind. My thoughts today have made my work pleasant: six hours at Talleyrand, and at odd moments my mind wandering back to that summer and winter the T.s spent in the house at New Road.' I went back to my earlier diaries – which I never read – for the enchantments of those walks with C. 'Those old diaries of mine (I am ashamed of them) read as if they were breathless with activity. They are full of work at school and reading at home, and of plans and hopes for getting to Oxford. They aren't worth much, nor do I suppose these later volumes are.' Forthwith I destroyed the first half-dozen of them, kept mostly in school exercise-books.

This has been an evening such as I enjoy most: after a rainy day, when the sky still has some ragged threatening clouds, and a cold wind is up. I trudged uphill, when the sunlight had already gone from the slades and plains and lit only a few housetops and chimneys ... It was still early when I left the Carn, so I tramped down the road towards school, and back again through the village. A muffled peal of bells was ringing when I turned homewards.

One evening at Charlestown I ran into

an interesting old fellow of a councillor, called Tresidder, who has spent most of his life as a schoolmaster on the north coast. He originally came from the West, and has the typical face of the purest Cornishman: small and dark, with high cheek-bones and sparkling eyes, deep-set in the head. A thoroughly active type, bubbling over with interest in all kinds of things. We started on the subject of dialect, thence to Charles Lee and his

Widow Woman, which I have never read. He remembered the starting of the *Cornish Magazine* in the 'nineties, with Charles Lee and H. D. Lowry among its contributors, Q being Editor. His main interest was the flora of Cornwall: throughout the summer he has been making trips twice a week with a friend who is making a collection of Cornish flora for the authorities at Kew. They already have one, but want another to exchange with Riga. Strange meeting of extremes! This week he had been to Ruan Lanihorne for some sedges, and to St Enodoc for a great buttercup.

On a later September Sunday, hearing that the new Bishop, Frere, was to preach at Lanlivery I walked the whole way to hear him – a couple of miles on beyond the four to Luxulyan. Coming down through the quiet, resting countryside I suddenly heard the bells ringing from the tall tower to evensong – somewhat to my surprise; for I knew that the parish was at loggerheads with the eccentric vicar and I didn't expect that there would be any ringers. The vicar was an Irishman mouldering away in that roomy Georgian vicarage, who spent most of his time writing letters to the *Western Morning News* and sending exceedingly odd contributions to the Deanery Magazine. My friend Bruce McFarlane once penetrated into the vicarage with Charles Henderson, to find a very Betjeman figure: the old clergyman's hair was tied up in pink ribbons and he spent his time making violins – which didn't play, of course.

But the new Bishop had brought the parish together with their vicar, at least for his visit. The church was fairly well full, the altar ablaze with candles, and the vicar had even raised a couple of scarlet-cassocked choirboys to attend as acolytes upon his lordship. Bishop Frere appeared in great simplicity – no cope or mitre, merely a black chimere – and preached a simple, pastoral sermon. Just, one would have thought, what the parish needed. Not so the parish: as I passed out through the porch I heard one farmer say to another, 'E'es, a nice simple sermon; very simple.' What they evidently wanted from a bishop was something more impressive: something they couldn't understand.

Before I returned to Oxford, I had another exciting letter from Q inquiring for my acting version of *Troy Town*, which Fowey Grammar School thought of playing at Christmas. So I chased around to school after it, ransacked the archives for the remains of the typed copies and managed to put it together again.

On looking it over, I felt that despite the drawback of the play's lack of action, it was not unworthy of the book. The structure of it is regular enough and minimises the melodrama which is what *Troy Town* has for action. The plot is the least essential to the book, and so in the play it is merely described by the characters instead of being forced into the limelight. The ending, when I read it again, quite moved me: I left it unobtrusive; it seemed truer, and a little pathetic, that way.

On the other hand, just before my return:

3 October: A relapse of two days, during which I have done nothing. I've been unwell again and last night had a harassing time of it, instead of quiet sleep. Whether the excitement of good news, or merely an indigestible dinner, is responsible for it, I don't know. Perhaps it is that I am quite run down again after the unceasing work of the vac.; because, with the exception of a fortnight at most, I have worked regularly seven hours a day on average. I haven't the mental energy now to read a difficult book or write notes on it or even letters.

There was the enemy, lying in wait.

VI

Third Year: Last Lap: 'Schools'

EVERYONE who knows Oxford knows that taking the Honour School of Modern History seriously is a great strain – more than, probably, any other Final School. It involves so much reading, interminably: there is no end to it. The Greats School – the classical school, based on Greek and Roman literature, history, philosophy – is divided in two by Honour Moderations at half-time. So that it is not such a burden. In the History School there was a preliminary examination at the end of one's second term, just to keep one up to the mark; after that there was the long stretch ahead of two years, two long vacations and a term – rather like the endless, unpunctuated succession of Sundays after Trinity that had bored me as a choirboy.

This long passage gave people plenty of opportunities to lose themselves, and not come up again. I found it hard going, for I had not been taught much history at my small Cornish school, unlike the History Scholars of my time – the Etonian and Wykehamist Collegers, the Connollys and Birleys and Pareses, or even a plain Dulwich Scholar like McFarlane of Exeter. I groaned under the burden; I thought I should never see daylight. Yet, curiously enough, it doesn't seem to have occurred to me to repent of my choice, or to repine at my tutors for pushing me into it. Indeed I was grateful to them: I thought that they were looking after my best interests, even if I were disappointing their expectations by being somewhat unprofessional. The fact was that I was working away, even if at something other than what they expected. And I gave myself a double burden, by carrying on my literary interests, both in reading and writing – never enough to satisfy my insatiable desires – *pari passu* along with all the history. It never occurred to me that carrying on like this might give one a nervous breakdown; but it must have encouraged the ulcer.

Anyway, the long, intense, concentrated work of that Long Vacation in Cornwall made all the difference; having been for so long behind, I was now abreast. So far from reforming my ways – unlike the professional Birley, who never put a foot wrong, or made any contribution to general undergraduate activities, so far as I ever heard – in the new term I was to give up a good deal of time to the chairmanship of the Labour Club, and the next vacation to writing a long poem for the Newdigate.

As for tutorials, it occurred to our tutors to couple Roger Makins, who has had such a grand career of public service, along with me: I suppose it was thought it would be good for us both. Roger was immensely distinguished to look at even then, very lofty with prominent bony nose and slightly Mongoloid cast of features; very alert and intelligent, with a quick, engaging sense of humour. But I don't remember anything interesting being said, and the truth is that I was rather bored by Masterman's tutorials: he was more like a schoolmaster, seeing that we got our quota of work done. Had he any intellectual interest in the subject himself? I doubt it, or he would have written about it. For want of such an interest and rather than be bored, once and again I held forth myself – and caught J. C. and Roger catching each other's eye. All the same, Masterman did his duty: he saw that we worked. He used to inflict two essays a week on us: I never could get more than one and a half, or one and a bit done, with all the rest there was to do.

Feiling undoubtedly had a living interest in history, and was at this time bringing out the first of his volumes on the Tory party, in which I was loyally interested – without being a Tory, of course. (I even went so far as to spend 18s. on that volume in Parker's, feeling as if I had dived off into very deep water.) David Cecil used to say that Feiling gave him a real, romantic sense of the past – he had told him of the feeling it gave him to come in at Tom Gate the sense of all the history that had flowed in and out of it, the Civil War, the Restoration and Charles II going forth in his coach to surprise the Oxford Parliament with its dissolution, John Locke and the Revolution of 1688. I am sure that this is so, for it all appears in the last of Feiling's books, *In Christ Church Hall*. These essays, he tells us, 'originated in a thought recurring each autumn, that this was the most memorable day of the University year when, dining in Hall on the first night of the Michaelmas term, one looked down at the hive stirring with yet another generation who came from every sort of home and every province of the Commonwealth, to make or mar.' There upon the walls, lit up shadowily by the lamps upon the long tables where we sat, or occasionally flickering in the flames of the great Hall fire in winter, were famous Christ Church men on all sides. 'For three centuries the foreign affairs of the realm were largely directed by men who once sat here. In that gallery there has been much glory and tragedy, if, among ministers, one thinks of Carteret and Shelburne, Grenville and Canning, Salisbury and Rosebery, or take from the ambassadors' ranks William Wickham and the first Granville, Dufferin and Lyons, without trenching on our own controversial age in Halifax and Eden.'

If this was what Feiling was thinking about, he didn't communicate much of it to me. But that was hardly his fault, since for much of our time together we were bogged down in the Middle Ages, and he was not a medievalist; neither was I. In my last year Feiling recruited a professional medievalist to the staff, in E. F. Jacob from All Souls. For a term's revision of that immense tract from the Dark Ages to the Renaissance – when I woke up and began to take notice – I went to him. The kindest of men, at this time he was very shy and that made me so; I remember sitting on the edge of my chair while the esoteric (and latest) treasures of the Manchester School – like Matthew Arnold's corded bales – were uncorded or tangled up, as the case might be, before me. Dutifully I chased off to the Codrington Library and sat there in the afternoons from two to seven, until my bottom grew paralysed on those Chippendale chairs, reading the interminable Tait and Tout. Never a question on it all appeared in the Schools.

With all this on hand there are far fewer entries in the Diary this term than when I was alone to myself in Cornwall. For a whole month after getting back I made no entry: 'each time I have wanted to, I have had so much reading to get through that my conscience (my 'Nonconformist conscience', as Otis says) held me back.'

7

Otis was a new acquaintance who had come into my circle, a junior: clever, with a jerky, neurotic manner, tall and spotty, malicious – perhaps pardonable in one so young, though not really attractive. Great things were expected of him: they did not come off. He had the advantage of already knowing German, he was a professional historian who won a University prize; he was well informed in the new literature and was (I think) the first person who introduced me to Eliot's literary criticism, lending me *The Sacred Wood*.

Eliot's poetry – after all, the more important side to his work – I already knew for myself. I read 'The Waste Land' with much excitement to Wadleigh, whose response was favourable enough, though the real enthusiasm of his mind was for the humbugging delights of ethics that had little appeal for me. Poetry and politics, history and literature – such was my simple make-up, incapable of losing myself in the Non-Sense Land of metaphysics and theology, and not much given to wasting time over moralistic cant. Hard work, duty, achievement – do the best one could – as much control over oneself as one could manage, make oneself do what one willed, stick to one's friends, give enemies back as good as they gave – I don't know where I picked up this not very exalted code from, but it served me in good stead. Rather more effectively, I observe, than the probing into ethics of the more high-minded Wadleigh kind; and I must own, I thought that rather vulgar – better to keep it to oneself.

Something that came into my mind from the past gave me

a sudden feeling of happiness. I believe it was the thought of Mrs Arthur Coode, that proud (and comic) old relic of Victorian days at home, which interposed itself between me and Rousseau. I have just left off at the chapter, 'Que la Souveraineté est Inaliénable'. Well, let it be; in my present mood I don't much care. The awful sense of duty that has kept me away from my Diary, from writing poems, from thinking of the things that are the very stuff of my life is away (not far away) on holiday. I suppose it's good for me to nail myself down to solid reading, but I wonder how long my mind will stand it?

Twice lately I thought of an impression that would ordinarily have been an idea for a poem. Both times – in Balliol Hall this morning when a sense of the drabness of existence overwhelmed me for a minute, and last night in a lecture-room that I entered alone when it was dark except for a strange light that fell about the room and gleamed upon the chairs where it fell – I put away both impressions as if they were temptations. I might have allowed myself to get excited over them, and then I could have thought of nothing else. I suppose such a deliberate action of the mind is economical of time and energy; but it does not give much real satisfaction ... It's getting late; perhaps I'd better get back to 'Que la Souveraineté est Inaliénable.'

There were consolations, however, as always in Oxford.

26 November 1924: This best-loved of moments has arrived, when I have a few minutes to myself before some friends arrive for tea. The kettle is on the fire, and the tea-cups set out on the little table. What is more, darkness has set in early, so I've turned on the light, before the curtains are drawn for the night. The avenue into the Meadows is shining with rain; the trees outside my windows stand up like gaunt ghosts. I shall be sorry to leave it all, as I must at the end of the year.

At this point my friends arrived, Jacobs of Hertford and Levine of Magdalen, of whom I saw a good deal at this time – he was on the committee of the Labour Club – and we had a pleasant tea-party. Later that night,

I have just come back from Exeter with an annoying sense of a lost opportunity. F. P. Wilson, a don, gave a delightful paper on Shakespeare's London, which left not much room for discussion. Only two people spoke at all, and I, on being asked, modestly refused: too nervous. Now I am regretting it, for I had several things I really wanted to say. I swear that in future I will not forego such opportunities through pandering to my nervousness. I felt positively ungrateful at making no contribution tonight, though I was there as a visitor. Well, now, rather breakdown than such weakness.

It is curious to me now to remember for how long I was afflicted with this nervousness at speaking in public. It came from extreme self-consciousness, and made me very vexed with myself; for there were frequently things I much wanted to express and discuss. Here is a matter over which I find the modern generation at an advantage over ours: whether in Britain or, still more, America, students have far less self-consciousness and have no hesitation in getting up and exchanging ideas. Good thing! That evening I had been John Garrett's guest, specially asked because of my literary interests; he must have been disappointed with me, and I never got to know F. P. Wilson until many years later. How my fellow-undergraduates made me Secretary and Chairman of the University Labour Club, President of the Essay Club, when I was so nervous a speaker, I can't think: I suppose I made up for it by being aggressive in private. I took it as due simply to willingness to work.

From this November dates the first of the letters home that my mother took to keeping: pretty simple they had to be; my parents didn't find it easy to read handwriting. This one is mostly about my Labour Club activities – no use confiding to them my troubles with Tait and Tout, Rousseau and Aristotle. (Aristotle would have meant to my mother, as secretly to Victorian women, his book on child-bearing: unmentionable. But I knew that that book was secreted in her chest of drawers in the old home. That was what the sage meant to the people.)

The work goes forward merrily enough. I have been reading all today; then tomorrow night is the Labour Club meeting. They tell me I have made a good Chairman and have run the meetings well. It is great fun, though I am always rather nervous. One night the Master of Balliol College [A. D. Lindsay], who has just been appointed and is a great Labour man, came and spoke. Last Friday we had the new Labour woman M.P., Miss Wilkinson, who wasn't bad. Another M.P. the week before – a splendid fellow, an Irishman whom I got on well with; he came and had breakfast in my rooms next morning. As far as money goes I have managed all right. Shall be able to get home without pawning my shirt. Am not so tired this term as usual; still it'll be nice to go home.

Here were my impressions of a couple of our speakers recorded in the Diary. E. F. Wise was an able Cambridge economist who had proved himself as an effective administrator during the War, and had probably overworked himself, for he died in early middle age. With his capacity and experience he would have added one to the small band of able Labour ministers; as it was he became one of the larger band of promising Labour men snuffed out before their full time, Evan Durbin, Stafford Cripps, Aneurin Bevan, Hugh Gaitskell, John Strachey. I thought Wise

a charming man, with varied experiences of the post-war conferences at Cannes and Genoa, of Moscow (with the rush of hundreds of nude Russians to bathe in the river at the first approach of summer) and of running war-departments, such as that which made sausages when the butchers refused to. I thought of him as a sort of Labour Keynes; Otis was struck by his points of likeness to Hugh Dalton. Perhaps the Cambridge economists conform to a type; one's impression is of a practical balance one can have confidence in. The more G. D. H. Cole type, still more that of Palme-Dutt, gives one no assurance as to its real competence.

That, at any rate, was not far off the mark.

Andrew McLaren was of quite another kind, a very recognisable one to me. He is the generous, open-handed Irishman, with force and imagination. But the force is dispersed by lack of practical sense, an insight into what is practical and what is not. At dinner he insisted on paying for us all and throwing wine into the bargain – wouldn't hear of my not taking any: so I did and was quite eloquent at the Club afterwards. The train he went by was rather crowded, so he travelled first class. I don't suppose he has any means except his Parliamentary salary; he's married and has a family – so the Irish generosity appears not so generous after all.

(I don't know whether M.P.s were provided with first-class railway vouchers in those days; but I wouldn't have dreamed of travelling first-class, nor do I still.)

'My mind's energy has been so absorbed by my work and the chairmanship of the Labour Club that I have had no time for living to myself' – or for poetry. Social life, engagements for meals, continued on a more subdued scale: lunches with Feiling and Rawlinson, teas with John Kirkwood, the celebrated Labour M.P.'s son, with a new Christ Church recruit to the Labour Club, T. B. L. Webster, who was to become a distinguished classical scholar; with my fellow-historians, Fellowes-Brown, on his way into the Church; Whitlam-smith, on his into the consular service; with Otis, Aikin-Sneath, Robin Burn and dear Tom Lawrenson, who gave me a birthday tea on 4 December at the Moorish Café. Then there was my Indian friend, Swamanathan, and another Japanese acquaintance, Professor Saito. I found time for only one musical session, Palestrina's 'Missa Assumpta est Maria' at New College, and one or two visits to the Playhouse to see Synge.

2 December: An extraordinarily chaotic evening such as I do not like, however interesting its events. Mrs Beazley came to tea – if that isn't too euphemistic for a visit at which she neither drinks tea nor eats, though others do. We talked, perhaps somewhat uneasily, until 7 p.m.: of poets, of politicians (for whom she has an abhorrence), and I read some poems. Robert Graves and a crowd of other people then followed; dinner at the guest-table in Hall – a distraction being Oakshott's absence, though we had waited for him – and a meeting of the Essay Club. Graves's paper was all about the analogy between poetry and politics: the Right, Centre and the Left. It failed to arouse much discussion, it was all so new and strange to our ears. There were things in it, however, with which I disagreed; and I had an interesting, though disjointed, talk with him before and after the Club. A queer, charming fellow; I think I understand him. His craze for analysing motives and psychological phenomena must be due to that slight mental unbalance left over from the War. If that doesn't get the upper hand of him,

he'll do great things. My Japanese professor was also present; this apparently is the last occasion on which I shall meet him. He has left me with a rare privately-printed thing of Lascelles Abercrombie, and a notebook so beautiful that I dare not use it.

Today I have spent pots of money on books, far more than I can afford. The fact is I got £5 out of the Bank to take me home: 30s. of it went west today. However, I have *A Shropshire Lad* to show for it. I read this to Wadleigh, who appreciated its point:

> Into my heart an air that kills
>   From yon far country blows:
> What are those blue, remembered hills,
>   What spires, what farms are those?
>
> That is the land of lost content,
>   I see it shining plain,
> The happy highways where I went
>   And cannot come again.

After the memorable twenty-four hours I had spent at Pendower in the summer, I wrote the elder son of the family, whose memory had surged up in my mind. Now for the last week-end of term he came down to stop with me.

Sunday, 7 December: I've just seen C. off at the station. He has been here since Friday night, and we've spent most of the time sight-seeing and talking. It's always a little lonely when a friend goes away; it's all the more lonely because it's C. who has gone. He hasn't altered much; I suppose it's I who have changed since the days – three years ago? – at St Austell together. But it wasn't strange or awkward when we met again, after all that time. We fell into the old ways and talk. On Friday night we sat up till two, on Saturday night till one. He has been happy to be here, and it makes me glad that he came. It was all so pleasant because we had a short time together; if we lived in one place for any length of time, the glamour of it would vanish like anything else ... When I came back from the station, the moon was up and there was a gleam of light along the cupola of Tom

Tower. And St Aldate's bells were ringing, in the street outside rather loudly, but once inside the gate they seemed so far away; the echoes threw back a soft undertone as if the bells were muffled.

On Sunday we had gone out to Woodstock, a favourite excursion, to see Blenhcim Palace: in at the town-gate built by Duchess Sarah as a monument of her love for John, Duke of Marlborough, and then the splendid panorama bursts upon the view – Vanbrugh's monumental bridge spanning the lake, the vast house ending the horizon like a back-drop to a stage-setting. And one remembers that Vanbrugh was a dramatist before he turned architect. In those days one saw only the outside of the palace; we marched hungrily round like a besieging army, peering in at any cranny or crevice we could, to gain a glimpse of the esoteric ducal life lived within. It was not till many years had passed – and a great deal of work been accomplished – that I gained entrance into the Palace and on quite a different footing, as a guest of the family with Sir Winston Churchill, who was born there. (It was only natural that I should think back to the early days at Tregonissey, the 1910s, when Vanderbilts were as much in the newspapers as Churchills, and my father had walked into town to hear Winston as a Liberal speak in the Market House. An historian should appreciate these contrasts and transitions.) C. and I, on a dark December Sunday of 1924, ate our tea contentedly in one of those comfortable, satisfying cafés in the little town at the Palace gates.

*   *   *

In October our arrangements for the Labour Club had been upset by the unexpected precipitation of a General Election. The first Labour government, it may not be remembered now, had done moderately well. Ramsay MacDonald, in particular, had added much to his stature in the country by his handling of foreign affairs. Lord Eustace Percy, a truly independent judge, held that of all our post-war politicians MacDonald was the one most naturally gifted to be Foreign Secretary. I think this is only fair – and such is the malignity of politics that MacDonald held the Foreign Office for only some ten months. Instead, we were treated to a succession of Austen Chamberlain – not bad; John Simon – hopeless; Sam Hoare – who precipitated a disaster with the Hoare-Laval Pact; Eden – not strong enough; Halifax – who allowed Neville Chamberlain to run his own foreign policy, and that was ruinous to the nation.

At any rate, MacDonald in the first Labour government handled foreign affairs well. Roger Makins, who often watched MacDonald at conferences, once said to me that he had never seen him miss a point or give one away. The philosopher McTaggart, a fellow-Scot, said of MacDonald that 'his hands were literally calloused with wire-pulling' – a very good qualification for dealing with foreign affairs. After all, MacDonald knew more about them than other British politicians – not like Stanley Baldwin, who, in all the fifteen years of being the most powerful politician in the country, spent every September at Aix-les-Bains and could never once be persuaded to make the two-hour motor-drive to the League of Nations at Geneva. If we are now saddled with, paralysed by, the Welfare State, the Conservatives have only themselves to thank: in the 1920s and 1930s they showed themselves unworthy to rule a great nation. In the 1950s and 1960s they have made a better showing, produced better people; but this, too, is like the malignity of public affairs, for it is too late now. It doesn't much matter any more; the real decisions are elsewhere, and we are out of them.

But MacDonald's government existed on a shoe-string, or, rather, since it was in a minority, by sufferance of the Liberals, who were themselves divided between the Asquith and Lloyd George wings. Neither of the historic parties could accustom themselves to the idea of Labour governing the country, and they did not mean it to continue much longer. As usual Russia gave them their opportunity. MacDonald had negotiated a treaty with Soviet Russia, which involved a loan to purchase British goods. This provided a good plank on which Conservatives and Liberals could come together to oust the government. At this moment the Communists came, characteristically, to the aid of the Conservatives. The *Workers' Weekly* had come out with an article calling on soldiers and sailors not to use their arms against members of their own class –

as if any such circumstances were likely to arise in Britain! Pure
fantasy – but it enabled the Liberals to dissociate themselves from
the 'extremist' courses of MacDonald's government, and Baldwin
to execute a characteristic smart manoeuvre by lining up the Conservatives with the Liberals to vote the government down.

MacDonald did not resign, but decided to appeal to the country.
I think he genuinely thought that he had a chance of improving
Labour's position, if not of winning a majority. The Tories, with
the Liberals aiding them, and the Tory press saw to that: they all
ganged up to keep Labour out, as they did again in 1931. In about
a hundred constituencies the Liberals stood down to avoid three-
cornered contests and put the Tory in; in some others, including
Mr Asquith's constituency, the Tories stood down to keep Labour
out. There couldn't be any doubt of the result. But to make doubly
sure, five days before polling day, the Tory press panicked the
electorate with the affair of the 'Red Letter'.

The famous Red Letter was a routine communication from Zinoviev as President of the Third International instructing Communists
to work for the overthrow of the existing institutions of this country, as of other capitalist countries. What else? Wasn't that what they
were supposed to be doing anyway? Was that news to people? The
letter was minuted as a routine matter in the Foreign Office – and
then someone communicated a copy to the press. MacDonald was
away electioneering and in no position to stem the tide of idiocy
that swept over the British public and overwhelmed the Labour
Party.

By this trick the Tories won 413 seats in all – a clear majority of
211 over all others. Labour came back with only 151 seats, against
their previous 193. The once-great Liberal party returned a mere
40 – several of them only by the aid of a pact with the Tories.
Serve them right. But observe the electoral facts underneath the
seats in Parliament: $7\frac{3}{4}$ million Conservative votes, $5\frac{1}{2}$ million
Labour, 3 million Liberal. The Conservatives, with their immense
majority in Parliament, were still in a minority in the country.

This now-forgotten election of 1924 was historically important,
perhaps momentous. It put an end to the political uncertainty –
there had been three elections in two years – of the post-War

period, and also, alas, to its hopes. It put an end to any effective Liberal party in British politics. Liberals went on encumbering the scene, refusing to recognise the facts of life, wasting their time and other people's, depriving the country of the services of a number of able men – as a remnant still continues to do. But there hasn't been any point in it since 1924. Henceforth, the main struggle in the state would lie between Conservatives and Labour. Thus, too, the election of 1924 marks the beginning of the modern period in our politics, with its contemporary rhythms and issues.

It was the beginning of the twenty-year run, virtually, of Tory power that ended with the second war and the Welfare State. The Tories were really in a minority in the country throughout that time; but under Baldwin they were marvellous at the humbug that bemused and befoozled a stupid electorate, until they woke up and found themselves having to fight for the nation's existence all over again in 1939. As if humbug and cant were not enough to lull the electorate into a false sense of security, when it came to election time they had a bag of tricks with which to panic the people – the Red Letter set a good model in 1924, followed by the Gold Standard panic of 1931, and Mr Baldwin's fake appeal over collective security in 1935. They were past-masters at internal political manœuvring – while the prime interests of the safety of the state, and all the people whose lives depended on it, went by default. They can never be forgiven for it – certainly not by the historian who thinks in terms of the England of Elizabeth and William Cecil, of Oliver Cromwell and William III and Marlborough, of Chatham and the younger Pitt, of Gladstone and Edward Grey and Winston Churchill, whom *they* kept out as long as they could. Unworthy, unworthy, unworthy – it was my fate to grow to maturity and attempt to make my contribution to the country whose history was the inspiration of my work under *these* people!

*   *   *

But we are only in 1924. When I got home to Cornwall I was amazed to find people still talking about the Red Letter, and to find out what a sensation this nonsense had made in their 'minds'.

I could hardly believe my ears. I had a lot to learn yet on the subject of collective human idiocy – about politics, about religion, about sex. What they think on such matters is almost always nonsense.

For the first fortnight at home I read hard, six, eight, ten hours a day: 'a two-volumed *Life and Times of Cavour* by a long-winded American, Thayer, G. M. Trevelyan's *Garibaldi's Defence of the Roman Republic*, two volumes of congealed Ward on nineteenth-century Germany, and Browning's *Strafford*.' Then suddenly one Sunday, deviating, I started off on a longish poem about Byron for the Newdigate. Never having tried to write a long poem, I regarded this as an experiment:

> A man grown old before his time: a man
> Whose splendour of youth burns dimly now and wan,
>
> Yet bursts into a momentary flower
> Of flame, as the embers in the evening hour
>
> Leap suddenly to light, and all the faces
> Gleam in the dusk out of their shadowy places.
>
> For such was the last glow of high endeavour
> As on the threshold of his journey's end
> He stood, and all his comrades caught the light
> Upon that pallid brow and in his eyes.
> And such the image that I have pursued
> Down the mind's dark echoing corridors:
> Of one who stakes his all upon a venture
> Made to retrieve the irretrievable,
> And therein finds an ultimate content.
> O, to leave the dead, the wasted days
> That like a sad, slow funeral procession
> Wind wearily across the blighted land,
> To leave them and forget, and seek to find
> Only the unknown hills and the certain end.

Having begun that Sunday, I went on. (No more history, especially beastly Economic History I was *supposed* to be reading for Collections at the beginning of term. Would there be trouble, disappointing my tutors again?) For the rest of the vacation I was writing the poem, along with a paper on Carew's *Survey of Cornwall* to read at the Zion Guild, of all places. (My father as a boy had attended this chapel, belonging to a brand of Nonconformists, Bryanites, peculiar to Cornwall. I had rarely been inside it.)

Two days before going back to Oxford the long poem, some three hundred lines of it, was finished.

> 14 January 1925, after midnight: The work is over and the poem finished. It has filled my waking thoughts and a good part of the nights during this last week. In the end it got on my nerves, so that I am as relieved as I am proud that it is done. All preparation for going back to Oxford has made way for the poem, and no work during the last fortnight have I done at Economic History for Friday's Collections. But I would rather have done the poem and no work than *vice versa*, even if it doesn't get the Newdigate, which it is good enough for. I feel confident that it is a good poem, though I shall feel less sure later.

As usual, in the excitement of composition I wasn't capable of criticising it. Looking at this piece of juvenilia now, after many years, I see that it was a genuine poem, no mere academic exercise, and that the subject had caught hold of me. It was really about Byron's last journey and his end, descriptive in character: what else could be expected from its extraordinarily unsophisticated, if all too sincere, author? There was more of Carn Grey and the hills and moors where I walked than of the mountains of Greece, where I had never been. (Nor have I still.) The poem was simple and sentimental; all the same, it was not orthodox, it had its own originality. It was written mainly in blank verse, but with passages of rhyming, disjoined couplets, like choruses, at intervals; and in these were modern half-rhymes, which I liked. How would the Newdigate examiners like these? Wouldn't they fall for something more conventional?

However, I knew the poem's quality and went back to Oxford, for once, well pleased. Not until Collections were over was I free to tackle my Economic History – the Hammonds' *Village Labourer* and *Town Labourer*, Cunningham's *Growth of English Industry and*

Commerce, Lipson's *Woollen and Worsted Industry* – all the horrors. I mustn't give the impression that I disliked the whole of Economic History, but I care less for the woollen and worsted industry.

Much more fun was going up to 'the Broadcasting House' to read another poem with the poets. And, to add to my pleasure, I discovered unexpectedly that the *Oxford Magazine* – the dons' paper to which Q had contributed as a young fellow – had published a little poem of mine that I had forgotten all about. In London my old choirman friend, Booth, looked after me and made all the arrangements I should have been incapable of making in the daunting metropolis. I paid my first visit to the British Museum – thus belatedly! – and was fascinated by the wonderful realistic reliefs from the palace of Assur-nasi-pal. 'Bought a card there for mother, and on coming out heard a multitudinous clamour of sparrows in the eaves, so loud that I heard it above the rumble of the traffic.' (Louis MacNeice made good use of that in a poem of his.) Booth – I always referred to my friend respectfully as 'Mr Booth' – took me to a rehearsal of the London Choral Society where I was much impressed by the beauty of Elgar's part-songs – rightly: they should be performed more often than they are – they have much more of the juices of life in them, more genuine inspiration, than many more fashionable works, cut flowers that do not last.

'At the B.B.C. I didn't read at all well; all the earlier poets read at such length that Graham Greene, Monkhouse and I were reduced to short time.' The result was that I was rather rushed and felt doubly nervous. 'Besides, I didn't like reading before all the others: if I had the room to myself, or with one friend, I should like to give a long reading from all my poems. Perhaps I may some day.' (That day has not even yet arrived.) I learned on this visit that Graham Greene, formidable competitor, was in for the Newdigate, and had written a 250-line poem on Byron during the vacation. For 'he read an extract from it tonight, which I liked as a separate poem, but not for the Newdigate. He has dealt with Byron from the point of view of women and love, and to that extent is a much truer picture than that I give.'

Next week I had tea with Graham, but I have no memory of it. What I remember is the extraordinarily youthful appearance with the curly flax-gold hair and the odd strangulated voice, speaking from his Adam's apple as if he had difficulty in producing the voice. Most of all, one was struck by those staring, china-blue eyes, wide open to the world. Later on, those eyes came to have an expression as if they had looked on some nameless horror, into all the horror in life – an impression in keeping with his books after he went down from Oxford and came to maturity. At this time he had not the sophisticated maturity of the Actons, Quennells, Brian Howards – any more than Evelyn Waugh had. It is significant that those were the two who had genius and had so much farther to go than the others. For genius has nothing to do with sophistication or smartness; indeed, one observes that it is often accompanied by naivety (witness Beethoven, Schubert or Brahms) – understandably, for that is an accompanying evidence that they are looking at life and experience with new, surprised eyes, with a freshness and unexpectedness of vision. One thinks of the naivety of the early Shakespeare, of the first comedies and histories, and *Venus and Adonis*, written when he was twenty-eight, no longer young for an Elizabethan.

Next day I lunched with Roy Harrod and had Geoffrey Grigson to tea with me. In spite of our common interests in Cornwall and literature I do not think that we clicked – it is surprising that we did not quarrel; but he was a freshman, we were both very immature and had not yet developed our fighting spurs. That night I went to hear Emma Goldman at the Masonic Hall. Who was she? – some eminent old war-horse of an American anarchist, I fancy. I am surprised by the amount of social life I got in in those unreclusive days: dinner with ever-kind and fascinating Mrs Beazley, tea with the no less kind and constant Rawlinsons, and now with Mrs Feiling; lunch with Mark Thomson, dinner with Levine. I made a new Indian friend, Krishna, who came to tea with me and together we went to the Playhouse. And I had now made the acquaintance of Mary Coate at Lady Margaret Hall, then engaged on her researches into Cornwall in the Civil War. How much I enjoyed those walks across the Parks, the first snowdrops and crocuses out in the carefully tended verges, later the prunuses and flowering cherry and crab-apple, in early summer the chestnuts swaying with their load of candles white or red. There we sat over tea in her roomy, book-laden room, each of us brimming over with talk about Cornwall, history, politics – for she was a life-long Tory, as against my Labour views with a Tory temper underneath.

Nor was Cornwall forgotten: whenever I had a moment, back I went to it in mind. '28 January: What with eight hours' reading and writing today, plus a cold in the head, I feel in the mood for scribbling rather than for any more Industrial Revolutions. Most of the day I have been reading economic history, and all the after-noon I spent in writing letters.' I had been greatly impressed by *The Cherry Orchard* at the Playhouse, especially by the end, the idea of shutting the old house up; 'and when the shutters are closed outside the windows, the old retainer who has spent all his life there in its service gropes through the darkened rooms and finds that he is left alone there to die.' It made me think of a similar idea in Haw-thorne and the memories of the shut mansion of an old Colonial Governor. I was reminded still more of a shut-up mansion at home: Duporth House, built by Charles Rashleigh in Regency days, in its hollow looking to the sea, and with that rocky beach all to itself from which it takes its name – meaning dark beach.

During the vac. I went to the sale at Duporth House, because I wanted to see and feel what the old place in its desolation was like. There were books in the sale, but I hadn't any money to buy them. From the path that follows the cliffs from Porthpean to Charlestown [now fallen away and no longer followable: it was beautiful under its tunnels of ivy, sloe and wild plum, white with blossom in spring], Duporth always seemed so forlorn and deserted. It, too, was shuttered in part, a rare thing for a Cornish house. The stone front with its bays always looked a sad grey, with streaks of green where water had dripped from the eaves or the sea-spray had beaten. If one solitary line of smoke rose from its chimneys among the trees, it seemed all the lonelier. Then the place had such a queer story, with its asso-ciations. Canon Hammond tells of the ghostly striking of a match in the hall; it must have seen strange doings in smuggling days. There is a convenient lane, now overgrown and disused, that leads down to its private beach, a place as gloomy as its name.

On the day of the sale I got into the house for the first time, and was not disappointed: there was such a neglected air about it all, as if nothing had been done to it for the past fifty years. And I dare say nothing had, for the Hodge family were as poor as church mice. It was pretty squalid, with antiquated furniture and hangings piled about, and with the faded coverings and broken chandeliers on the floor. A crowd of people pressed from room to room with the auctioneer, and at last settled down in the dining-room where there was a mass of plate to be sold. I wandered by myself in the drawing-room and library, which look out on the grass sloping down to the trees, the lane, the sea. All the shelves in the library had been emptied; but I found an account book of a Northamptonshire squire from, I believe, Tollerton Hall. It began with the man's marriage about 1687 and was crowded with entries from cover to cover. There was a set of bound files for Stannary papers for the Tywarnhaile division, in which St Austell was included. So I lazed away all my afternoon; when dark was coming on I went up the drive to the gate on the main road and so home. Duporth, I hear, offers attractive building sites for villas all down the slopes to the sea. The house itself has been bought by a successful china-clay magnate, who intends to renovate it and fit it up with every modern convenience. So there's much the same that might be written about Duporth as Chekhov wrote about Madame Ranevsky's house and ancestral cherry orchard.

This long entry, written when I should have been at the Industrial Revolution, gives rise to some reflections. Duporth provides the first instance of my fixation on a house, which has been a recurrent theme through my life – as with some others. Or perhaps the first was Tregrehan, which loomed so romantically, all shut up within its Italian garden and environing shrubberies, behind the lives of my mother's people at the lodge-gates below. Then came Duporth, similarly sequestered and deserted, which I would eye upon my solitary walks across the cliffs from Porthpean to Charlestown –

what would I not give to live there? Another, and later, fixation was silver-grey granite Luxulyan vicarage, Georgian and eastward-facing, down in its hollow among gleaming rhododendrons and silver-trunked beeches. (Bishop Hunkin once told me that, if only I would come into the Church, I should have it.) Along with all these Naboth's vineyards there was always, rarest and most beautiful of all, Trenarren in its enchanted valley where I (sometimes) now live.

It must have been their appeal to the imagination that made me long to live in one or other of these houses. Instead of that I lived in a vile, cramped council-house, surrounded by other people. I wonder I put up with it as long as I did – illness all through the 'thirties, I fancy, or I'd have got out of it long before. By then I was too ill, and too much wrought up by the politics of the 'thirties to bother so much about it. But, earlier, I am not ashamed to say, I was mad (in the American sense) with vexation at not having been born in one of those country houses, into one of those families: I knew that my make-up was much more in keeping with that background and those who had created it.

For my heart was backward-looking; my mind was engaged by the contemporary world, but I was not of it – it yielded nothing but misery, anger, contempt, scorn, shame, humiliation, in the end despair. In my tastes I was already an addict of the cult of romantic decay. One could live, imaginatively, fruitfully, in the past. In the present the bungalows and villas for superfluous people arose around one. Oh, yes: the slopes of Duporth towards the shining sea have been engulfed all right, in the years since I eyed the grey house, built by a man of imagination, across the untarnished cliffs. And all round the fringes of the estate, too, the green and fertile fields swallowed up. While the estate itself is given over to a holiday camp, the house engulfed in bungalows and army-huts and sleeping accommodation for trippers – for this is the age of the People. The People can have it. For oneself, one can always hide, or abscond to America.

Even yet I have not fulfilled my intention of writing about Duporth – though this experience had some little echo in a poem of the name, published in Oxford, which was also reprinted among the early pieces of *Poems of a Decade*. If only I had been able to retrieve a few scraps from that long-ago sale, the old squire's account-book, or the Stannary papers of Tywarnhaile, or one or two of the portraits that went for a song and were picked up by townspeople in St Austell! Still more, if I had been able to possess the place, cherish it, make it my Cornish opposite-number to Harold Acton's 'La Pietra' – but I might just as well have wished for the moon. All I can say is that, if it had been mine, it would not be a holiday camp today.

Meanwhile that term, in February, my enemy was gaining on me and several days I was really ill.

Sunday, 8 February: Am just back from tea with the Rawlin-sons and am for the moment too excited with all the things we talked about to sit down calmly to an essay on the Star Chamber. And when I went into my bedroom to wash my hands just now I had an idea for a poem, from seeing the pale light on my face reflected in the glass, with the boughs of the trees swaying eerily across the reflection. Suppose if they were gashes across the face in the mirror? The other night a new and different idea came into my head. It was while I was walking around and around my room at four in the morning, with perfect agony eating out my insides. It took me several days to get over it. What these attacks are that come and go, and make my life unbearable, I don't know. I think of all sorts of deranged things when I am actually in pain, and afterwards take it lightly and forget about it. I was so mad as to think of a poem about Pain itself – of the agony, and the wearing down of one's strength bit by bit; and then, worn out, being prostrate as if in suppli-cation to a God that hears. The pain effects what the man in no other circumstances would have yielded. It was rather a morbid imagining, but the whole strength of it must lie in the bitter-ness of the conclusion, where the poem ends with the man appearing to have submitted, when really he hasn't.

I had plenty of opportunity to observe the phenomena of pain in the years that were to come, and did eventually make poems out of the experience, printed in *Poems of Deliverance*. But not yet. I kept hoping that the last attack would really be the last: hadn't I had my operation? Hadn't that put things right? I put up with what I called 'indigestion' without taking enough notice. There is no entry in the Diary about the bad attack that is referred to in my Engagements Book, for it meant no work. But I find on '18 Feb.: 7 hours' work. Ill. 19 Feb.: Ill. 20 Feb.: Unwell. 21 Feb.: Unwell.' But next week the enemy was back in strength again and I was driven beyond endurance to protest. Protest to whom? There was no one to unburden myself to but the Diary. '26 February, 4.30 a.m. In agony again. Nothing for it but to walk round and round the room. Good God, what is the matter? Scarcely a night of unbroken sleep for a fortnight. Pain by day and by night.'

Long experience now would enable me to diagnose that these periodic attacks of excruciating pain meant an ulcer, and the fact that the pain came at the end of the process of digestion meant that the ulcer was in the duodenum. But I knew nothing about that then. Whom could I consult? I hoped against hope that the operation had cured me; each time I was better I thought it was for good. But I couldn't have afforded another session with the doctor anyway. Any first-class doctor diagnosing the trouble – it was years before I found one – would have rusticated me and put me on a strict diet, perhaps insisted on my putting off Schools for another year. Out of the question: I couldn't have afforded it, my scholarships – on which I lived – would have come to an end. So I plodded on doggedly.

The week after that dreadful fortnight I find:

Tuesday, no – Monday night. Yet another essay on the stocks: this time about that wretched middle-class Revolution, about which the books (as on every other point of real historical importance) are meaningless. Have been in a wretched state for the last week; apparently that concentrated bout of reading did for me. The pains I suffered night after night were excruciating, and now I am left weak, but convalescent. The paper I was to have read at Exeter mercifully cancelled. Two essays yet remain my portion. Have been dreaming about home in a disordered way for some time; always it's something has happened to father or mother. How distant those days are becoming, and it is only at moments that I know them to be, as they are, irrecoverable.

A fortnight to go, during which I picked up my pace at reading again – 4 hours, 6 hours, 9 hours, 7 hours, 9 hours, like someone in training for a race (but winged) – before I was home once more. On my way down in the train I noted in my I.L.P. Diary:

> Going into the West. Still water under trees: open spaces of downs, hills that meet the sky; and sudden in a lull, a bird's song. Light and shade falling in folds along the distant hills. A solitary haystack that stands four-square to the winds. A familiar nook: a shallow pool ringed by great elms. And here a barren place made beautiful with white flowers thickly sown. A lone signal that beckons like a scarecrow in the gathering dark. Lights in harbour like a flight of birds.

There were my consolations, my inner life.

*   *   *

Arrived home for the Easter vacation before Schools I tried to achieve the clock-work regularity that had been somewhat broken, though not entirely, by illness in Oxford. Here were the evidences of overstrain.

> Thursday about the 28th of March. [Actually it was the 26th.] I feel rather crazed in the head and am willing to put up with Baldwin's *King's Council* no longer. I ought to go for a long tramp to Luxulyan or along the cliffs ... Overwork in Oxford and during the fortnight I have been at home (witness the absence of entries in this Diary) must account for my present state of mind; devoid of initiative, my brain has become the passive register of the conflicting ideas of mediocre historians on points that nobody minds and developments that don't in the least matter. It looks as if I am to feel all love of poetry dry up within me; I read Flecker during breakfast this morning without real enthusiasm and my head hasn't buzzed with ideas and plans

as it usually does when I walk the roads in the evening. The truth is that I have been trying for a fortnight to live a sober, well-regulated life: three or four hours' reading in the morning, a long afternoon's exercise, then three or four hours' reading at night.

I added, innocently, 'it's enough to turn one into a *petit bourgeois*' – I suppose I meant, living the clockwork life of a clerk in an office.

I was now reading Macaulay, and that history was gaining on my mind is clear from the positive reaction to him as against the passive reaction to the third-rate, of which so much of an historian's reading consists.

> I feel moved at every other paragraph to protest and disagree; my copy of the *Essays* is larded with lines and queries and comments and notes ... That luminous common sense that is his chief quality surprised me by its convincing conclusions even more than its corresponding superficiality disappointed me. There are places, particularly in the essay on Hallam, where he seems led astray by the very obviousness of his outlook: it is all so straightforward and simple to him, but there are things undreamt of in his philosophy ... I was ill in Oxford last term, but I believe I am getting much better now.

There follows a conscientious list of my history reading during the past fortnight: besides a volume of Macaulay's *Essays*, Swift's *Conduct of the Allies* and *Drapier's Letters*, and Leslie Stephen's biography of Swift; G. N. Clark's *The Dutch Alliance*, and Holland Rose's *Napoleonic Studies*; Dean Stanley's *Memorials of Canterbury*, R. L. Poole's *Illustrations of Medieval Thought*, and Baldwin's thick, congealed *King's Council*, from which I profited little and at which I repined.

I don't think it occurred to me that there could be such a thing as a nervous breakdown – which was precisely what was happening to my fellow-Scholar, Emlyn Williams, and of which he gives such a vivid description in that other Christ Church autobiography, *George*. Amusing, he makes it, with his head turning round with such earth-shaking considerations as 'the early history of the French

Partitive Article cf. Sneyders de Vogel' or 'the equivalent of "quam ut" is "que que", sometimes found in Old French.' Actually I didn't know Emlyn Williams at all well, though we both lived in Meadows, I at one end and he at the other, on Professor Lindemann's famous staircase. Nor, when we met, did we click. For, I am afraid I was a prig and a fanatic – or whatever the reader of this book may decide on the evidence; and I considered that sprigs of the working class in this alien environment should give no points away to the enemy, should be serious-minded and hard-working, if possible, members of the Labour Club. This was far from Emlyn's view of life, as readers of his enjoyable autobiography will readily perceive. He was taken up by everybody and had a gay time at the O.U.D.S. and everywhere. I am ashamed to say that I much disapproved – he was my junior by a year – and regarded his breakdown and leaving college with a total lack of sympathy. Working-class lads simply didn't do this kind of thing. I was quite wrong, of course, and he was quite right to follow his genius. He hasn't a more sincere admirer now than I am, both of what he has achieved as a dramatist and of his gifts as an actor.

My fears that poetry and the imagination would dry up were belied by the poem 'Duporth' –

> Into a quiet, lonely place I come,
> A coign of cliff, a lane that drops to the sea –

occurring on the very next page of the Diary. Along with notes for a poem 'Before Storm'. 'The strange, green light reflected in the windows that I pass going up the hill. The stifled noises ... only a few birds that sing. The lines of gorse glow darkly rich in the threatening light. Silence settles down like a veil over the land. The first heavy drops drum.' I constantly returned to the idea of a poem on the quarry at Carn Grey: but 'I must save up this idea in my head till the summer and I am home again; it will be a comforting thought all through the horror of next term and the Schools. A good title for a book it would make ... ' There follows a string of projects for three books, each of them a good idea and not one of them even as yet accomplished, so I will say nothing about them. But how extraordinary it was that my head should have been so besieged with projects clamouring to come to birth, and so long ago that even in a full hard-working life I have not yet got round to fulfilling them! Then – Good Friday, 1925 – 'I am apt to be seduced into thinking about them, when I should be considering pre-Conquest feudalism.'

A few days later:

> I am digressing from Stubbs' *Constitutional History* to note another piece of work which must have my attention during the long summer months when I come home again: a blank-verse poem on the house at Duporth, a companion to the last I wrote. Which reminds me that 'The Old Woman by the Fire' has not yet had its companion-piece about the old man in a room full of the scent of sweet peas. There are three poems I have definitely in mind to write. I like to think of them all accomplished as I have imagined them and brought together in a book. But I wonder what the cool prospects are? I heard from Graham Greene a day or two ago, and he said he liked the last poem better than anything else I had yet written. Moreover he's got a book coming out with Blackwell on May 1st.

Evidently there was an intense conflict, such as I had not remembered, going on all the time between ideas for poems and projects for writing constantly bubbling up and the strict control necessary to get all my historical reading done for Schools. What would emerge from the tension? Inevitably the poetry, from the point of view of time, was driven to take second place; yet never in my heart's estimation – and, strange to say, it never did dry up.

This Easter the amenities of family life – which (like Francis Bacon) I have come to detest – took a hand to add to one's worries.

> 7 April: Great trouble in the house ... A heavy blow in our news from George in Australia: Dossie [his wife] has left him, and for the moment all the heart has gone out of him. Sold his farm which he had worked up for two years and was just getting into order. [Now worth a small fortune, of course.] His letter sounded crazy enough: I hope he won't do anything desperate. This is a new variation on the theme of family incompetence,

and in the same direction as the revelation with regard to Len which knocked me out last vacation. What will come next?

It has only just occurred to me whether the shock of this revelation – anyone tougher, less sensitive and vulnerable would not have been so shaken by it – might not have been connected with the savage attack of ulcer shortly afterwards in Oxford. It was a cruel introduction to the facts that underlay the surface of adult married life, and it corroborated the disrespect I had felt for human beings and their pretences ever since childhood ended and adolescence began. I never have had much *respect* for human beings – affection, yes: an attitude corroborated by my intensive reading of Swift and my temperamental affinity with him. I remember agreeing with a vet. at home not long ago, who said that he had more respect for animals. Quite right: they don't make such a mess of their lives. And this, in spite of the fact that human beings are endowed with reason, to make something of. And what do they mostly make of it?

This revelation, which connected our family story with the most romantic spot in Cornish history and had always elicited my probing childish questionings did not increase my admiration for heterosexual relations or my appreciation of their consequences. But, curiously enough, whatever trauma one suffered, it did not loosen the ties of family loyalty. We had been a secure and somewhat ingrown family unit, in my childhood living much to ourselves. The shattering of the shell of security accompanied the process of growing up – a painful process for me, intellectually precocious, humanly and socially retarded. It did not occur to me to break away from the family in the normal human way, as my brother and sister had done to form their own. My mother and father had at least given us the benefit of a stable and secure family background, if one of intense reserve and no show of affection to us whatever. I never remembered a quarrel or a cross word between them, or any mention of sex, let alone a bawdy word, in front of us. Old-fashioned, Victorian working-class respectability: much to be thankful for.

I perceive now that all this was founded on my father's adoration of my mother, much more remarkable a person than he was, besides being strikingly beautiful: incandescent pallor of complexion, black wavy hair now turning grey, exquisitely formed mouth and nose, small shell-like ears, blazing eyes, coarse working hands. I suppose that all his life he was under her spell: she made him a good wife, as wives go, without ever being in love with him. He was an un-remarkable-enough working chap, and when I was a growing boy I hadn't much cared for him. The effect of the shattering of my security was to make me draw closer to him; there was an innate delicacy in our relations, so that we never exchanged more than one sentence over what had thunderstruck me, and that was his word, 'Now you see for yourself how things are.' I grew fond of him, though there was precious little we had in common, except extreme impatience of temper; as he grew older, I extended protection to him as he had done for me as a child, and looked after him. My mother, not without her own motives, saw to it that I did not forget his birthdays; and with my increasing illness and precarious hold, as it seemed, on life, he became more and more fond of me on his side. Simple working man that he was, he had much more capacity for affection than my mother ever had; but she had re-ceived a mortal blow to pride – no fault of her own – and it had turned her to stone.

As for my brother and sister, they were unremarkable enough, too: they turned after him, were very like his side of the family, no doubt of their paternity. With my innocence and limitless ambition, it did not occur to me that they were very ordinary people, like everybody else: not in the least above average. I ex-pected them to achieve something in life, as I intended to myself; it was merely another step in the process of growing up, another breach in the walls of security, to realise – though I could never accept – that they would achieve nothing. One of them ten years, the other five years, older than I, I remained behind at home the guardian of the family solidarity, keeping them in touch with everything, writing all the letters – my parents wrote with diffi-culty – and sharing their burdens and worries, needlessly, super-fluously. It never occurred to me, so much their junior, that they might have shared mine. Here was I, before going back to Oxford for my last term as an undergraduate, Schools before me: 'a few days of lassitude following upon a too strenuous week; also I fancy the news from George has demoralised me along with the rest.'

*   *   *

The summer term of one's Schools was indubitably the last lap. I went back on April 24th into that clime which Emlyn Williams describes as the enemy (my enemy was nearer home). He writes, 'walking into Christ Church in the warmth of early evening, I saw the Oxford summer as my enemy. The late April sun lay across Tom Quad, brushing the Cathedral spire like a blessing; and from all sides windows winked on to the spacious grass, calm tolerant eyes mellow with the gathered wisdom of centuries. The sight should have smoothed my spirit, but I zigzagged across with no more sense of where I was than a fly making its way over a framed Canaletto.' As if I had not experienced, was not to experience year after year, the lush, erotic suggestiveness of the Oxford summer myself. But, away with such thoughts: this was the summer term of Schools!

So, on May Day,

I have taken up my pen in sheer despair at reading. For one question, not even an essay, I have read hundreds and hundreds of pages: it is a sort of disease. The whole of Coulton's big first volume on Monasticism, Armitage Robinson's *St Dunstan*, a good patch of Davis's *Medieval England*, a futile essay by a Miss Cooke on twelfth-century religious reform, and what else? I wish I were at home again, and I've got a cold coming on. Joad is speaking at the Labour Club tonight: shall I bother to go? All which means that I must return to malt and oil.

The dichotomy between history and poetry continued.

I have settled down at my desk to apply myself to the Final Act of the Congress of Vienna. But, looking out of the window at the trees where the birds have been flitting about all day and are now piping drowsily among the leaves – it is too beautiful: I ought to be writing a poem on the procession of the day as it passes before my window. It's very hard to submit to a dull round of diplomatics, especially when I can hear Newman below me playing passages from the Preludes and Fugues, and even more tantalisingly from Beethoven.

This was Sidney Newman, the organ Scholar, on his way to becoming a distinguished musician.

One Sunday later: 'two subjects hold me most unwillingly from Prothero's *Statutes and Documents,* that passionate object of my desire: a descriptive poem about just such a summer day as today has been. All humanity turns out in the streets, the gay and sparkling, and also the deformed and the cripples who are wheeled out to take the air, and make one shudder to pass their carts.' It reminds me of the daily ritual I used to see years later from the window of my hotel near the Plaza del Sol in Madrid, of an exquisitely beautiful girl being wheeled out each morning on to the balcony above me across the street. Lovely, frail, fair creature, perfection of colour and grace – it was only on the second morning that I realised that hers was a vacant beauty, a helpless idiot girl.

At this time I was more and more fascinated by the idea, the thrill, of fear as a subject for poetry. 'Sunday, 17 May: A solitary call that startles me from lost thoughts: was it in my mind or in the air? A voice that I have heard before and, though long time forgotten, brings back the farthest memories of departed childhood. The cry was a cry of despair: what was it that tore at my heart?' Or again, 'Late at night, after finishing Webster's *Foreign Policy of Castlereagh*: For a poem of Fear: plunging one's hands into a basin of cold water, the shock of the thought that it might be into a bowl of blood. Lady Macbeth. Laughter runs down the walls!'

I suppose these were evidences of overstrain, much like Emlyn's obsessive 'the tendency to denasalise nasal vowels began in the sixteenth century, while the flectional system ...' However, his nervous symptoms were hardly from overwork. I was jogging along at an average of seven to eight hours' solid, too solid, reading a day. I had given up social life that term, went out to lunch or tea only occasionally, and, when acquaintances came up to my rooms after Hall in the evenings, I put them firmly out at 9 p.m. and sported my oak.

As the horrid hour of Schools approached I did very little new, last-minute reading, but gave myself up to revising the work I had done, essays, book-notes, lecture-notes. This stood me in good stead, and, as a tutor later, I always insisted on the importance of revision, bringing up to scratch what one already knows, instead of a feverish mugging up for lost time.

I ambled about to a few lectures. One sparsely attended course by H. W. C. Davis I have reason to remember. (He had been chosen to succeed Firth as Regius Professor, instead of A. F. Pollard, whom, the most eminent and forceful product of the Oxford History School, the Faculty would not have at any price. Just as subsequently, when Namier had achieved that position of eminence, the Faculty opted for someone else. It is symptomatic of the inferiority of our time that Oxford has gone in so easily for second-rate options.) On 'Saturday in Eight's week: A bad hour's work and a bad lecture. Davis was at his most reactionary, and upheld Francis Place with his middle-class Political Union as against William Lovett with his Trades Union: Place was indubitably far-sighted compared with Lovett.' Next week the small audience in the Schools was treated to more of this: the political ideas of the Radical Roebuck were up-graded as against those of the Chartists which were depreciated. I had had enough of this and snorted loudly. At this Davis halted in his tracks, his steel spectacles rose upright on his nose, he fixed me with his ice-blue stare, and said in his frostiest manner: 'You evidently disagree.' This had never happened to me before, and I wished the earth would open to receive me. But I realised that the only thing was to go forward now, there was no line of retreat. So I said that just as the ideas of the Chartists were the product of their environment so Roebuck's were the product of his: the Chartists could hardly be expected to subscribe to them. The Professor paused, and then said slowly, 'That represents a degree of historical scepticism with which I do not agree.' The crisis was safely passed; however, I had made my point. Though the point has little importance in itself, it is some evidence that history had gained its own grip on me, that I was disturbed by the intellectual problems it raised.

Before the ordeal of Schools another body-blow was delivered me. Masterman came up my stairs to congratulate me on being awarded *proxime accessit* for the Newdigate. I was furious; I would rather have had no award at all. I was certain that mine was a good poem, and that just because it was different and original it had not been chosen. It would be an obvious move now, gentlemanly and polite, to say that I was wrong and that the examiners – Garrod and A. D. Godley and Farquharson and the rest – chose the right poem. What they did was to choose the obvious poem, in conventional, orthodox, Swinburnian metre:

> There is an altar builded sure
>   In the world's deep heart, in the heart of time;
> There is a worship shall endure
>   Though temples moulder in dust and shine;
> Though old gods perish and faiths decay
> The shrine of Freedom shall stand alway,
> And men shall serve her with passion pure,
>   With deeds and daring and echoing rhyme.

This piece that carried off the prize was by an unknown Canadian Rhodes Scholar, also of the House: E. W. McInnis. No mention of the poems they sent in was achieved by either Graham Greene or Emlyn Williams, while mine was awarded a *proxime accessit* to this work of art. So much for the judgment of Oxford dons on a matter of art – the dons who in our time have garnished Oxford with the New Bodleian, the works of Sir Hubert Worthington, the new Selfridge's put up by Magdalen on Magdalen Bridge – the President of the College being Slade Professor of Fine Art, and a member of the Fine Arts Commission.

It did not console me that Q in his day had also been awarded a *proxime* – probably to some competitor never heard of again – and later referred to the Newdigate as 'a mere academic exercise'. What I cared about was that all my plans for the summer, conditioned upon getting that prize, were overset. I had hoped for

a free long vacation, the first in which I could have allowed myself a real rest and recuperation, after years of solid plodding and no relaxing of the mind. I might have put in a short visit to Brittany such as I have often dreamed of: no more than three weeks and inexpensively, so that I might have something worth while to hand over to father and mother for my keep. And now, what can I do? I feel like a rat in a trap: just the same sensation as I had before getting enough scholarships to bring me to this place ... But it will only be what they expect at home: father knows that the harder you work and the more seriously you take your responsibilities, the less reward you are likely to get. He has spent his sixty years in ceaseless work, beginning as a cart-boy at nine, and winding up with harder toil than ever in digging clay out of the soil now ... What is inevitable, though how soon it is to come I fear to say, is the complete disablement of father and mother; both of them I shall have to provide for when the time comes.

This I accepted unquestioningly, and without resentment.
Truly, the iron had entered early into my soul; and all my experience of life has corroborated it. At least it serves as a prophylactic in ill times.

*   *   *

One consideration shed a ray of comfort on the gloomy scene: at the time of my taking Schools – on which my whole future depended – I was in good health, the ulcer quiescent. But fancy a lad of twenty-one, anxious to do the best he could, having to be grateful that his guts were not going to be gnawed away and his chances ruined! So far from being a fortunate man, as some people think, I could curse and curse again at the luck that has been mine all through life. If I have ever won anything, it has always had to be wrested from the teeth of circumstances, by my own efforts. It has never been *given* – certainly not by other people, who have shown again and again that, if they had the chance to withhold something I wanted, they would. No: the very fact that a man wishes to do his best, is anxious to make his contribution, is in itself a motive to frustrate, to stop him. Very well, they can have their way: I have no contribution now to make, either to their well-being or their ill-being. I do not care either way.

Before going into the Schools, sacrificial victims, we were dined and wined by the dons. Feiling invited me to lunch at his red-brick house in the Iffley Road – I remember being struck by the Victorian presence of a large plum cake at the end of the meal. Jacob invited a number of his pupils to lunch at All Souls, the first time I had penetrated that venerable institution – as to the purpose of which, since it had no undergraduates, I was a bit vague – except for some lectures in the Hall. But I have not forgotten Arnott's delicious summery *mousse de jambon*, which became more familiar later. For me the Dons' dinner was just a nuisance, for, unlike Emlyn – who seems to have revelled in dressing up and changing his clothes, treating himself to a second, more fashionable suit of evening clothes, for he was better off than I – I had none. I had

> spent the afternoon with David Cecil, having a tremendous conversation in which arguments were merely rhythms. The evening was a time of ignominy and shame. I had to rig myself up in borrowed plumes from a multiplicity of sources: a dress-suit from Low, shirt and collar from Madden, studs and tie from Thomas, not to mention unsuccessful attempts upon May and Otis. I felt myself to be a fraud, and for once sympathised with Americans of the Mid-West objecting to the addiction to dinner-suits in the East as contrary to the rights of man. I have hurried back and divested myself of such clothing, and am now writing with a good conscience in pyjamas and dressing-gown.

That was evidently all I cared for the Dons' Dinner, and indeed I remember nothing else of it. I fear I must add to the other characters of the author of this book that of horrid Puritan. How different this was from his fellow-collegian, the author of *George*, who was 'riding the waves, and plunged into shopping. It had to be faced that my dinner suit was no longer *à la mode*, and for Commem, which I was determined to sample, you had to have tails. I told myself, and Miss Cooke, that two new outfits would be an investment, true, and that Oxford tailors were so understanding that could pay next term out of scholarship instalments.' Here was difference between a Welshman and a Cornishman: such a mode of thought was utterly beyond me. I ended my long struggle as an undergraduate not a penny in debt. Commem! – the Commemoration Ball – I should as soon have thought of going to it as of scaling Mount Everest.

As the testing time of Schools approached I found myself, unexpectedly, delectably cool and well: at concert-pitch. No last-minute delirious staying up all night with a wet-towel around my head trying to make up for the nights spent at the O.U.D.S. or, for that matter, the Labour Club. I went to bed early, I slacked off, going out into the Meadows to sit under a tree with my notebooks open before me, the punters gliding by with their precious cargo of female flesh, the ripple of sexy laughter under the green waterways.

What does it matter about the actual examination? I have forgotten almost everything about it – except that all the lugubrious time I had spent on Tait and Tout was utterly wasted, since that blest pair of sirens did not put in an appearance. On the other hand, I was able to make good use of reading in Victor Hugo which I had done years before as a boy at school. Simply for the record, I may say that in those days there were eleven papers of three hours each, morning and afternoon, spread over six days with a Sunday interval in between. It was a pretty hot, gruelling test, as the Final Honour School of Modern History at Oxford has always been – having to carry all that in one's head over three years. But, mercifully well in health, I took it all methodically: every evening after a day in the Schools doing a little brushing-up for the papers next day, no more, bringing quotations up to the surface of the mind for use, and so to early bed.

When it was all over I could not remember the date. 'Somewhere about the middle of June: I have been sunk deep in the Schools for the last week. The freedom of having finished with it all is so glorious and I felt at the beginning of the afternoon that there were so many things I might do, that I have done nothing at all. I might have walked up to Shotover, but instead have shut myself in my room with my oak sported.' It seems rather a curious thing to do. I have myself up nostalgically to thinking of home and Miss M., one of the young mistresses at school: 'how far away it all seems when I used to go for walks with her last summer up the hill to Carn Grey,

8

across the moor and down to Garker, sometimes on to Crinnis and home through the woods. It won't be long before I shall go over all that ground again, but not with Miss M. The very name as I write it seems unfamiliar, still stranger as I say it with my lips. Besides she isn't Miss M. any longer: she's Mrs M. now.' Life had moved on for someone, leaving me as usual much where I had always been. Emlyn Williams's idea of life led him into the free flow of it – proper for a dramatist; my idea, watching the current go by me, observing it, noting every movement, those who swam as well as those who went under – was appropriate for the embryo historian. The historian's development takes so much longer, but our fates were being decided for us.

Young as I was, the sense of the flow of time was not only already with me but always with me.

It's all very queer: only last summer, and it might have been ten years ago. I wonder if the summers will pass over me like that always, like a river that goes on and on and there is nothing that one can stop and cling to. I remember this curious feeling once when I was having tea at Professor Wright's. He was saying how, in the years before the war, he used to have a punt and go up the river: that was when they were living in Mesopotamia. It all seemed so far away as he said it; he must be over seventy now, and I wondered what he thought as he went back twenty years in his mind.

To me then it seemed an aeon; I don't suppose now that to old Joseph Wright it meant so much. I have only just remembered the point of that far-away experience. Whether it was the magical effect of the phrase, 'living in Mesopotamia', or no, I was suddenly overwhelmed by the sense, to become so familiar, that I had been through it all before: the very same table, the people in their places, the room, the atmosphere. But when? And what did it mean?

It is extraordinary to me how people take the mystery of the passage of time without imagination and without protest, their lives running out in the procession of the seasons, as in the garden below me now that has moved on to blood-red peonies spilling their petals upon the path, the doctoral scarlet of poppies, the variegated flags blue and gold. Somewhere in my poems there is a phrase,

A time will come and I not be ...

All my work, all my writing, has been a protest against the ineluctable onward march of time towards one's extinction, an attempt to erect a barrier, something to hold on to in that ever-rolling flood. As I write this Sunday evening of June, Trinity Sunday, the bells of New College begin their mnemonic appeal across the garden, the notes flitting in and out the dappled shadows of the mulberry tree beneath which Warden Smith used to give his vanished summer tea-parties. Some may think, with the hymn, that only religion offers the promise of the conquest of time, but it is no less an illusion.

I perceive now, forty years after, the real reason why I had locked myself in my room that summer afternoon when I was freed from Schools.

And now I am leaving this room: I can't realise it now that I have been here wandering around the whole afternoon. But when I came back from the Schools, where I have practically lived for a week, I suddenly realised that I was leaving this room not to come back to it, and that it didn't belong to me after all. It's very hard to think of it with somebody else installed, with different pictures and the chairs re-covered, and perhaps a new arrangement of things. I have been very happy here; it is all very beautiful; but nothing stays. I am not worrying my soul as to what I have done in the Schools, nor do I much think of the immense disappointment of the Newdigate, but only that I am going away, and that these days that I have lived here are irrecoverable.

Apropos of these curious tricksy experiences of the mind, two are much associated in my memory with my room in Meadows. It had immensely heavy Victorian sash-windows: if one were to fall on one, one might have been killed or at least seriously injured.

One of those summer evenings I had my head out, looking out in a vacant mood of despondency and resentment. Suddenly it occurred to me, suppose if the window should fall? Such was my mood that I said to myself, Let the damned thing fall! The thought passed from my mind; I went on looking out and then drew back un-thinking – all in a second. The moment I had drawn back, the window crashed. What alarmed me was not so much that the window fell as that the instant before I had said, deliberately tempt-ing fate, Let the damned thing fall! I have never been able to explain it.

Once again, in a vacant mood one grey afternoon, it suddenly came into my head that if I went down to the Library I should see the two young assistants of the Library in each other's arms. I went down – and there they were, disengaging.

These odd, quasi-psychic experiences happened, I noticed, when I was off-colour, the mind rather vacant. It is the less to be wondered at that medieval and primitive people are so liable to the pheno-menon of possession.

Before I went home there was another fling at the circumstances that so tied me by the heels. 'I had to refuse an invitation from Jacob such as I should most have loved to accept, to go on a reading-party with him in Scotland during September. Otis is going, but where am I to raise the money with which to go?' Scotland! I might as easily have got to Timbuctoo.

*   *   *

Schools over, I was by no means through with Schools: the Viva Voce loomed ahead at the end of July and intending Firsts were well advised to prepare themselves for that further ordeal, caulking leaks, filling in gaps, strengthening the weak spots divined by our enemies, the examiners. I gave myself a fling by reading such things as Huizinga's *The Waning of the Middle Ages*, Graham Wallas' *Human Nature in Politics* and *Our Social Heritage*, the Goncourts *Journal*, W. P. Ker's *Essays in Medieval Literature*, and then went gloomily back to the grind once more.

At once the protest follows – a familiar rhythm now. I had begun writing what was to be a longish poem, 'The Village'. But

I cannot run abstract historical reading along with sensuous poetry. Inspiration isn't lacking, but it comes in mere hints, and I cannot keep up any long flight when at the same time I read as much as six or seven hours at Longmans' *Political History of England*. Several nights when the moon has been rising over the shoulder of the house across the road, I have had in mind a poem about moonlight over the woods, but I haven't been able to get beyond two or three lines ... I cannot write this poem until I can give myself up to it; much less can I finish 'The Village' and begin on 'The Quarry' and 'Lantellan Church', which is to be the age-long poem I have carried in my head about Luxulyan church and the coolness after the long hot walk across the moor, and the scattered sounds of life outside, so undisturbed and unchanging through all the centuries. How splendid it will be to give myself up for weeks to reading and writing poetry! I shall read Bridges and some Tennyson and Malory, and I shall write the things that have been running through my head and out into this Diary for the last year or so.

To clear the decks, 'the early volumes of the Diary, to the number of six in all, I destroyed in a heap the other day ... The first volume must have been begun about 1917, and I took eight years to destroy it. At that rate it will be sixteen and a half years before it comes to the turn of this volume.'

Alas, for my plans! Things took an unexpected turn with my Schools result, so 'The Village' remained a fragment, to be published only in *Oxford Poetry* that year. The two other projected poems of some length were never written at all – they went into limbo as sacrifice for the All Souls Fellowship; however, by a backward kick, three other not very satisfactory poems survive in the Diary from that summer.

One July morning I gave up to haymaking with father in Neddy's meadow; the afternoon I spent reading Graham Wallas on our tiny patch of lawn in front of the house. In the evening, while I sat at my open window upstairs trying to go on with 'The Village', 'a very near neighbour came out to mow his lawn with fiendish energy.

Then the rain came on, which I had prayed for to drive him indoors; unfortunately it drove someone else in across the way: the result has been a pitiful half-hour at the piano at all sorts of elementary versions from popular music-hall revues.' Such were the amenities of living in the middle of a council housing estate: I really *hated* living with the people all round one, but there was nothing to be done about it. Living so much at my upstairs window I could hear all the noises of the road, the maniac noises made by children playing and even the endearments of their hardly more rational parents going to bed.

The moment I came home another blow struck the family full in the face. My sister Hilda wrote from California that 'her little Reggie, the only one of her children whom we knew, died three weeks ago, in the night of Friday June 18th: that must have been towards the evening of Thursday, the day I spent restlessly after my week of Schools. They buried him early on the Saturday morning; he was just seven years old.' It was a propos of this that my father had one of those telepathic experiences so well known to old Cornish folk – like the striking of the dumb clock in the kitchen a Tregonissey when his youngest brother, Cheelie, was killed in the mine in South Africa.[1] At the time of the little boy's death my father, not given to dreaming, had an intensely vivid dream of his daughter in great trouble, and saw her with the child on her lap.

She wrote a broken-hearted letter to us, and we all spent the morning half-dazed, in a sort of incredible dream. How the troubles thicken about us; I wonder what will be the next thing to strike home. Oh, the infinite love of God – what a monstrous lie it seems and is! ... But how primitive all that is: it is only an inversion of faith. It will be a worse day when I come not to mind at all, when I accept with my heart what I already do with my brain, the knowledge of the heartlessness of things. It means that one will have become impervious to feeling, at heart dead. All the morning while I thought about the poor child and his mother, the church bells were ringing as if for church on Sunday. I thought of earlier Sunday evenings in

[1] Cf. *A Cornish Childhood.*

autumn, when Hilda used to go to and from church; and then of the months in the winter after the Armistice when she brought Reggie across from the Scilly Isles. My head aches; I have been writing to her and thinking about her, and been reading over and over Bridges'

Perfect little body, without fault or stain on thee.

I let that entry stand as evidence of how a simple, unphilosophical family took the ills of life, myself taking things too hardly, as usual. Not that I disagree even now with the rebellious sentiments expressed, except to say, wearily, to what point? And also to add that the rebellion, as I saw even then, was superfluous, since there was no one and nothing to rebel against. When one thinks of the numbers of books on the insoluble Problem of Pain – C. S. Lewis and the rest – one reflects that it is only insoluble, or even a problem, to those who assume an all-wise and all-caring Providence and are then surprised at the infinite ills experienced by its creatures. It would be enough to make one sympathise with William Empson's old-fashioned resentment at Milton's deity: if one believed in Milton's deity one would have every reason to be resentful. In truth, there is no problem, for the assumption is superfluous, indeed primitive, belonging to the childhood of the race. My family were simply children, with one member of it emerging strangely, incongruously, out of that state.

Coming into Los Angeles from the airport the other day, the bus passed by the gates of Inglewood Park cemetery, and I suddenly realised that that was where my sister's promising little boy was buried.

The day I went back to Oxford for my viva, 27 July, was little Reggie's birthday: I remembered it. Next morning in the cool, shadowed Examination Schools with its marble-paved hall that has echoed the feet of so many thousands of anxious examinees, they were a distinguished lot of examiners one had to face: G. N. Clark, E. L. Woodward, F. M. Powicke, E. I. Carlyle and the formidable C. R. Cruttwell, with a tongue like a whiplash, in the chair. I was very nervous. It fell to me to be viva'd by G. N. Clark, and he was kind: he rapidly turned the viva into something that interested me,

Celtic art in Roman Britain, and I at once lit up over the then recently discovered Desborough mirror, with its beautiful whorls and spiral linear decoration. Did he know it? It did not appear that he did, and after a few polite exchanges my viva was at an end. I could hardly credit my relief when I found myself once more out on the cold hard marble. A formal viva meant a definite class without any question. At once the familiar state of anxiety supervened: this meant that I had got an absolutely safe and sound Second. I could hardly bear to leave the building, it all seemed so sickeningly inevitable; I even hung round for a bit, in mute protest at its inevitability, and then slunk off.

The next three days I spent in the Bodleian, working away at material that should make a fascinating Cornish book – I won't say what, for I still haven't got round to completing it, forty years after. The day before I was due to go home I was summoned to All Souls by Jacob, who put an end to my anxiety by telling me that I had got a good First. I don't know whether those eminent examiners got out the right results, but there we were, some fifteen of us in the First Class, when the class-lists came out, out of some two hundred and seventy candidates. There was the inevitable, the infallible Birley, who couldn't put a foot wrong if he tried; there was Denis Brogan, who was already a graduate from Glasgow and some three or four years senior to the rest of us. There was K. B. McFarlane, who had been viva'd for his First which was in question; there were Roger Makins and I, who had been taught together and were, it transpired, among the best Firsts of the year. The History Scholar at the House got a good sound Second – so the dons had reason to be specially pleased with Roger and me. More interesting were other names that appeared, to become better known since: handsome Antony Knebworth, of whom his father, Lord Lytton, wrote such a touching biography, Scrymgeour-Wedderburn and Graham Greene, all together in the large and cosy bed of the Second Class. In the Third, the surprising name of the Brackenbury Scholar at Balliol, C. V. Connolly, and Lord Dunglass to become better known as Lord Home, Foreign Secretary, and at length, after translation back into the House of Commons as Sir Alec Douglas-Home, Prime Minister of Great Britain.

Nothing about this in the Diary: I have had to get it up from the University Calendar. Of course I was immensely relieved and pleased: going home in the train, reading Lansing's *Peace Negotiations*, I trod on air. It was very agreeable receiving all those letters of congratulation from the dons and being told several times over 'we are all proud of you', especially from those who had seemed a little doubtful before. Most delightful were letters from nice Jim Byam-Shaw, whom I didn't know very well (apparently Emlyn Williams did), and from friendly Canon Cooke:

> I gather that you intend to come up here for another year, or at any rate to read for the English School. It is a happiness to think that I shall see you again and talk over common interests and the things which really matter, i.e. Hebrew metres, plain-song and Cornish poetry. Now take my advice, and away with dull care, and be out of doors and open your chest to the moor-land breeze and your mind to the simple, big things – 'those mighty hopes which make us men'.

Away with dull care, indeed! My First in the History Schools gave a further twist out of the literary course I had set myself; the dons were already arranging another lap for me. The Diary is full of the Cornish book I had in my head and for which I took the opportunity of my *viva* to get some work done. Now –

> everybody has been very nice and appreciative, and Jacob and Feiling have been bricks: they want me to try for an All Souls Fellowship. And I really will work for one. It means doing another foreign period, and I'm without a book here. So it all brings an end to my dreams of any real achievement this summer. I am incapable of writing poetry, thus overburdened and intellectualised – though I came to a conclusion tonight on my walk to Carn Grey which should enable 'The Village' to develop on its own lines, when I can really settle down to it.

This was evidently what I really had at heart.

VII

All Souls

So here I was let in once more for one of those long vacations in Cornwall with nothing to do but work, the mixture as before. It had, however, a slightly different inflexion: I was not working to a dreary syllabus, I could please myself more, the reading less regurgitative, more sophisticated and mature. Moreover, I was turning to the Renaissance. Hitherto I had been a nineteenth-century man – French Revolutions, the Congress of Vienna, the Concert of Europe, Bismarck's Germany; now I was turning back to the fascinating borderland between the Middle Ages and modern civilisation. This appealed more to me; here, for the bulk of my historical interests, I was to remain.

I gave myself a little fling to begin with, reading Paul Bourget's evocative *Sensations d'Italie*, since I couldn't go there, and *Monsieur des Lourdines* by Alphonse de Chateaubriant, a Breton writer who failed to fulfil his early promise, in the dreadful 1930s when so much went under. Then I turned to my, rather superior, reading for All Souls – such books as Leslie Stephen's *English Thought in the Eighteenth Century* and Edwyn Bevan's *Hellenism and Christianity*. The latter aroused a very positive reaction:

what a curious atmosphere it breathes; I shall be relieved to get back to the stolid rationalism of Leslie Stephen. Bevan began magnificently; but such essays as that on the Gnostic Redeemer made me suspicious, and I was appalled by the argument of 'Christianity and the Modern World'. The awful sentimentality in the concluding propositions about love gave me every sympathy with Lowes Dickinson's view of love between God and Man as ridiculous and repulsive. Perhaps it's my fault, though;

I am coming not to be able to read books about God and Christ and religion: the atmosphere is so strained and unreal, the tone so vulgar. I have been put off by the end of this book; in the rest there are striking ideas, and I should like to feel that I have grasped what is best in it.

There follows an entry that shows I was thinking things out for myself; sketchy as it is, it provided a basis for my thinking and a point of departure for further explorations.

The gist of my objection to the philosophy of religion is its method. Granted the two elements of the known and the unknown, out of these the religious compound a whole, which they call ultimate Reality = God. In the light of this hypothesis they turn back and re-interpret what is already known to our experience, investing it with a significance not properly its own. They make the equation $a + b = x$, when we only know what a is. They not only lend an interpretation to b, but give a new and unwarranted interpretation to a, in the light of x. x is really pure invention; we don't really know any more than what we began with, a. It is both impertinent and dishonest to lend a new interpretation to what we know already in the light of the concocted hypothesis. The more honest method is the anti-metaphysical: taking one's stand on known experience and knowledge to explore into the region of the unknown, continually pressing to expand a at the expense of b. We can see this process going on with great rapidity, and immense extensions of knowledge being made, in the new physics and astronomy, as also in anthropology and psychology. This outlook of mine which, transposed into other terms, holds good of historical method, has its parallels and developments in all subjects that I think about. So that I feel my outlook is attaining consistency, even if the above is badly expressed. Which I suppose it is.

Unprofessional as this is, it was in keeping with the school of analytical philosophy that was shortly to develop at Oxford, under the aegis of my junior at Christ Church, A. J. Ayer. With its marked anti-metaphysical stand, it abnegated the claim of the old Oxford-German philosophical school to queen it over the other disciplines – the assumption that I had found so intolerable in a Wadleigh. Now the other disciplines were free to think their own thoughts, provided that they thought with accuracy and precision, and to work out their own appropriate methods.

I began to apply this increasingly to my own disciplines, history and political thought. I was reading the woolly Ernest Barker, with his strong tendency to humbug, on Aristotle and, 'more pleasurably, writing a note on "The Bankruptcy of Aristotelian Political Thought", showing how it all reposes upon a basis of class-division which it doesn't make explicit. So the whole scheme becomes just a calculation how to keep the possessing class in the saddle. This is most apparent in Aristotle's treatment of changes in the constitution – much the most significant in the light of events today, yet no light is given on it.' I think here, too, there was an unspoken criticism of my tutors, one of them setting up to be a kind of philosopher of Conservatism. If I had heard the intellectual case for Conservatism properly expounded, on its historical basis, with the proper functioning of a class-system made explicit and candid on the basis of people's differing pyschological aptitudes and the differing functions of different social groups, I should have had difficulty in resisting its truth. For it is obviously true, and it has always been clear to me that Burke's view of society is roughly right, far more profoundly true than any doctrinaire rationalism of the Left; for people are not rational, and we know it. To deny this simple psychological truth is either insincere – as it has been with many figures of the Left, Joad and G. D. H. Cole, for instance – or deluded, as with the lunatic fringe, who are incapable of recognising facts. G. D. H. Cole, whom I came to know intimately in later years, knew what fools human beings are, none better; but used to defend himself to me by saying 'We must go on as if they were not'. What is the point of that? Any effective and true view of society and political conduct must proceed on the basis of a true view of human nature. Conservatism always has the advantage of that asset; but its theoretical strength was never made clear to me by my tutors: I had to find that out also for myself.

For light relief there were the antics of the *villageois*.

A curious meeting with Johnny Go-fitty [his nickname] in the village: a pathetic, nerve-wracked cripple of a man, with a natural grievance against life and a muddled fervour that derives from the Book of Revelation. His language teems with the imagery of St John the Divine. I shan't forget his state of excite-ment at a quiet hole-and-corner Labour meeting we once held in the basement of the Primitive Methodist Chapel. Still, per-haps it was more appropriate than my missionary secularism. Tonight I was buttonholed for a subscription to the Fighting Fund, though what or whom it fights it is hard to say. Of course he wouldn't hear of taking money: my name in a book would do. I gave him a shilling, in the confident hope that tomorrow his wife will spend it in candles and tea. Perhaps this is too cruel, but what can be expected from these wretched people drives me to despair. I expect nothing from them: if Labour wins a majority, it will be just by accident. If their interests are flagrantly exploited before their eyes, the working classes can be relied on to be stampeded by some cry into the fold of the exploiter.

This was precisely borne out: as it had been in 1924, so it was to be in 1931 and 1935. 'Perhaps,' I continued, 'when their very exis-tence is threatened, they may open their eyes. I believe that the existence of us all will be threatened; perhaps only the merest brutes, living from hand to mouth, will survive.' One can hardly exclude that possibility now, though then one hadn't the prospect of the nuclear age in mind. I concluded, 'When I think of the helplessness of leaders in the face of our problems I can hardly sit still in my chair and go on with "the work at hand".'

Well, there is little of that to retract or withdraw. People would not wake up till 1940, though given plenty of warning and danger-signals. By then it was too late, too late for this country, to hold the position in the world to which it was accustomed, lost by its govern-ing class, followed by a bemused and lazy people.

In mid-August there befell a small family chore, with its own appeal to the past.

Tonight we have been saying goodbye to the last pillar of the old village. Mrs Courtney belongs to father's generation and is his cousin. For fifty-seven years, with a very few years' break, she has lived in the village, owning the old houses in Back Lane and where Granny Rowse used to live. Her husband worked ever since their early married life in South Africa; all her children have emigrated one by one; last winter her mother died, and since then she has lived all alone, except for Tiny, the Pomeranian, and Kate's cat.

I was on friendly terms with this swarthy connection of ours – she was so dark that I wonder now whether she had not gipsy blood in her veins – and used to call on her and hold sedate conversations at the gate, with immense cushions of white arabis and boy's love growing on the wall in spring.

When I last saw Tiny and the cat, they had got past themselves with age. The cat scarcely moved from her armchair by the fire; she had grown too fat, but her black coat was as soft and silky as ever. Now they are both gone, and for the past month there has been nothing in that house to keep her company. I expect she could see Kate and Sam in every corner of the place. I could, when I called to see her there in the spring of the year. Now she's leaving it, and going out to her children in America.

She spent the afternoon and evening with us, and then I went up the road with her. I expect she could see all her life in the place, as we walked up the hill to Tregonissey: childhood and youth, apprenticeship in the town, all the bustle of dressmaking in a shop, a hastened marriage and a quick succession of children; then five years in South Africa, all the rest in the village again, rearing her children, marrying them and watching them go overseas. Nor is that unlike the life of so many other Cornish folk. I went back to the village tonight, past our old house and my bedroom downstairs, past the window Sam has tapped at on other Sunday nights, up the court where my feet felt for the rugged stones they knew so well, up to her gate where we said goodbye. I asked her to remember me to Sam, who was a good sort, and Kate, whom I used to take to church on Sunday evenings during the war. How Kate loved the cat and Tiny and our Neddy; she wasn't afraid of Jack Loam's ferrets or even his snake. A good-hearted girl, now she and her man, a groom, are settled on the Long Island estate of a New York family – I think Whitneys. She will never come back again to the village where she was born.

Turning my mind to the Renaissance I was now reading Burck-hardt's *Civilisation of the Renaissance in Italy*, Armstrong's *Lorenzo de Medici* and *Charles V*, Bridge's *History of France, 1483–1493*, Pirenne's *Medieval Cities* and a couple of volumes of his *Histoire de Belgique*, a couple of volumes of Creighton's *History of the Papacy*. For light relief I read Newman's *Apologia*, Renan's *Souvenirs d'Enfance et de Jeunesse*, Keynes's *Economic Consequences of Mr. Churchill*, Belloc's *The Servile State*, Russell's *Problems of Philosophy*. One day I got up to as much as twelve hours' reading, six at Pirenne and then in the evening Bury's *History of Freedom of Thought*. Sometimes I went off somewhere for a whole day by myself, spending one day happily on the ledra at Trenarren – no penetrating into the house then; another day at Carn Grey, reading Dante's *Vita Nuova*.

My friends faithfully rallied round. One day Len Tippett and I walked all the way to Bodmin and back. Then the constant Booth came to stay in the town. In September

for more than a week I have been reading Boswell's *Johnson*, though it has been interspersed with other readings and frequent visits to the beach with H.B.B. … Boswell has been everywhere with me this week: at Trenarren, where I read him on the bank while H.B.B. bathed beneath; at Porthpean, where I read for an hour and a half while H.B.B. and Bacon went out in a boat (which I refused), and at intervals while half-asleep on the sheltered seat in the drowsy part of the afternoon. And now I go to bed, feeling much as Bozzy felt at the end of the great play. But perhaps this is only late-night sentiment, and will vanish with morning. Already I hear the cocks crowing!

Once more I find myself writing at midnight and returning to the old conflict.

14 September: A wonderful quiet midnight. I have come back from Carn Grey to refresh my mind with a change of reading, from Pirenne to Walter Raleigh's *Milton*. What accomplished writing it is! and coming to this after weeks and months spent with lesser historians, I have been smitten with regrets. But even while reading Raleigh my mind has wandered off to a poem on Midnight, when all the house is so still I can hear the clocks ticking in the rooms; and all outside is so quiet that I can hear the sound of the sea running in on the beaches two miles off. I fancy I can follow it from Crinnis to Charlestown, and then to Duporth and Porthpean. Not long ago I heard the bell chime from among Duporth woods. Perhaps the sound like surf running is as much the wind among trees as a high sea.

Thus this volume of Diary came to an end with a familiar theme. It was time to go back to Oxford and sit for the All Souls Fellowship.

*   *   *

I came back to go into lodgings for the first time, and this I didn't much relish. Perhaps it was on account of that that I can hardly remember anything about it, though this may also be due to the fact that I was unwell again, under attack from the enemy. So there isn't much in the Diary, but from this time my parents sometimes kept my letters. To them I wrote simply and directly – no point in consulting them about doubts and difficulties.

I am installed at 5 Whitehouse Road [off the Abingdon Road – an area to which House-men resorted when they went out of college]. I am rather unhappy at not being in college, as I loathe all changes. But my digs are quite nice and comfortable, and it is very homely to be in the same house with Tom Lawrenson. We are going to have meals together, and that will make things a little cheaper. But for the moment I ought not to bother about anything until the All Souls exam is over. I have seen several of my friends walking about the college, and they are quite thrilled at the All Souls business ... Be careful of yourself and don't overdo the cleaning. Tell Len to look after his Arithmetic, and the Lord will look after him.

The point of this was that little Len had a good deal of natural intelligence, and a distinctly artistic bent, but he was also easy-going and charming and idle: without somebody behind him he would get nowhere. I was determined that he should get a scholarship to the grammar school, and by a combination of coaxing and bullying – and occasional tears from him – I saw to it that he got one.

I don't think I had a very clear idea of what All Souls was, or what it stood for, or how it was constituted, or of its eminence and distinction in those days, when, armed with a letter from the Dean of Christ Church, I waited in the ante-room of the Warden's Lodgings to be called into the silvery presence of Warden Pember. Next day the examination began – my life to date, it seemed, had been nothing but examinations – and it lasted three days in the dark autumnal Hall. I didn't know who my fellow-competitors were – a score or so of young men who had done well in the Greats, History and Law Schools – except for Roger Makins, McFarlane of Exeter, and a brilliant Balliol man who was tipped as likeliest: J. R. Hicks. (Mercifully, the unsinkable Birley was not a candidate.)

At the outset I was confronted by a very uncongenial essay-subject, excogitated by about the ablest Oxford man of our time, Cyril Radcliffe: 'Possessions.' What was one to make of that? All very well for a lawyer, but I had hoped for something more literary. Nothing of my love of literature was called forth by this rebarbative theme; discouraged, well-nigh daunted but more vexed, I turned it into an essay on property – Aristotle and all that – with some psychological reflections of my own. It never once occurred to me – the inner censor operating far too deeply – to go into all that the lack of possessions had meant in my own life: the restricted opportunities, the brick wall all round one, the deprivations – no theatre, no art, hardly any music, no taste, no furniture, no art-objects, no anything of value – the perpetual frustrations, the humiliations (of which I was even more conscious), the incessant struggle, the resentments piling up, the illness, the undiagnosed enemy. What an unwritten essay was there! I doubt if it would have fetched those elderly gentlemen in that ancient house of learning. Anyway I am writing it now.

In my memory it all seemed to be history, politics and law – and that was the inflexion of the college, its flavour and colouring. There was only one question that gave my particular literary interests an opening – on the current tendencies of English poetry – and I made the most of that. How could I 'discuss the English country house *either* in architecture, *or* in literature'? I had hardly ever seen one, or been inside one, let alone shared its life – that most agreeable of all lives, now rendered practically impossible to live by the progress of civilisation, just when I have earned the right to live it myself. (It may be imagined how much I appreciate the Welfare State. But the joke is that the people, for whom it was all intended, don't much appreciate it either.) I fancy that this was a Richard Pares question, and he could have answered it from his knowledge of Jane Austen. He and David Cecil used to have tremendously detailed exchanges about the characters and events in her novels; but I was by nature a Brontë addict, not a Janeite.

Then there was the horrid experience of the All Souls *viva*. In the middle of our last paper, we were called out one by one to march down the long corridor to the dark panelled Common Room, where the Fellows were gathered ominously in the dim light of an October afternoon around the long mahogany table. Under all those eyes one was confronted with a series of passages in foreign languages, to translate one at sight. (No wonder David Cecil the year before had taken one look at it and saying, 'I'm afraid I can't do it,' fled from the room.) I stuck to my chair amid the encircling gloom, feeling confused and hot and foolish under all those eyes, but stumbled somehow through and out. Altogether I felt I hadn't done myself justice.

This was followed by the worse ordeal of having to dine on Sunday night in Hall as the Warden's guest – I could willingly have been spared that, togging myself up once more in borrowed plumage. There I was, seated at high table on the Warden's right, opposite me the Senior Fellow, Sir Thomas Holland, impenetrably deaf, almost blind, skeletal. He might have been the subject of one of Warden Pember's own stories – of the ancient *émigré* Archbishop after the French Revolution, who used occasionally to come down to Talleyrand's dinner-table and sit there like a mummy, eating and drinking nothing. One day a guest turned to Talleyrand and said, 'Pourquoi Monseigneur ne répond-il pas?' Talleyrand took one look at the Archbishop and said, 'Parce qu'il est mort depuis cinq minutes.'

True enough, there turned up as the sweet at dinner the famed cherry-pie, which was reputed to be the social test at All Souls: what did one do with the stones? The only candidate who completely passed that test dealt with it by swallowing them all – but he did not live to be elected. Archbishop Lang told me of the terrible solecism of the candidate whose ready-made white tie – in those days guests wore white tie and tails – fell into the soup. One way and another I would much have preferred to be let off – wine was a bother, too: I didn't really like it, but was afraid to say no. However, Warden Pember was kind and turned the subject to Cornwall, which I welcomed like an unsteady ship coming into port. How bored he must have been! – but he can hardly have been more bored than I was by this *corvée*. By the end of the evening, what with the wine and the chatter and all the smoke, the horror of cigar-smoke in addition to everything else, I could hardly hear myself think. I sank into a coma attended to by kind Keith Hancock and Ernest Jacob, dear Reggie Harris and Richard Pares.

At this juncture in my fortunes David Cecil was kindness itself: he upheld me and spent a good deal of time with me. I find that I dined with him the night after the ordeal at All Souls, but I was so exhausted that I haven't the least memory of it, where or how or what we said. And, in fact, that week I had more or less of a collapse, and had to go to bed ill. I think it was owing to the state of feebleness to which I had reduced myself, the nervous exhaustion on top of everything, that I have no memory at all of those autumn weeks in Whitehouse Road: it is just as if it had never been.

However, from my letters home, which my parents were now keeping, I find that I had had a return of what I thought was 'that appendicitis-pain. It didn't last long, and wasn't half so bad as the old attacks; but it quite bowled me over and I had to go to bed. I spent the rest of the week there, and had the doctor to see me; I thought it safer, though more extravagant. And I think that enforced rest will do me good; though I should hate to think it meant I was going to have little attacks like that.' Alas, this was precisely what it did mean. On the other hand my finances were put right by 'a letter

from dear Sir Arthur Quiller-Couch, with the usual £15. Now isn't
that all right? And wasn't it good of him, just when his eyesight is so
bad? ... Out of this I shall pay Aunt Bessie at last; I hope she isn't
tired of waiting.' Evidently I had had to borrow from her to get
back to Oxford. Out of this acquisition to my wealth 'I have at last
got a dinner-suit: a beautiful fit and only cost £5 10; then there's
shirt and collar and studs and silk scarf and cashmere socks all extra.
What tomfoolery! I think it's all very foolish to be dressed up like
that just to eat a meal.' (I note a very different reaction from
'George's' attitude to dressing up – proper for an actor – in Emlyn
Williams's autobiography.) As for the white tie and waistcoat and
tails demanded by All Souls, 'isn't that worse than ever? I shall feel
smothered under it all. I have a growing sympathy with father's
vexation with collars, and difficulties in doing them up.' (From boyhood I often used to do them up for him.)

Now that my ship had come home, I was able to repay good old
Aunt Bess with something extra, Jimmy Bacon his couple of pounds
with five shillings added, and a pound note for mother – 'a present
for you to get a pair of stays and some flannels for the winter'. But
'wasn't Q an angel? If he hadn't turned up trumps I should have
been down and out and unemployed. But do you know how his
sight is failing? I find he's got coming out a big book which he has
worked at for the last five years, and I dare say it's too much for
him.' (This was the *Oxford Book of Modern Prose*, which he gave me
with a handsome inscription, when I went home that Christmas.)
'This is a long letter, but I had better say no more until I can give you
definite news. I'm not really resting, you may guess, but reading
much as ever; but I'll look after myself, and I feel fairly well now that
I've been bad. Mind you all look after yourselves; and if you have
half a crown to spare, buy some malt and oil for father. He loves
medicine, I know; he ought to be up here to drink what I don't like
and won't take.'

Meanwhile, what was happening at All Souls? – Not a murmur
penetrated the profound silence. I once ran into the Balliol favourite,
and dared to ask if he had heard anything; receiving a discouraging
shrug from that shy, laconic man, I fancied a rebuff. From my next
letter home: I learned at tea with Feiling that

I have done well at All Souls, and am definitely in the running for the Fellowship. But there are two other strong men against me, and how the election will go, nobody can quite tell. If I don't get it, Feiling was considering other possibilities; he talked of my having a research studentship, a semi-donship at Christ Church, worth something over £200 a year and rooms in college free. That was very handsome and kind of him to have thought about my future in that way; but he talked about that so much that I felt he had some inside knowledge from All Souls that I wouldn't get their Fellowship after all. And, of course, I would a hundred times rather get that than a Research Fellowship at Christ Church. Still, you never know how things will turn out; perhaps, after all, Feiling doesn't know. And, apart from that, he will move the Christ Church authorities to provide for me during the next three years.

While in this state of suspense – though, curiously enough, I was not even considering any other prospect than that of All Souls – I was up and about again, going for walks and talks with David Cecil, reading *Tom Jones* and Tawney and Trotsky. I spent most of the last day of October with David: 'he told me his plans for a story he is going to write; I was really thrilled about it, as he told it me this evening walking up and down the Broad opposite Blackwell's. Then we went in and stayed a long time, and I suddenly missed him. Queer to find he had flitted in that way!' It was my first experience of David's odd absent-mindedness, or a curious absorption that made him forget everything around him – a characteristic inherited from his famous grandfather, the great Lord Salisbury.

One evening I went to the Jowett Society to hear Eddington speak, who was all the rage then; his book, *The Nature of the Physical World*, had immense *réclame*, he was spoken of with veneration as a new Daniel come to judgment. I fear I was not properly impressed; the truth was that I didn't much like this mixture of Quaker quietism with unintelligible physics. It didn't much speak to me, though I dutifully did my best to struggle through his book. My brain was brimming with something else.

I am reading Trotsky's *Literature and Revolution* at the moment, and with the ardour of a disciple; but that is only the climax to my own thoughts on the matter of late. The materialist conception of history haunts me day in and day out; it is an obsession. I can think of nothing, but my historical theories come in and colour whatever I am thinking about. All my friends must be bored at my constantly bringing it into all discussions; however, I can hardly help myself. Is it a sort of madness; or is it that I am mentally tired out, and must have a rest? I have no doubts that it is true, and that I have found a philosophy that gives me intellectual satisfaction. But may it be that the effort of construction (for that's what it amounts to: I have to piece out each step for myself; there is no guidance to be had, but only stray suggestions which have to be made consistent and systematised) is too great a drain on one's energy? Perhaps I ought to have a rest; but how to do it? My brain goes on and on like a steamroller, and there's ever more stones in the way to crush into order. There's German and Italian to learn; philosophy to read; my own lines of historical criticism to work out; besides the old schemes for poems and writings which, though laid aside, have always been nearest my heart, and never more than at this time when it is becoming inevitable that I should throw in my lot with the historians, and when I have been straining every nerve to make myself competent as a historian.

Here was a programme of work! But at this very moment I was assailed by 'the old doubts whether this awful concentration on academic work, which has been going on unrelieved for the past three years (and with especial emphasis the past eight months) will not end in the atrophy of the imaginative in me.'

There are no entries in the Diary for the next three weeks: in the interval I had been elected to the Fellowship at All Souls, along with Roger Makins.

*   *   *

Both All Souls Fellowships going to House-men, both historians – neither Greats men nor lawyers – was something unprecedented, and the Christ Church authorities were correspondingly pleased. (The elections to All Souls, being competitive, offer a barometer to the intellectual standing of colleges in the university. Before the 1914 war there was a majority of Balliol men at All Souls; between the wars New College took the lead and All Souls came to have a Wykehamist flavouring. Christ Church has rarely achieved an election to All Souls since.) Headlam who, on becoming Bishop of Gloucester, had been re-elected at All Souls, ran along to Christ Church with the news. I was summoned to the Deanery – and purposely that morning had refrained from shaving, by an obscure superstitious impulse: I suppose in order not to seem to expect good news. Dear Tom Lawrenson had lighted a candle for me in the church of St Edmund and St Frideswide – so perhaps that decided the election.

That evening I dined at the guest-table in Hall with Godfrey Elton and Aikin-Sneath. Elton wrote up this first election of an All Souls Fellow from the working class in an article in the *Daily Herald* – symptom of the social transformation of our time, etc. So my election was news, and there followed a hail of congratulations – votes from the Cornwall County Council (so niggardly in its university scholarships), from the Truro City Council (very good of them), from the St Austell Urban Council (which felt it ought to follow suit), and so on. I don't think anybody had been elected from a Cornish school before – or has been since. One small triumph registered, for it was in an area where I had had so much reason to be sensitive – the financial. I now had to invest in an objectionable full evening suit, tails, white waistcoat and all. Finding a suit that fitted, I offered to pay by cheque – I hadn't the cash. The shop-man wanted a guarantor. Inspiration came to me: 'Would a Fellow of a college do?' 'Certainly, sir,' he said. 'I *am* a Fellow of a college,' I replied. It was my proudest moment in the whole business.

Coming to live in All Souls meant moving into an upper-class mode of life, intimate and gregarious. It was rather a strain, though there were very few of us living in college – what with gloomy old Rydar, the butler, whom I thought of as a Uriah Heep, the stern Calvinist Manciple, who had been trained at Balmoral and whose chief detestation was the Junior Fellows, and changing every night for dinner in the dark-panelled, candle-lit Common Room. On the first night I dined as Fellow, my health was drunk in champagne according to custom. I preferred water really, but was consoled by Archbishop Lang by whose side I sat, who sympathetically said that he was a water-drinker too, and then added in his stately manner, 'but on special occasions I give myself a dispensation'. This went down very well with me and I appreciated the kindness that went with the intuitive sympathy: he was not much appreciated by the middle generation of Fellows, but from that moment he had an admirer in me, and as time went on a feeling of affection. He was at his best to and with young men.

The full nature of All Souls and the extraordinary distinction of its membership at that time dawned on me only gradually, as the grandees – Viceroys, bishops, Cabinet ministers, public figures (Lawrence of Arabia the most remarkable, if the most withdrawn) – came down for week-ends or assembled in state for college meetings and gaudies. During the week there were very few of us: Roger for the first term or so, then he went to Germany to learn the language for the diplomatic service. Richard Pares had gone off to the *Liverpool Post*, thinking of a career in journalism; Reggie Harris had a teaching job somewhere. Keith Hancock, whom I liked from the first, was living in college. So was Sir Henry Sharp, an eminent Anglo-Indian Civil Servant, who had been secretary of the recent University Commission: yellow-skinned and much-wrinkled, he had lived so long in India that he looked Indian – as whites who visit China come to have a Chinese look. He had no, or only a rudimentary, sense of humour and a mechanical, mirthless laugh on three deliberate notes. General Swinton, newly elected Professor of Military History, was another character: the talented author of *The Green Curve* when young, he had had an important part in the development of the tank and nursed an almighty grievance – as well he might – at the too little and too late use of this winning weapon in the first war. (His daughter, coming out of their house in the Woodstock Road, was killed by a tank in the second war.) The General had a warm-hearted, affectionate nature and a sense of fun; but I was astonished by his habit of shamelessly telling the same story three or four times over to the same audience: I had never met anything like it.

Then there was venerable-looking old Spenser Wilkinson, a far better military historian and a far greater bore; also sweet-natured and kind-hearted. He had a celebrated story about being arrested and imprisoned in Cracow, guaranteed to last ninety minutes: politer members of the College had been known to pale at its onset, but he never got round to trying it on me. A journalist of the old school, well acquainted with Europe and especially Germany, where he had relations, he boasted a brief acquaintance with Sarah Bernhardt and was not averse to having it thought that he had enjoyed her favours. On my first meeting with him, after lunch one day, he said portentously, 'I see from your papers that you are not very good at foreign languages. Let me advise you: when you go abroad, take a dictionary to bed with you.' No doubt he was right; but when I perceived the bearing of this excellent advice, prig that I was, I was much put out. Other, less worldly, professors were in and out to lectures and meals – Oman, R. W. Lee, D. H. Macgregor, Holdsworth, Coupland, W. G. S. Adams; Lionel Curtis was much in evidence, and of him I grew very fond. And we saw a good deal of Woodward as Domestic Bursar, responsible for our creature comforts.

The Diary records how I felt in myself about the change.

18 November 1925: The last three weeks since I came here have been so hurried and busy as to leave no time for reflection or any kind of inner life. I have never led an existence so externalised and occupied only with circumstances ... I have felt so frozen during these weeks. The excitement of getting the Fellowship, of arranging to come in and shifting my things on a handbarrow through the streets, and for the first few days of living in two places at once: it was all too much for me. And since I have settled in, I have been re-creating myself by talk and listening to talk, lunching and dining out, and meeting all sorts of people.

I added, significantly enough: 'But that isn't going to give any real satisfaction. Next term I shall arrive at a way of life which will achieve more in the way of work, while using the social amenities of the college to give savour (and no more) to the existence which I shall live to myself.'

There follows the plan of campaign I intended to follow. 'I am going to read Marx's *Capital* during the vac.' People can hardly imagine now what a mysterious Everest this was to us then, or what we hoped to get out of it. 'Krishna has lent it me, together with a students' guide which may be helpful, though not a thing to rely on.' (Who was this Krishna? Not Menon?) 'I intend to make myself a proficient Marxist, and a proficient historian. For the next five years I shall devote myself to laying in a stock of knowledge which will serve me throughout life. I am going to learn German and Italian; and next long vac. I shall therefore spend in Germany. It seems a grand prospect, but I have an eye open to the danger of dawdling my life away in the comfortable society of dons and their families ... The curious doubt that haunts my mind is whether this turn in my fortune doesn't coincide with a turn in my development. It seems certain that my work will lie in the direction of history; what sort of result will that have on my desire to do creative work?'

The first people to take me up and launch me out into the family life of my new colleagues were the dear Adamses, who lived on one of the outlying spurs of Boar's Hill, then still mostly dingles and copses, bluebells and birdsong. They lived next to Chilswell, the famous home of Robert Bridges, and not far from the Masefields. Masefield had had a private theatre built for him in his garden, for the performance of verse-plays, his own and others'. This particular evening, 21 November, we went to see 'Ross's *Evil* (not very good) and Gordon Bottomley's *Gruach*' – characteristic name for this Celtic twilight stuff.

Shortly after I was bidden to tea by the Masefields: 4 December, it happened to be my twenty-second birthday.

I set out late as usual, with not a bus within half an hour, and with a thicky snowy fog over all the land. The bus caught me up and took me as far as the turn halfway up the Hill. A friendly baker, who is baker-in-chief to all the poets, carried me in his trap along the next stage. I sat shivering with cold and fear of the horses's stumbling in the frozen road, while the baker dictated to his boy the sales of bread at the houses. He had an outlook on the poets from an amusing angle. At the Masefields' wife and daughter were most in evidence. Masefield himself appeared before tea: a shy man, ruddy, frosty, sailor's complexion, simpleness of manner and mind, it seemed. He talked a little of Cornwall and the Roseland: was there good bathing at Pendower? And of an exhibition of Revolutionary portraits he had seen in Paris recently. Nothing memorable; except that, talking of the fate of clever unbalanced women who went mad – like Mary Lamb, Maggie Benson – he said it always seemed so 'tragical', when ordinarily one would say 'tragic'. After tea, more of Mrs Masefield on Count Keyserling [who had an inflated reputation with his *Travel-Diary of a Philosopher* at the time] and Christ; a typical woman's stance: it was goodness that mattered and this is unaffected by circumstances!

This was very much contrary to my view of things.

Coming back the four miles from Hill Crest was an exciting game. Pitch darkness outside the garden-gate: I could hardly find my way to it, or find the latch when I got there. Everything was so still as to be listening; the thick bushes looked like figures huddled up in the shadows. The trees loomed white, powdered with rime, passive and motionless with not a sound in the air. My feet crunched on the flakes, and when I ran my steps echoed behind me along the road. I felt as if I were being followed by the Old Man of the Cairngorms. When I got into the main road there were lights and occasional bicycles; and so by running and walking I got over the miles in short time. Even so I was none too early for the little dinner-party Jacob held in his rooms at Christ Church, with Dawkins and David Cecil as guests.

The wintry scene of that first visit to the Masefields remains with me still: wood-fire, candle-light and scones, the somewhat precious atmosphere of cultivation Mrs Masefield created around her. Even then I appreciated the point of her role in protecting her famous husband from intrusive bores, but didn't she also cut him off from life, the seed-bed of poetry? Rather a dragon, really – though not such a formidable one as Kipling's wife, nor such a horror as poor Hardy's first spouse. One of Mrs Masefield's phrases has stuck with me as revealing: Irish herself, of Huguenot descent – at any rate the daughter of Nicholas de la Cherois-Crommelin – she could not understand 'how the Irish *contrive* to be so uneducated'. Herself read Keyserling. One summer when they took Sentry, the tumble-down Georgian rectory at Mawnan – abode of old Father Leverton, a character in Charles Henderson's menagerie – Charlie took me over to call. Mrs Masefield said, very impressively, that they had been having such a good *read* the past fortnight. 'And what have you read?' I said in all innocence. Confronted with this direct question, poor Mrs Masefield couldn't remember a thing – until she faltered out, 'Oh, Santayana and such.' Charlie laughed at this the whole way home.

I fear I was very simple and direct, with no return upon myself; I cannot think how people put up with me as they did, for I had masses of friends. (As I still have, in spite of the deliberate quali-fication I have imposed as the result of unfortunate experiences at the hands of some. Very easy to get yourself demoted from the rank of friend to that of acquaintance, if you misbehave.) Here was Dawkins, for example, who was a member of Common Room and used to come across from Exeter a good deal. To me he was not an eccentric celebrity, the 'blubber-lipped Professor' of Corvo's description – I had never heard of the horrible Baron or of the Prof's curious experiences in Crete and the Greek Islands. Nor did I ever make one of the Prof's circle, nor even quite see the point of the Prof, let alone make a cult of this weird old satyr with the eldritch scream of a laugh and predatory teeth such as one sometimes sees on a Greek vase. His uncle, John Doyle of All Souls, had left him a large house in North Wales together with, most improbably for Dawkins, a pack of hounds. I accepted Dawkins as part of the *décor*, I never sought his acquaintance – or anybody's, for that matter.

Next day,

we were a merry company at tea round the smoking-room fire: Blagden, Harris and Makins, in addition to Sharp, David Cecil and me. Reggie Harris gave an excellent rendering of a dentist's drill, one of his many accomplishments, in addition to being able to sing all the parts in Bach's B minor Mass, many of them in falsetto, and saying Mass with the mantelpiece for altar as a French priest would say it – *per saecula saeculor-ewm*. David very funny about the man who ate the *Daily Mail*, a lunatic he once met in a train. At dinner Dawkins was added unto us: with whom I talked all the evening. First, about dreams, as at tea; then coincidences and tokens; my curious experience in reading the cards before Ian's wedding; later, punctuation according to sense and according to rhythm, Doughty and early alliterative verse, the Baconians and old Burton, of whom and of Osler, old Francis of Christ Church Library has a story.

Such were those winter amenities in the 'twenties. In the later 'thirties, Dawkins, who was essentially a-political and had no under-standing of politics, was a vehement Appeaser and had the hardihood to splutter hotly in favour of this nonsense to me. He strongly disapproved of my anti-Appeasement line – as did so many of the people who were so obviously, so fatuously, wrong. And – such was the sadness of those dividing days – I ceased to speak to him.

*　　*　　*

The mention of the Cairngorms reminds me that it was Roger who first took me to dine with the Buchans at Elsfield. John Buchan told me of the Old Man of the Cairngorms, and his own frightening experience coming down from the mountains one evening, with the sound of footsteps echoing behind him: he ended up running. This was the first of many visits to that hospitable house that became so familiar, the family that were as friendly as they were gifted, with whom I have kept warm contact ever since. Of that first visit I remember the drive through Marston, then bowered in elms, still a village though on its way to being spoiled, up the steep hill to Elsfield and the Scotch-baronial-looking house at the end with the view down the broad slopes over Otmoor. How well I remember that square library, walled with books, the blue-crystal chandelier, the portrait of Ralegh over the fire-place. There was John, with the spare figure and grave face, slight lisp and parsonic manner, whose interest in interesting people of all kinds and classes – he found them more interesting than uninteresting ones – was obvious and endearing. Amid the handing round of silver dishes at dinner, he suddenly said to me, 'Do you know the Duchess of Marlborough?' One might as well have asked, did I know the Empress Catherine the Great? – she was as present a figure in my mind. 'Do you mean Sarah, the great Duchess?' I said; in fact he didn't, but we talked about her instead. I fear that my innocence must have been more formidable than most people's sophistication.

David Cecil took me out to dine at Garsington with the famous Lady Ottoline Morrell – she wasn't famous to me: I had never heard of her. Curiously enough, I was less nervous and self-conscious in this milieu, perhaps because its very exoticism had a levelling influence or put it out of this world. David thought it about the most beautiful house he knew. I had never seen anything like it: there was the drawing-room with its panelling painted deep coral, as a background for the Venetian dye of Lady Ottoline's looped and coiled hair. There was the thrust-out lower jaw of John's portrait of her under the enormous hat, the extraordinary way of speaking English as if it were Italian, the sibilance of the flowing gown she wore, the exotic scent of the room. Of this first occasion – for I shortly came to know the house better, the pictures and drawings by John, Mark Gertler and Paul Nash, the terraced gardens described by Lawrence, the hall with the door in the panelling through which Aldous Huxley saw the footman vanish with the tray of steaming viands for the frail beauty upstairs who ate nothing, as in *Crome Yellow* – I remember nothing, except Lady Ottoline's adherence to an old-fashioned habit of having tea brought in at nine o'clock, which I much appreciated: an unexpected link with simple life in the village at Tregonissey.

*   *   *

What, meanwhile, of my own life to myself in my room – the joy of a room of one's own?

'22 November. All this morning I have spent in the happiest way, marking shirts and collars and things up in my bedroom. I am emerging from the stunned state of mind which has prevailed over me here, in which I have taken everything very much for granted. Looking back over the last three weeks, I seem merely to have come upon the future as it lay in my way and nothing unexpected has happened. (So much I recollect from the curious phrasing of Eddington's ideas that night at the Jowett Society.)' I was becoming much attached to my rooms, an upstairs set in the Old Quad: somewhat dark and gloomily panelled in the time of Charles I, dolphin-hinges on the press in my bedroom, with a view on one side upon the Warden's garden and across to the long range of Queen's, the other dominated by the spire of St Mary's, to me always Newman's St Mary's.

Now Keith Hancock was going back to Australia, and I was sad at this. I had grown fond of him in the short time we were in college together. He had finished his first book, *Ricasoli and the Risorgimento in Tuscany*, which was conceived as the other side of the diptych to Trevelyan's too endorsive picture. Hancock had the idea of making himself an interpreter of Britain to Australia, and of Australia to Britain; and later wrote the best general book on his home country. We made a pact to write to each other, and I was able to get several of his pieces into *The New Statesman*.

26 November. We had a quiet farewell supper together in my room; I lit the candles on my mantelpiece in honour of the occasion. The first meal I have had in my room – the room and I are less distant after it. Hancock felt on leaving as if he were leaving a family. He wouldn't be reminded of the old Fellows whom he may not see again – Johnson certainly [the Chaplain], and apparently Johnson felt so when he said goodbye. I told him, if ever he came across another Rowse in Australia, to scrutinise him for my brother. At eight o'clock we went down to the gate and I saw him off.

My rooms were coming to accumulate associations for me and I to identify myself with them, when I suddenly received a chastening shock: they held within them a most sinister, and quite recent, memory. One sad grey afternoon, when one felt at one's lowest, one of the Fellows casually told me at the foot of my staircase the story of the mysterious and unexplained suicide there: the quite successful and attractive young Fellow who had quietly gone out one day to purchase a length of rope and hanged himself from the wooden beam over my bed in the bedroom. I don't think I should have minded so much if I had been told beforehand; but I had begun to identify myself, as always, with my rooms and now I felt that they were contaminated. 'I feel now as if I don't belong here, but am only on sufferance', I wrote in a long entry after two days of disturbance of mind. Worse than that, I was frightened: 'it has been a perfect terror to me to be in it these last two nights, and to go up into it during the day-time. I fear it most of all now when the day draws in early in the afternoon, and there are ugly shadows each side of that beam.' There beside the door-handle was a remnant of red sealing-wax, from when the room had been sealed up. I was the first to inhabit it after this dreadful association.

I had always been a prey to night-terrors from childhood, and peculiarly susceptible to the atmosphere of places. Here was something to live with! – for it never occurred to me to give up. It would probably have been better for me if I had; for, already overstrung and illness on me, I have often and often lain in that bed at night, my heart pulsing out of my body, suddenly awakened in terror, turning on the light and waiting for my fear to subside.

But I wouldn't think of shifting to another room: never give up, never give in. I inhabited those rooms for some fifteen or sixteen years, until I succeeded Lord Salter in my present rooms, and G. D. H. Cole succeeded to mine. By then I had exorcised the other presence.

Curiously enough, I had quite a different hallucination about those rooms, not at all baleful, rather a jovial one – perhaps it was that the memory was a real one, the hallucination fancied. It was a visual one: I often fancied a figure coming out of the little room I used as a box-room upstairs. It was always the same figure: a tall Fellow of the time of Queen Anne, long curled locks on his shoulders, a full-skirted coat and *jabot*, high riding-boots; always holding a guttering candle in his hand, he emerged with a rolling gait, tight. Where on earth did this cloak-and-sword figure come from? The image of him was quite a constant one, never varying: who can he have

been? There was nothing in the least sinister about *him*. I did not let
my mind dwell on the other figure.

Before term ended we had a college tramp across the fields to
Kidlington – an institution that has died out in my time, not only,
I fancy, because there are no fields near Oxford to walk across. Six
of us went, Edgeworth, Geoffrey Faber, Sharp, Swinton, Lionel
Curtis and I. Edgeworth had been a member of the original Tramps
led by Leslie Stephen, not without murmur on account of his pace
and refusal to consider obstacles. (In that like G. M. Trevelyan, who
just walked through streams and ditches.) 'Edgeworth was in great
form: there ought to have been a Boswell at his side. Roger and I
have sworn to record some of his sayings.' But in fact his style was
very difficult to catch: it was not Johnsonian but early Victorian.
Owing to his being the child of an elderly father, his immediate
family memories went back, incredibly, to the reign of George III.
His great-aunt was Maria Edgeworth, who reproved him for saying
Brighton instead of Brighthelmstone. When I pointed out an article
on Mrs Siddons in the *Revue des Deux Mondes*, he thought that there
couldn't be anything new to say about her; for that it would have
been necessary to know her, as indeed his grandfather had done.
Apropos of modern poetry and older people's dislike of it, he remembered a generation that disliked and never came to appreciate
Tennyson.

What was characteristic of his talk was a certain obliqueness: it
was difficult to get him to say anything straight out. On being
invited to go down a steep hill into some attractive gorge, he couched
his refusal in these terms: though he couldn't disguise from himself
the fact that the pleasure of the descent would be great, the corres-
ponding ascent would considerably detract from that pleasure. Not
for nothing was he a mathematical economist, with a refined
apparatus for measuring marginal utility. It may be imagined what
difficulty Edgeworth had in explaining where the college rears were
to General Swinton on his arrival, and what amusement this provided
for the soldierly sense of humour. Edgeworth would hand me an
article he couldn't be bothered to read with, 'You look into it,
Rowse, and extract the gist of it; and with your historical mind
present it to me.' Himself had been well based on the classics; on his

9

single journey to America, suffering agony from sea-sickness, he lay most of the time in his bunk reconstructing more than half of the *Iliad* from memory. He was the only person I know who has read Voltaire's *La Henriade*. He used to say that he 'liked the duplicity of things'. The only subject on which I got him to express a direct and decisive opinion was that Marx was no good as an economist, and this nettled me.

That distant December day it was 'an invigorating tramp over the frosted fields and in a nipping air'. Curtis gave us lunch in his old thatched house by the river – 'beautiful, but not like the creeks of the Fal' – at the quiet end of the ancient village of Kidlington, just beginning to be ruined, and now a disgusting suburban sprawl. There, in the inter-war years, he paddled his canoe, reared his ducks, planted his willow plantation, cut up his timber, reconstructed the boy-scouting, out-of-door life he had known in his South African years – in the intervals of vaticinating about the British Common-wealth, writing such works as *Civitas Dei* and regurgitating blue-prints for the universe. Besides being a most remarkable man, who had had a fascinating life, he was a great dear. If only, instead of all those pamphlets and blue-prints about what should happen, he had written an autobiography, what had really happened to him! ... It was the only book worth his writing, and this he would never do.

I came upon an essay on 'Autobiography as Art' by Arthur Mac-Dowall, one of the few literary Fellows, whom I was yet to meet. A man of extreme sensibility, he had had a breakdown and was very frail. It was owing to him that D. H. Lawrence had such perceptive and sympathetic treatment constantly in *The Times Literary Supplement*, MacDowall reviewing his books there as they came out. He wrote an excellent book on *The Art of Thomas Hardy*, whom he knew – and told me early some of the queer things we all now know about Hardy's first wife: how she had a psychotic jealousy of his work, thought that she too had genius, wrote reams of rubbish and considered that he stole his ideas from her. What a *supplice*, for a man to have to live with that!

Going home to Cornwall for Christmas I had a nasty experience myself of the ways of women. 'A horrible letter arrived from the M.s in Montana: as an ironical Christmas greeting it must have been meant. Written by a younger daughter, to my mother, it was obviously inspired by her mother and contained just the sort of charge which rends families and makes people miserable.' There had been a great deal of local fuss about my winning the Fellowship, resolutions of the councils, an interview with my parents whom a journalist got hold of, much to my annoyance. All this transpired to the family with whom we had been on such close – too close – terms in old days in the village, now emigrated to Montana. It was more than the woman could bear, transported with jealousy, contemplating the talents of her own likely brood. I read the letter to my mother, then tore it up and burnt it, so that no evidence of it should remain; but it added renewed strain and dubiety to my own make-up, increased the sense of insecurity, provided another trauma and was followed by another attack of ulcer. I dare say that may have been due in any case.

But is it any wonder that I have no relish for family life?

VIII

New Acquaintances

HILARY TERM, 1926: how well I remember the clammy cold of the Thames valley in January and February, the shroud-like touch of the sheets I returned to from the cosy warmth of Robartes Place! The new term brought with it my first experience of teaching; not that that transported me with excitement – that was reserved for my inner life – but I was interested, and made most of my tutorials lively. Not all of them, for it takes two to make a tutorial. My first pupil was a Benedictine monk from St Benet's Hall, then under the rigorous discipline of the ascetic Father McCann. My pupil, a nice chap, now at Ampleforth, would come to me at eleven in the morning dropping with fatigue: he had been up since some unearthly hour, five or five-thirty, singing the offices in choir, or whatever they do. My other pupils came from nice, normal St Edmund Hall, and were a hefty, hard-working, average lot. One or two of them made rather better than average careers subsequently.

A. B. Emden, admirable medieval scholar and most devoted to the well-being of the Hall, which owed everything to his public spirit and scholarly taste – in return for which he was once passed over for the Principalship – gave me my first chance at teaching. I rather think I owed this to Cruttwell, who failed to conceal warmth of heart under a lacerating tongue. When I first came to All Souls I was afraid of him and the whiplash he wielded – until the day came when I stood up to him and gave him some of his own back. From that time on we became friends, in the end more – comrades in illness, having a good deal to bear, taking our invalidish walks together. I never knew until after his death that he considered the way I put up with illness 'manly' – in fact it made me still more impatient and resentful; and at his death I was astonished to receive a handsome legacy. (You could have knocked me down with a feather; it made me all the sadder that he should have died.)

One other *quondam* Fellow, Kenneth Bell, who was constantly in and out of college from Balliol, alarmed me by his blustering, bullying banter. He also had to be stood up to – when I discovered that he too had a heart of gold. It is interesting that these two men with such sharp tongues had exceptional kindness of heart; they were in fact both gifted and highly neurotic, and came to sad ends before their time.

Kenneth Bell wrote hardly anything, except reviews, to warrant his gifts: I suppose his life's work was his pupils. He certainly wasted himself a lot. Cruttwell, who was an excellent military historian, among other things, wrote a first-class History of the War of 1914–18. It was a pity he did not live to chronicle, or give us his commentary on, the second as it went along – he had a penetrating mind on military affairs.

He was an extraordinary character, with his misogyny and his idiosyncratic vocabulary – he had a Swiftian attitude and manner of speech. I forget the full Cruttwellian categories: the ordinary female dons were 'drabs', the more emotional ones 'breast-heavers', the usual teaching dons, men-folk, were 'hacks'. Richard Pares and I used to lead him on to further flights of humorous exaggeration, all in inverted commas, of course: this Swinton did not perceive and so didn't relish. He, too, feared Cruttwell's tongue and still more his disapprobation, for Cruttwell had no opinion of him as a military historian and thought him useless as a professor. I rather think that I must have over-compensated my original trepidation and followed in Cruttwell's wake in habits of freedom of speech.

Certainly some compensation, if not over-compensation, was necessary to offset the acute inferiority-complex I suffered from in regard to so many things – going out into society, mingling with people, making a speech, or – still worse – with regard to writing history, historical research, publishing poetry. How odd it seems in retrospect! G. M. Trevelyan once said to me, 'We thought you were never going to begin,' and then added generously, 'But, my goodness, once you got going … !' I told him how much illness was responsible for holding me up, and it greatly increased the sense of inner isolation, cutting me off from normal ways of life, throwing me further back upon myself.

Here was an offer from C. K. Ogden to write a little book on Historical Materialism in either the *Daedalus* or the *Psyche* series he had invented. They were quite famous in their day, with Bertrand Russell, Julian Huxley and J. B. S. Haldane starting off the former, I. A. Richards, Malinowski and Joseph Needham contributing to the latter. My first reaction to it was that I couldn't do it. 'Now where does that awful sense of inferiority come from? I should like to track it down and extrude it from my mind.' I could only persuade myself that if I couldn't write up to the ideal of the book on history I should like to produce, there were not many people who would do it better anyway. So I made myself do it. And so it was with everything – *making* myself do it against inner feelings of incapacity or inferiority.

The little book turned out better than might have been expected. And for this reason: though I had the ardour of a neophyte about Marxism, which I was discovering for myself, I would not go a millimetre in my declarations beyond what I really thought to be true. I had reason to be grateful subsequently, for, unlike so many Marxist converts, I did not commit myself to propositions impossible to maintain. So the booklet – it was no more than an essay – served to clear my mind and also pointed the way to future work even if the work was a long time in coming. When I re-read the book twenty years later in preparation for *The Use of History*, which developed the position more fully and said what I thought about the subject after the experience of writing history, I found that luckily I still agreed with it all. When I came home to Cornwall, I was surprised to find that my good old friend F. R. Pascoe, Secretary for Education, and his son, who became a very able industrialist, confessed themselves incapable of understanding it!

C. K. Ogden, who had taken me up and of whom I saw a certain amount until T. S. Eliot came into my life and took his place, was a very odd man: not really my cup of tea. The co-author with I. A. Richards of *The Meaning of Meaning*, he was celebrated for his war-time editorship of *The Cambridge Magazine*, which he made the forum of unpopular causes, pacifism, neutralism, pro-Germanism defender of Russell upon his expulsion from his Fellowship at Trinity. (It should provide an interesting historical source.) Ogden thought of himself as a latter-day Bentham, which in a way he was: a calculating machine of pleasures and displeasures, or, rather, utilities and disutilities. He was a great eccentric, and when he stayed with me at All Souls used to provide himself with pink wax ear-stoppers to extrude all noise in order to sleep at night.

I dare say now that that was not so odd as I youthfully thought, for Lang, Dougie Malcolm, Richard Pares and others found the bells of Oxford sounding the hours all through the night troublesome. They never bothered me. The wax ear-stoppers remind me of Herbert Spencer, another pleasure-pain calculator, also a hypochondriac, who, on meeting the young Grant Robertson, after twenty minutes of it, took out his ear-stoppers and applied them firmly, saying 'You are interesting me too much'. Robertson, who was a prodigious bore, though otherwise a great dear, told me this himself in all innocence.

When C. K. Ogden became world-famous with his invention of Basic English, he played a characteristic trick with his world-public. Besieged with requests for signed photographs, he bought up the stock of a Victorian photographer somewhere in Cambridge for a fiver; with the result that in various parts of the world, New Zealand, Japan, Hong Kong, the United States, South America, devotees of Basic English possess authentic autographed portraits of the pious Founder, but all of them different – some with mutton-chop side-whiskers of the period, some with goatees, full-moon or spade beards, or merely curled and waxed moustaches. Ogden was a singularly hairless man himself, so bald as one wouldn't believe; it was the kind of joke that he appreciated, creating confusion in the minds of the faithful.

I was ingenuous and silly enough to part with him, though it was from a sincere impulse: a Cambridge utilitarian calculator, all psychology and the measurement of impulses, he wasn't my type. I was all history, politics and poetry, and the time shortly came when I told him so, that he didn't share enough of the aesthetic values for me. This was true. Ruthless and uncompromising, really I hadn't much sense or consideration. Now I am sorry – and yet still not so sorry as I should be!

An ageing reactionary of whose opinions I disapproved, Charles Whibley, surprisingly pleased me more. Why was this? 'He is really ludicrous to look upon: so diminutive, perky and pot-bellied, with a double chin running into dewlaps, petulant lips and an absurd eye-glass. He's rather like a child. His perversity of opinion goes so far as to be merely amusing and quite harmless: in his self-indulgence appears the essential innocence of his outlook on life. His bright little eyes, though now somewhat glassy, are still wide-open and round with wonder at the world. One subject he talked about gripped me among all the trivial clevernesses of Common Room talk.' He talked about the subject of Pain, and how it could be a stimulant. This chimed in with what I already knew from experience: it kept one on edge, keyed-up, alert and sensitive, even if it isolated one within oneself. It was a world of its own, with its own phenomena. I had noticed in my own, now frequent, attacks of acute pain, 'how at night, when the brain's control was taken off the nervous system, the unity of one's self was broken into. I have lain in bed thinking that the pain didn't belong to me, but was somehow outside myself. An image came to me one night: it was like sitting in a brightly-lit theatre, watching the course that the pain took, somehow dramatised into events on a stage.' I wanted to make a poem of this queer experience; I had much more of it before I did. But here was an unexpected affinity with Whibley; it is the affinities that count. Whibley was a friend of T. S. Eliot: I was on my way to Eliot.

Meeting G. K. Chesterton that term, however, meant nothing to me: he was disappointing. Obviously he hadn't prepared his speech and had nothing to say to us: the only interest of the performance was to observe how he managed to keep going on a few worn-out jokes and stale paradoxes. G. D. H. Cole, who knew him well, told me that Chesterton was never the same man after his breakdown during the war. I think there was another element in the folding-up of his inspiration: his genius throve on the whimsical, kindly irresponsibility of the Anglo-Catholicism of the early 1900s, of which I was early enough to have caught a whiff of incense. Chesterton's cult of paradox flourished in that eccentric and endearing ambience. Belloc's pulling him into the arms of Rome put his wayward spirit into a strait-jacket, while their silly cult of drink – odes to wine, the rolling English drunkard, and what not – helped to debilitate the talents of both of them. As an adolescent I had enjoyed the very bearable brilliance of Chesterton's earlier work; his later work held nothing for me – nor for anybody else. While Belloc never had anything in him for me at all – except for a few of his poems and epigrams. It has always shocked me – in the way that nothing else shocks me (certainly no moralising humbug) – that a man should have written so much about history without caring whether what he said was true or no. G. M. Trevelyan used to describe him to me as a liar. He was.

On the night of the Purification of the Blessed Virgin I dined with Dawkins to meet Walter de la Mare, whose poetry I particularly loved – I placed his magical poem 'The Listeners' alongside 'Christabel'. Nothing impressed me so much as the extraordinary stillness of his personality, the inner quietude, perfectly natural and unforced, for outside was perfect courtesy and charm. Next among the poets I was bidden to tea by the great Robert Bridges, who had rather an alarming aura: whether it was that he was the Laureate – an otiose halo which he carried with an air – or his magnificent leonine appearance, tousled white hair and aggressive beard, or his way of snorting at any faltering nonsense (and he had a good deal to put up with from doting ladies), but he was an impatient and gruff man, a spoiled child of fortune.

The denigration of Robert Bridges by people unworthy to loosen the latchet of his shoes is a curious phenomenon: it may partly be in reaction against the over-estimation of him in his own, rather academic, circle in his life-time. Bridges is absurdly under-estimated now, as his friend Hopkins is over-estimated. Both were men of genius; to admire one does not preclude the other: only fools think like that (there are many about, especially among literary critics: compare Housman on that subject). In fact, the alarming element in Bridges's presence was owing to a quality I have come to associate with genuine greatness – both G. M. Trevelyan and Churchill possessed it, as Bridges also – a shattering, sometimes unnerving, integrity of spirit that expressed itself in uncompromising, sometimes rude, directness. And this came out when something that touched their real (and lofty) standards of value was in question. Ordinary people, with their pathetic little compromises, their readiness to shuffle where things that really matter are concerned, in the interest of appearances or something second-rate, naturally find this daunting.

I have watched this in operation, often with Trevelyan, sometimes with Churchill, once or twice notably with Bridges. One day at tea at Chilswell he was showing an undergraduette a picture of a Chinese horse. It wasn't really good. The old poet asked her what she thought of it. She didn't seriously think, but gave a conventional answer, anxious to please: 'I think it's a beautiful horse.' This was fatal: 'I d–don't think it's a beautiful horse,' the old man thundered, with his impressive stutter when roused, 'I think it's an *Aw-ful* horse.' There was a consternated silence, while I registered not to serve up any cliché-reactions in future. Nevertheless, I was caught out myself some years later. I was back from Dublin, where I had met the remnants of Irish literary life – all that were left after Ireland's attainment of self-determination: A. E. (George Russell), Oliver St John Gogarty, Frank O'Connor, were still there, Yeats away at Rapallo, Joyce the perpetual exile. (In the city which the world of art and letters saw through the eyes of the author of *Dubliners* and *Ulysses*, not one of his works was to be seen in the bookshops, as in the bad old days: now, under self-determination, Catholic censorship operated.)

Bridges, now in his eighties, was writing his life's work, *The Testament of Beauty* – I dare say he had left it a little late. When I went up to Chilswell, he was then much excited by Joyce: he had been reading *Portrait of the Artist as a Young Man*, and 'I find J-Joyce's aesthetics are *m-my* aesthetics.' Readers of that wonderful work will remember the long argument about aesthetics which, however much in Scholastic form, works out that the apprehension of the world and experience as beauty is their final redemption, the only lasting value that transcends time, environment and circumstance. This was the religion of Proust, as of Ruskin (however muddled and muddied by morals); it was Joyce's religion (after the dross of doctrine had been drossed away), as it is mine. It was also Robert Bridges's, and the whole message of *The Testament of Beauty*.

The great man was agog with excitement to know all I had heard about Joyce in Dublin and what kind of man he was. When I reflected on what I had heard about him from Gogarty (the original of Buck Mulligan in *Ulysses*) and others – the seedy sponger Joyce had been, the habit of biting the hand that fed him, the ingratitude, the unscrupulous writing-down of friends – well, youthfully, I didn't like to tell the Poet Laureate in all his dignity what I had heard. So I hesitated: 'Well, he's a queer fish, you know.' At once the flame leaped: 'I d–don't need you to tell me that: I can see that for m–myself.' I didn't in the least resent this snub from the great man; in fact, I quietly laughed to myself, as I have done since at being ticked off by G.M.T. or Winston, for it is just the way I feel myself.

On the main spur of that elevated country (in both senses of the word), Boar's Hill, lived Gilbert Murray and his wife, Lady Mary, one of the daughters of the intolerable, and intolerant, Rosalind Countess of Carlisle – all of them hopelessly gone to the good. One of their good works was to ask me up to lunch, at which Lady Mary, an aggressive vegetarian, asked me whether I would have some delicious nut-roast, or some of the deplorable bird (I think, a partridge). I preferred the deplorable bird. Dear Gilbert Murray, what a lot he had to put up with in life! – and how nobly he put up with it, never a word of complaint, no souring of that essential sweetness of nature, no dimming of the light of reason and rationality in him. What was wonderful about him was the saintliness of his nature, the transparent living of his life by a moral code of reason more elevated than any reliance on religious sanctions or beliefs. For of the latter he had none. Brought up as a Catholic in the Australia of his childhood, he matured to the life of reason – but few can have lived it as he did. Devoting all his life, with his exceptional intellectual gifts and perceptions, to public service and good causes, he was the nearest to being a Saint of Rationalism one will ever see. On that subject, it was an essay of his that confirmed my disbelief in the religious nonsense – for, intellectually, it was nonsense, however charming and poetic and nostalgic – in which I had been brought up.

G. D. H. Cole, a militant Rationalist, was very far from being a saint of Rationalism – and also much less rational, by the way. It was with him and Margaret that I had met the Murrays, at the Coles' house in Holywell where they lived briefly on Douglas's return to the university of which he had been a brilliant, if controversial, ornament. Lunch with the Coles was to me far more daunting than lunch with the Murrays, or the Bridgeses or even Lady Ottoline. Why? It was partly that I looked on Cole with some adulation as my leader; but it was much more because of the brittle, friable atmosphere of the Coles together, sharp and needling, no warmth or free flow of feeling. I suppose that that was inhibited, would have been thought sentimental in their advanced intellectual circles, but it would have made for greater social ease, besides being more polite. Anyway I sat there utterly paralysed, acutely self-conscious, acutely uncomfortable under the barrage of such sophistication which nothing seemed able to please. For years I never felt at ease with Douglas – the fact was, he wasn't at ease in himself; until, in later years, he came to reside in All Souls as a Fellow during the week, away from the company of the uncompromising Postgates, all of them extremists of one sort or another. And then one saw what a dear Douglas Cole was, under the bitter, defiant, supercilious exterior: a nature rather starved of affection – much more moderate and reasonable, too, away from all those fellow-travellers egging him on, and even capable, at times, of sensible compromise.

Early this year, too, I met Attlee and R. H. Tawney. Tawney's personality made an immediate impact, even if it were a trifle too noble to be true. There was a regular cult of Tawney's nobility and high-mindedness among these people, particularly in the Workers' Educational Association, for which he and Cole did so much. Ethical high-mindedness, that middle-class virtue, never much appealed to me, a genuine son of the working class, and I don't think that that atmosphere of veneration in which he lived was altogether good for Tawney. As for Attlee, he was the least impressive – and the least out to impress – among public figures at a first meeting. An ardent young Labour intellectual would have thought much more readily of Cole or Tawney as a leader; but there the young intellectual was wrong.

The figures that were to form such a part in my life, the animals in my particular menagerie, were coming together. All unknown the future was shaping itself for me.

At the end of term I went to give a W.E.A. lecture at Stoke-on-Trent. It was the first time I had ever seen or set foot in an industrial area.

*　　*　　*

Apart from meeting all these people, what about my own inner life, which mattered so much more to me?

News from home was that Grandmother Vanson had died, and patient, silver-voiced old Grandfather would not outlive her more than a few days. Strangely enough, a moment before writing this I happened to look up the family Bible to verify the phrase apropos of the denigrators of Bridges – 'the latchet of whose shoes I am not worthy to stoop down and unloose' (Mark 1. 7) – when by a kind of *sortes* I came upon their birth-dates: Edward Vanson, born 13 November 1842, Elizabeth Vanson (born Goynes), 21 February 1844. I find these simple inscriptions more affecting than all the profound thoughts in the world, for they enclose a life and its course; just as I am not in the least interested by what people think, or suppose themselves to think, compared with what they do and what happens to them. There speaks the true historian, who reveres the fact rather than any theory.

Readers of *A Cornish Childhood* may remember the character of my formidable grandmother (after whom I take), with her sharp tongue, her instinctive generosity, her domineering ways, bossing her numerous children and grandchildren much like Queen Victoria, with whom so much of her life was contemporaneous. And they may remember – as Gerald Berners always did – my description of the beautiful background to their lives, the park at Tregrehan, the sunken Italian garden of the house with the colonnade looking on to it, the house always shut up and deserted, from the upper windows the view down over the dark-green woods of Crinnis to the cliffs and the sea.

How appropriate it was that my grandparents' lives should come to an end within a few days of each other: they had married young, had never been away from each other for a day, their lives had grown intertwined with each other like something growing in their woods, the holly and the ivy. Dominated by her all his days, mutely adoring her far more vital and charged personality, he did not wish to go on a day without her. All was rounded and complete, nothing to repine at. They were buried together in the little churchyard of Biscovey, at the top of familiar Lodge Hill at the foot of which they had lived so much of their lives. There I used to visit them all through the years of my boyhood – was indeed rather a favourite with the grandmother of whose sharp tongue and imperious ways her other grandchildren stood in awe. Now, in the Diary, I remembered 'those golden evenings at Tregrehan, with the pheasants strutting under the trees in the park, the light falling along the boughs and under the leaves; and Granny coming out in the cool to sit for a while in the corner-seat, while Grandfather dug up potatoes or pottered about among the rose-bushes.'

Edgeworth's death, which occurred about the same time, affected me more.

> The college without him is empty and almost unimaginable. How I have missed him during the few days he has been ill. We were very much together, as we were by far the most regular residents ... I respected and venerated him. There were ways in which it was possible to get near the emotional element in him; I found quite early on that we had a bond of sympathy in Ireland. For, though he was reticent, he had a real feeling for Ireland, and seemed grateful, as he was certainly responsive, to my appreciation of the Irish poets.

A few days later I was recalling his image

> just as he was on that afternoon walk in the Parks when the snow on the ground was thawing. I remember how he turned to me with that remote, unknowing look in his eyes, as if he were thinking of something else and conversation with me was a game that could be carried on by rote, it had been played so many times before with others.

I suppose his hold on life was slackening, but his attention had always been oblique, courteous but curiously discontinuous. The ambivalence in him may have come from his disparate parentage, ascendancy Irish on one side (was there not a place named Edgeworthstown?), Spanish on the other. Some wit said of him that Francis was difficult enough to pin down, but Ysidro was the very devil. Old Arthur Johnson, the College Chaplain, far too downright himself, complained: 'I could not put up with the indefiniteness and the indecisiveness of him: never a straight answer to a plain question.' It was precisely there, I considered, that 'Edgeworth was as young as our own generation ... I always felt that I knew where he stood with regard to an opinion, after he had stated both sides and come to no obvious conclusion.' I went on missing him in the evenings in Common Room, for 'his was a mind that I had more in common with than any of the others that I meet there.' This surprises me a little today, hardened and toughened as I have been by time and circumstance; it may surprise the reader. We are not wholly right in this, however.

Keynes told D. H. Macgregor – Edgeworth's successor as Professor of Political Economy and a very Cambridge type – that for ten years he had received almost a daily letter from Edgeworth, and 'scarcely one without some gem of expression, some original phrase'. Among his papers was a whole budget of Marshall's letters extending over years; Edgeworth had put them in order and labelled the parcel 'Marshall on himself'. And then left instructions that his papers were to be burned. I rather think that Macgregor, who was not a man of much sensibility, did burn them. What a loss! it was one of those occasions where such injunctions should be piously disregarded.

Arthur Johnson, the Chaplain, for all his silvery appearance and the beautiful voice with which he read the services in chapel, was a testy old man and a bully – no wonder he couldn't appreciate Edgeworth. Johnson was an example of the fox-hunting parson, and he wrote an interesting book on *The Disappearance of the Small Landowner*, the class to which he belonged. In his earlier years he had had a raw deal, I fancy, having lost his Fellowship at another college on marriage, and had had to make a living the hard way by much teaching and coaching. This could not have improved his temper. He was the ringleader in the group of full-time tutors who made the great scholar, Firth's, time as Regius Professor rather unendurable after his aggressive declaration in favour of research in his Inaugural Lecture. They discouraged undergraduates from attending Firth's lectures – not that they were easy going for undergraduates anyway; they virtually ostracised him, the most eminent historian at Oxford in his day.

Johnson would take me for walks round Addison's Walk at Magdalen or in the University Parks to see his Siberian ducks, of which he was excessively fond. (I didn't want to see his ducks.) As we paraded round he would put me through third-degree with questions about my attitude on the test-question of the war. I have already admitted that I had been put all wrong about this by the Left Intellectuals – Russell, Goldsworthy Dickinson, Brailsford, E. D. Morel – and thought that this country was as much to blame for the war as Germany. I was quite wrong, of course, and after going to live in Germany for a time came to see better how things were with the people who have wrecked the twentieth century with their maniac bids for *Weltmacht*.

'Would you have fought for your country in the war?' the old man would say, demanding a plain answer to a straight question, as with Edgeworth. He was no more successful with me than with Edgeworth. I would begin posing certain conditions, if this ... then that, if that ... then this. '*Would* you, or would you *not*, take your country's side in the war?' the nasty old man would bark. And then, 'I want a plain answer to a straight question.' I must say he never got one: strung-up as I was, nerves on edge, all mixed-up about these issues, I was determined to think things out for myself. In future I rejected his invitations to go and inspect his Siberian ducks.

Johnson was not only a duck-shooting, fox-hunting parson, but a fighting one – very much a soldier of the Church Militant. I once saw him administer a ticking-off to Leo Amery, when he was a Cabinet Minister. Amery had said that the constitution of the British Empire was as indefinable as the Trinity. It seemed a harmless remark to me, but Johnson blew up: 'I would have you to know that the Trinity is a holy mystery. And your remark is a very improper one for a man in your position to make.' He stomped out in high dudgeon. Amery and I exchanged a smile. Perhaps it can be a little better understood why in life I have so straddled the fences, been really a cross-bench mind: Russell, Goldsworthy Dickinson, Brailsford and Company did not believe nonsense about the Trinity, though they did about the Germans and the war. The old Conservatives did not believe nonsense about the war, whereas they were apt to about the Trinity and religion in general. Why believe nonsense about either?

To be just, this rasping old man was not without a certain charm, when he chose. When I was very ill in the Acland, shortly after this, he came to see me. I was reading Renan's *Vie de Jésus*. 'I suppose you never saw Renan?' he said. I was enchanted: you might as well have asked me, 'Did you once see Shelley plain?' I was all excited to know if *he* had seen Renan, one of my heroes. Oh, yes, he had seen Renan when he came to Oxford to lecture, it must have been in the 'nineties – and then failed to give me any account of him, what he looked like, his voice or anything. I ceased to be interested: so like an ordinary human being – they hardly ever can describe to one a really remarkable person, appearance, habits, quirks and so on. However, I gather that Johnson took his duty as Chaplain seriously and was very sympathetic with Morrah on his way into the arms of the Roman Church. I shouldn't have needed any such attentions.

Sir Charles Firth, *per contra*, was rather a great man. He was a wonderfully exact, thorough and complete scholar: no one has ever known so much as he did about his chosen seventeenth century, not even Macaulay. In addition, unlike many pure research-scholars, he had a penetrating, an incisive mind, with a sharp edge: no illusions. He was a formidable man, had the appearance of a *grand seigneur* or someone out of his own seventeenth century with his crisp, white goatee-beard, the wintry sparkle in his grey-blue eyes. He had a very impersonal view as to the writing of history – as if it is possible to escape one's own personality, even in negating it, to jump out of one's skin – and this had an inhibiting effect upon his followers. On the other hand, he did encourage a great deal of worthwhile historical research in his time, as against the mere quantity of it in ours, much of it valueless.

Underneath Firth's formidability there was kindness of heart and an individual sense of amusement; he had inherited the public spirit and the generosity, along with his wealth, from the famous family of Sheffield steel-makers from which he came. He had a splendid library full of seventeenth-century rarities, which he bequeathed to Sheffield University. He was open-handed with his treasures and readily made them available to scholars. When G. M. Trevelyan was writing his *England in the Age of Queen Anne* he came over from Cambridge to profit from Firth's library. As they went round the shelves replete with rare Civil War tracts and what not, Firth observed to Trevelyan: 'You like writing about these old fellows?' George Macaulay Trevelyan replied, with enthusiasm: 'Why, yes: don't you?' Firth said: 'No: I only like reading 'em.' This was a characteristic piece of modesty, for, in addition to his immense reading, he actually wrote and edited a great deal – far more than any of his successors, except for Powicke, the only one of them to equal him in stature.

It was Firth, one evening when we sat together dining in Hall, who suggested that I make the Reformation in Cornwall my subject of research, which flowered many years later into *Tudor Cornwall*. At this time I had a perfect fixation on Newman, and in time read nearly everything of him, except the Sermons. I was much influenced by the sceptical implications of the evolutionary views of *The Development of Christian Doctrine* and by the still more sceptical conclusions to be drawn from the *Essay in Aid of a Grammar of Assent*. (No wonder Manning scented that Newman's intellectual influence was dangerous.) Let me make this clear. What drew me in Newman was his scepticism: in his late masterpiece, *The Grammar of Assent*, he used his subtle and refining logic to suggest how uncertain are the grounds of knowledge; and if we are so uncertain as to what we know, then why not angels? Why not the liquefaction of the blood of Saint Januarius? Why not the bodily assumption of the Virgin, or the Trinity? Why not any non-sense you choose to believe? Of course, the conclusion I drew was still further to reduce my respect for any metaphysics, any transcendental nonsense, and to confine myself to *common* sense, what was commonly and objectively verifiable in the realm of knowledge.

A second element in Newman's thought was no less congenial. In the *Grammar of Assent* he is not so much interested in *what* people

think as in what makes them think what they think, i.e. the psychological or other predispositions that incline them to take up the
positions they do or form their thoughts for them. (They are mostly
but reacting, not capable of real thinking, certainly not on any
abstract or general subject.) This was also in line with Bradley's
The Pre-suppositions of Critical History, which I was reading at the
time, and with what I was working out for myself. This sceptical
position as to the bulk of what people think has served me well
through life. It has meant an immense saving of time and energy –
when one considers the piles of nonsense urged and written about
theology (about the non-existent), religion, politics, morals, sex.
This saving of time is one reason, once I had turned the corner of
long illness, why I have managed to get so much work done.

This attitude, though less intellectualised and more empirical, was
shared by my closest friend in college, Richard Pares – and no doubt
it contributed to the economy with which he accomplished so much
in his too brief life. A long and intimate acquaintance with the talk,
and the ways, of eighteenth-century politics and politicians brought
the words 'nonsense' and 'cant' to his lips more frequently than any
others. A now younger, and still more sceptical, generation at All
Souls reminds me that there is such a thing as 'socially functional
rubbish' or 'socially utilitarian nonsense'. They are all too right: this
was the attitude of Renaissance Popes to religion. One appreciates
the fact in history, one understands that it is so; but why it is that
humans should be such fools as to believe what they do beats me.
And at the blithe acceptance of the situation by the cleverest among
my juniors I cannot help emitting a small squeal of shock. I suppose
it's almost as absurd as complaining of the weather. However, I do
complain of the weather, continually.[1]

[1] At the moment of writing this – August, in the year of grace 1963 – the newspapers record a characteristic event in an Italian village, where the villagers attempt
to lynch their parish priest, in spite of his working the miracle for them, on account
of his causing the face of their Snow Madonna to turn black. It appears that a
couple of local Italian emigrants to America piously wanted a plaster cast of the
Madonna to take back to the United States with them. They had contributed
generously to the *fiesta*, but the village said that as a result of the operation the
Madonna's face had turned black. So they proposed to make a sacrificial victim of
their priest who had permitted the thing to happen. Police reinforcements had to
be drafted in to protect him from their wrath; they rioted, burnt his car and

Somewhere in one of my numerous note-books I have jotted down some of Firth's sharp-edged dicta. But one of those evenings in Hall I remember: I was going on about the exquisite drawing of the young Newman by Richmond in the Common Room at Oriel. Firth was unenthusiastic – indeed no one was enthusiastic about the Oxford Movement at All Souls, though Geoffrey Faber wrote such a perceptive book about it. Warden Pember and Oman, who saw so little eye to eye about most things, were at one in their abhorrence of Puseyism; indeed Warden Pember handed down to me the tradition that Pusey had once betrayed a confidence he had learned in confession. The atmosphere of All Souls was of a Low Church secularism inclining to rationalism, in chapel Regency use with the northward position; whereas I, without believing anything, was passionately interested in the Oxford Movement and Newman, would have liked full ceremonial in that splendid unspoiled chapel. Firth was unmoved by my enthusiasm for Newman's profile and teased me by saying that he thought it a silly face. I thought this rather Philistine and insisted it was a beautiful face; to which Firth replied, 'Well, a silly kind of beauty, if you like.' I suddenly saw what Firth meant: there *was* something silly about Newman, the cult of his own chastity, for example.

A. F. Pollard was a Fellow when I came into college: his book *The Evolution of Parliament* was, I think, a piece of college research. I much looked forward to learning from this eminent Tudor historian, but must confess to a sense of disappointment: I learned much less from him than from Firth, Grant Robertson and Oman, or from Cruttwell and G. N. Clark in the next generation. Pollard was not wholly at ease in the society of All Souls; an able man, he had no charm, and I don't think that the grandees with their lofty good manners much cared for him with his. He would talk to me about the Tudors, but anyone who has studied his books will know that he had no subtlety of perception with regard to character, no sense of

---

damaged shops and property. 'The priest was stated to have been last seen in the early hours of the morning, taking the zigzag road down the mountain in a police car, with villagers running behind still shouting abuse.' (*The Times*, 8 August 1963.) Anthropology = the study of human idiocy: no limit to it.

landscape or beauty such as Trevelyan and Powicke had. He was above all a constitutional historian, with that passionate interest in Parliament which all Liberals of his generation had. Whatever I have been, I have never been a Liberal and, though I stood as a candidate, I have never been interested in the institution of Parliament as such, either historically or contemporaneously. I have never been moved, or even much interested, by the oceans of chatter in that talking-shop.

The reader may observe here as elsewhere, if he chooses, that in spite of my not fitting into any received category I may be more representative of the public – in my disillusionment with political parties and their bogus attitudes, the claptrap they talk, and in a certain withdrawal from public affairs – than those who are engaged and then complain of the public's indifference towards their doings.

This is not the place to speak of the college political grandees – the Viceroys, Foreign Secretaries, Cabinet Ministers, Law Officers, Editors of *The Times*; *ingénu* as I was, I was not yet aware of their ways: that did not come until the 'thirties.[1] But this term a professional politician (very much so), and an outsider (for he was a Labour man) was brought down by Coupland, who, as Professor of Colonial History, made it his business to keep in touch with the Empire-minded of all sorts. The visitor was J. H. Thomas, a man not very much to my taste; all the same I should have liked to get at him. Coupland kept him very much to himself,

while J.H. played bridge with great ardour and efficiency and drank an incredible amount of whisky. On Sunday night he spoke at the Raleigh Club, and I made a great effort to hear him. I broke away from dinner, and, in my haste to approach the Warden, had the misfortune to walk to the door in front of the Sub-Warden. Consternation ensued: one would have thought that an elephant had trodden on the Sub-Warden's toes. I was thunderously impatient at it all, but went to J.H.T.'s meeting and without permission. Thomas was not at his best, but he struck the right note for a club of imperialists, and they got on very well together. I asked one or two respectful questions, but

[1] Of some part of their activities I have written in *All Souls and Appeasement*.

refrained from probing into Thomas's socialist convictions. His lack of education and the disciplined mind has made him the worst sort of opportunist: any conception of a general objective has escaped him.

I was impressed by his knowledge of the facts of the job, but thought that he lacked 'real intellect and character', and looked like H. G. Wells, 'the incarnation of the common'. That week-end I had been at Garsington again, reading the poems of Patrick Pearse in the panelled parlour – 'what a revelation of an inherently nobler mind!' Celt for Celt, it was still poetry that had it over politics.

I had walked out to Garsington – 'along that road that was my first walk with Wadleigh, on my first Sunday in Oxford' – and found the house by day as beautiful as it had been by night.

Beyond Cowley the road hasn't changed a whit; but Cowley itself seems to have sprung up like a mushroom in the night. I don't remember that Morris's immense motor-works were there three years ago. Now they are being made still more vast: a large field was being ploughed up by steam-engines and long foundations of stone and brick being laid. On the other side of the road a motor-tractor was harrowing. What extraordinary activity: men going in and out of the works, hundreds of cars assembled, cars being tested on the roads, the men looking like so many children with their toys. One wonders how long the mushroom growth will last; while what goes on on the other side of the road has been from the beginning. The fields full of birds, never have I noticed such a chatter of chaffinches and rooks; in the marshy places big birds flying in couples and chaffing each other with their wings and strange whistling cries – they must have been lapwings.

And so to Garsington and that lovely house with its pictures and works of art, its memories of Lawrence and Huxley and Katherine Mansfield – much more to my taste than vulgar Labour politicians.

*   *   *

All the same, I was obsessed at this time by the idea of a Labour

University. I had been struck by Vinogradoff's reproach: 'if they [socialists] want a serious trial for their views they ought, like every other great movement of opinion, to strive for a commanding position in the domain of thought, and to justify the preponderance of the working class by its educational achievements.'[1] I was prepared to do my bit, if ever there had been any encouragement. And here, neatly exposed, were the two sides to my nature: on one side, what I conceived to be my duty, on the other, pleasure; my intellectual interests as against poetry, the sense of beauty, the arts. But which was my real nature?

To this end I was dutifully reading Newman on university education, Mansbridge on the older universities, Tawney on Secondary Education for All, reports of the Royal Commissions on universities, Maurice Dobb – whose acquaintance I was shortly to make – on Labour Research, J. F. Horrabin of *Plebs* on working-class education, looking into the history of the Workers' Educational Association, the National Council of Labour Colleges, Ruskin College. I find a rebarbative list of 'Books to buy in Paris' – Kautsky, Bernstein and Bogdanov, Marx's *Das Elend der Philosophie* and Jaurès, *Histoire Socialiste de la Révolution française*. But there beside this spiritually unnourishing stuff were Rimbaud and Verlaine, Rilke and Otto Braun's war-time Diaries, Burdach on Humanism in Renaissance and Reformation, Duchesne's History of the Church, and Wolfgang Gröger's translation of Alexander Blok's *The Twelve*.

My new life at All Souls meant no breach with my old friends, particularly those at Christ Church, to which I was passionately loyal and of which I was proud to have been a Scholar. Tom Lawrenson and I continued our walks, if less frequently; he and Burn came along to meals at All Souls, and even Wadleigh came more than I had remembered. I continued to see a good deal of my Exeter friends, Mark Thomson and more of Bruce McFarlane, who now had some senior studentship and was initiating those laborious researches into the finances of Cardinal Beaufort, which never worked out but left him our leading authority on the fifteenth century. (If only he had written more about what he knows better than anyone!) Young Otis I was carefully coaching along, for he was a

[1] Sir Paul Vinogradoff, *Historical Jurisprudence*, I. 83.

promising historian, and I hoped he would win a Fellowship at All Souls. 'What is the matter with Otis? ... He behaves in an extraordinary carping manner whenever a third person is present. When I get him alone he hardly dares even to differ in matters of opinion; when there are others about he jumps at the chance to criticise. What is the explanation?' Nevertheless, I did my best to get him elected next year at All Souls. When my early book *Politics and the Younger Generation* came out, he wrote a malicious review of it in the paper on which he was then a journalist. I thereupon dropped his acquaintance.

Here was a characteristic mixture of new and old acquaintance, among which both produced constant and lasting friendships.

Sunday, 7 March 1926. Breakfast with a crowd here, then spent all the morning drafting rules with a Labour Club committee. Lunch with Pares and his mother and Roger Mynors of Balliol. In the afternoon a walk through Magdalen and round the Parks with Archbishop Lang, most interesting talk and exhausting because of its interest [I was much impressed by Lang's early support for the W.E.A., and his experiences in social work as vicar of Leeds]. Bus to North Oxford, to tea with the Wrights and another crowd of people. Hurried back to my rooms and on to the hotel to find Booth and Jessop: unsuccessful, and so I ran to New College Chapel where they were, in time to hear the anthem. An enormous dinner with two meat-courses at the East Gate, and a frantic rush to the Cathedral to hear Charles Wood's Passion Music. I sat it out as long as I could, and then rushed out to avoid the ignominy of being sick in a cathedral. So I'm done for, for a day or two: in this state I don't look forward a bit to going abroad. I only feel like going home again; two months is long enough to be away from home. I want to go back and refresh myself at Carn Grey and Trenarren, and all the places that seeing Booth makes me think of.

Very much devoted to my old college, I went to the Censors' Dinner at the end of term, listened proudly to the record of the House and the doings of House-men in the past year. I dined at High Table in that grand Hall, of which Feiling has written, looking down from the dais upon the Scholars' table, so familiar from my own crowded and happy undergraduate years. I was now in a position to return some of the kind hospitality I had received: Rawlinson and Chavasse came to lunch at All Souls, Canon Cooke to lunch and walk. '11 March. Dear Canon Cooke has sent me a photograph of the exquisite Parmigianino drawing of Christ in the Library at Christ Church. I have set it up on top of the bookcase and against the panelling: it serves as a spell against the ghosts and the loneliness of this place.'

Where is this now? Alas, lost long since, along with other loyalties.

At last, after a term's teaching, I had the cash to go abroad for the first time in my life. But I was determined not to go until I had finished my little book *On History*, and that was harder going than I imagined.

Sunday, 21 March. I was displeased with yesterday's work. So many fine ideas besieged my poor head that it was hard to concentrate on the prosaic drudgery of the argument which is my book. At the same time a sense of duty to it prevented me from working up the romanticism which was going on all the time under the surface. Today, more satisfactory: as the result of a whole day I have produced about three pages. What hard going it is! I never thought I should find it so hard to write, after all the experience of this Diary. But the writing is in a different class, and I'm not sure that this isn't much the more congenial. A highly abstract argument freezes one, and yet I've plenty of ideas to go on with; and there's a rarified, exalted kind of excitement in working these ideas into logical form. Not a very human art, it must be the peculiar enjoyment of B. Russell, I fancy.

The book finished, I dedicated it nostalgically to the Essay Club at Christ Church 'for many evenings of pleasant discussion', threw my bonnet over the windmill and went off to Paris.

IX

Paris, the Christ Church Failure, Illness

IT is obvious how straitened and narrowly restricted my life had been, that not till I was coming to Oxford as an undergraduate did I set foot outside of Cornwall, and now not until I was a Fellow of All Souls – as against my student dreams of walking tours in Brittany – was I able to go on my first visit to the Continent. On the other side of the account, there was the advantage of being strongly, intensely rooted. I feel the value of that more and more today, in the rootless, shallow cosmopolitanism of our TV civilisation, the background of so much of contemporary literature the shiftless, seedy life of squalid industrial areas or suburbia. (Not so Hardy, or Yeats, or Kipling, or Conrad, or D. H. Lawrence. There is little enough in strictly contemporary literature – as against that of the 1920s and 1930s – that I really like or can admire.)

Now that I have come through, have survived, I would not have it otherwise – though I would willingly have had it otherwise at the time.

And thereby comes a curious sensation, the subconscious feeling that one's life has been guided, particularly in regard to the many, the regular, the invariable defeats that I have suffered at the hands of my fellow-men. So many roads have been blocked to me. Whenever I have put myself forward to make an active contribution to society, as I thought I ought to do – whether in my native county, in regard to my old school, my old college, my present college, in the university, in the public life of Cornwall, in politics, offering myself as a college tutor (I never wanted to be a teaching hack), or a professor (I never wished to be a professor), or as a political candidate (to have been elected would have been fatal) – nevertheless the fact is that whenever I attempted to do something other than I was meant to do, even as a matter of duty or in the public interest,

I have invariably been repulsed, rejected. It is a curious story, not without its psychological interest both for me and for others, not without its psychological consequences on my mind and character. It has made me, an affectionate nature underneath – readers may judge what they like for themselves – in the end, not in love with my fellow-men.

I suppose I ought to be grateful really for the road-blocks. One of the naturally gifted among my historian-colleagues at All Souls has said that there never has been a door opened before him but he has wanted to go through it. Many doors have been opened to him and he has passed through them; the result has been a somewhat disparate, discontinuous career, and he has not achieved the heights that he might have done as an historian, if he had been forced to concentrate on his one true talent. No doors were ever opened to me by my fellow-men, not one. If I have achieved anything it has been by myself alone; I can now, in my sixtieth year, claim that if I am depending on myself I can accomplish what I wish, produce the goods; if I have to depend on others, it is always withheld. I know why, and it does not put me in love with my fellow-men.

For myself, or rather for my work, it has been a godsend. Every other road has been blocked off, always, all the way along. It is as if I have been *made* to concentrate on that 'one talent which is death to hide', to fulfil my own true nature in my work, instead of turning down one of those inviting side-turnings so much easier to follow.

Myself, I never wanted a niche, nor really ever wanted a job, or even thought in such terms. I merely wanted to be myself, accomplish what I had it in me to accomplish to the best of my ability, fulfil the best in my nature in my work. I was always willing, my readers can see, to work hard: one already perceives how little geared I was to contemporary society and the way things were to go in my time. I'd have done much better to have been a Victorian, or an Elizabethan – theirs were values that I respect.

A curious woman once said to me that every man of genius struggles against his genius, tries to run away from it. Every time I have tried to run away, or even to deviate, I have been haled back and kept on the course. It is a definite feeling, even if a subconscious one, that I am aware of – as if guided, almost directed, drawn along the course. And I know well the explanation the religious would give of it. No reason to suppose anything of the sort – a quite super-fluous explanation. It is, quite simply, of the nature of genius to be obsessive: one is driven by a force stronger than oneself, or that is, rather, one's essential self. I could be driven, quite easily, beyond my physical or perhaps nervous strength, so great is the force, the drive within me. I don't have to do anything about it, merely see that it doesn't exhaust me, kill me – as it easily might.

The last sentence in André Billy's *Vie de Balzac*, that came out in Paris at the end of the war, much struck me. Balzac was fifty-two when he died: 'usé, épuisé par son œuvre, assassiné par son démon'. Or what about Shakespeare, dead at the same age? Nothing to re-pine at in the use of the word 'genius': it only means spirit after all, but a spirit that possesses one, drives one on. So far from having the transcendental significance the religious would give it, it is closely allied to egoism, the source of one's strength. Why make any bones about it? Everybody has his (or her) egoism, though usually with much less to be egoistic about. I am rather taken with Bertrand Russell's candour about this in his autobiography. 'It was a part of Victorian humbug to endeavour to conceal vanity. When I was young, we all made a show of thinking no better of ourselves than of our neighbours. Shaw found this effort wearisome, and had already given it up when he first burst upon the world.'

No doubt there will be critics silly enough to complain of the egoism of this book. But what is the point of an autobiography if it is not about the 'I' who is writing it? The only question is whether the 'I' is interesting.

At a deeper level than this is the marvellously searching diagnosis of Proust of the 'I' who writes books: not the exterior self, but the 'moi profond qu'on ne retrouve qu'en faisant abstraction des autres et du moi qui connaît les autres, le moi qui a attendu pendant qu'on était avec les autres, qu'on sent bien le seul réel, et pour lequel seuls les artistes finissent par vivre.'

True for me, I have chosen this as the epigraph for this book.

*   *   *

On April Fool's Day 1926, then, off I went on my first visit to Paris, to encounter no such initiatory experience as that which enlivens my fellow-collegian, Emlyn Williams's, autobiography. But then I hadn't his advantages. Though I read French almost as easily as English, I had had no experience of speaking it; nor, though I had a large acquaintance and plenty of friends, was I naturally gregarious.

Moreover, I went to Paris in a backward-looking spirit: it was the past that called, even my own past. For my schoolmaster friend from St Austell, Bacon, was there and he made the arrangements for me to stay at a very modest pension in the Rue Honoré Chevalier off the Place Saint-Sulpice. (I rather think he was teaching at a school at Jouy-en-Josas, where a fellow-master was Marcel Arland, then just coming into notice with his earliest novels, which I dutifully read.)

In the last weeks of term at Oxford I had been taken up by a distinguished figure of the undergraduate generation before me, on his way to becoming an eminent Catholic writer, a conscious follower of Belloc and Chesterton. He was very kind to me, evidently interested, and proposed coming to Paris himself that vacation. He was at the time much interested in Charles Maurras – the most unscrupulous and evil spirit among French writers of the time – and his dreadful *Action française*. I remember my new acquaintance arriving with Maurras' bulky *Enquête sur la Monarchie* (he was bulky himself) under his arm. To my consternation he proposed to stay in the little pension with me. This wasn't my idea at all – I was bent on seeing what I could of my old friend of St Austell days; but I didn't know how to deal with the situation. My new, and grander, acquaintance deposited his luggage in the pension, and we went out for my first walk into those endearing complicated little streets around the Place Saint-Sulpice. Suddenly I couldn't bear the idea of spending my precious time in Paris with a companion, and, while he was absorbed in a book-shop window, I slipped round the corner, ran for dear life around several other corners, and lost him. When I arrived back at the pension hours later, he had taken his bags away and I was happy again.

This was one of those outbursts of bad behaviour in my life that make me blush to recall. I am sorry now, though I wasn't sorry at the time. The acquaintance, not unnaturally, never ripened. In the intervening years we have seen something of each other, and maintained good, if sketchy, relations; but never have we spoken of my youthful *gaffe*.

However, that disposed of, I was free to enjoy myself in my own way. Paris in the spring of 1926, with governments rising and falling, and the franc for ever depreciating against the then so proud pound, so that life was cheap: one could get a good meal in many of those little restaurants on the Left Bank for half a crown, and buy books galore in their paper covers. That part of Paris, to which I became so attached that I have never been able to stay in any other quarter, was quite unchanged from the nineteenth century, indeed from the eighteenth: it was still the Paris of the French Revolution, the old streets shabby and unkempt, the houses peeling. It was unspoiled – before the Rockefeller Foundation in the goodness of its heart donated the ugly great building of the Faculté de Médecine, totally out of proportion to its surroundings, and the Sorbonne has followed suit. Everything everywhere is put out of countenance by the insane pressures of the twentieth century. One doesn't mind it erecting its monstrosities in new areas – Slough, Dagenham, the outskirts of London or Paris, New Jersey (where one doesn't have to see them) – but it is disheartening to see it ruin the best of the old with, as so often, the worst of the new. Look at the indignity of the third-rate buildings erected in the City of London in immediate proximity to Wren's St Paul's!

To me every acre of this old part of Paris was rich with its memories, historical and literary. Saint-Sulpice meant for me Renan: every time I heard those curious chimes, reverberating hollowly as if from a tomb, I reflected that those were the same bells he heard when a student in the seminary under the great Dupanloup. Our little street looked out to the garden of the seminary, at that time turned into a barracks. I did not know that Gibbon had regarded the heavy façade of the church, with its great columns, with enthusiasm as the perfection of the classical. I could not quite acclimatise myself to the unequal towers, and was amused by the current student-rhyme with its touch of surrealism:

Je hais les tours de Saint-Sulpice:
Quand par hasard je les rencontre,
Je pisse
Contre.

Lonely as ever, I liked best snooping among the bookshops under the arcades of the Odéon and taking my catch away to read by the Medici fountain in the Luxembourg gardens. And yet one could hardly be lonely here where everywhere was populated by so many familiar shades. Just below the Luxembourg was the house where Condorcet lay concealed during the Reign of Terror, to escape one day, be caught and brought back to the guillotine. (He had a progressive, an optimistic, view of mankind.) Here was Danton on his pedestal, orating to the mob as ever. In this little church near the Panthéon the Archbishop of Paris had been stabbed to death by a mad priest – there was the spot marked on the pavement, *En repos*. Down on the Quai Voltaire was the house unchanged to which Voltaire returned in triumph, after so many years, to Paris to die. All along the Seine were the galleries of the Louvre, extending from the vanished Tuileries – how one regretted that France never rebuilt the palace after the Commune, leaving the rhetorical pavilions, the pavillons de Flore and de Marsan, in the air embracing an empty space – to the old Louvre a quarter of a mile away. One saw the Empress Eugénie, always fearful that Marie Antoinette's fate would be hers, escaping from the Tuileries down the long length of the galleries to a postern in the old Louvre and the *fiacre* of her American dentist waiting to take her away. Or the thronging memories of the Louvre, the *tocsin* from the tower of St Germain l'Auxerrois giving the signal for the Massacre of St Bartholomew; or the fatally stabbed Henri IV being brought back to the Chambre des Sept Cheminées – one used to be able to see it in those days – to die. The historic memories of Paris were pretty bloody – what a contrast to sedate old London! Here was part of the fascination: one sensed the electric vibrancy under the surface, the brittle quality in French society, that there was something febrile about the Third Republic. But that was as it always had been.

There was this same electric current in French literature; this was what gave it its vivacity, its verve and sparkle. At this moment the literary scene was dominated by the personality of Gide – with the *Nouvelle Revue Française* behind him – and his questionable *mœurs*. There are some innocent, serious-minded remarks in the Diary, written in the purple ink I had bought in the Place Saint-Sulpice, on this. 'In company I always decry the stuff written about the modern malaise and inquietude; but I know in myself, no one better, what are the roots of this disquiet. But the gospel that I preach to others must serve for myself; it isn't enough to sit and enjoy the disquiet. Some solution must be found.' I sagely recorded that I didn't think that any solution along Gide's lines was possible, though it accorded with one side of my inclinations. 'But there are other inclinations also; it will involve a strenuous struggle to develop them. And *how* to develop them – when a stronger feeling than all others, that of my work in the future, runs counter to that development?'

I see now that the boy of twenty-two had hit on a profound choice in life: *either* one's work, *or* developing an all-round nature. If it came to that, as it did, I would never, at any time, have a moment's hesitation. Anyone, or almost anyone, can have a normal life, marry and have a family. Nothing exceptional in that; one may say of ordinary human beings what H. A. L. Fisher said of undergraduates: 'They recur.' To achieve anything different from the usual run, anything exceptional, requires exceptional measures. This was in keeping with the other side to my nature; whatever was propitious to one's work and achievement was to be approved of, what would be a distraction or an impediment to be discouraged. One had to put all the eggs in one basket – even at the expense of one's health: if this gave one extra-sensibility, a more acute nerve, sharper perceptions, perhaps it was worth the sacrifice. This was going too far, a morbid doctrine. But what was latent in my nature remained latent, and I am not in the least sorry; on the contrary I am very glad. When we went to bed at nights in the cramped quarters of the pension, looking out into the familiar proximities of an internal well, the two nice young maids of the establishment, taken with the young Englishman, would give him encouraging cries from their near window. The young man politely responded, but no advantage was taken.

Gide dominated the scene; *Les Faux Monnayeurs* had just come out; I bought and read it, as in time I read everything he wrote. At the same time he was no hero for me, and I never understood why he had quite such an importance for the French in those decades. It was obvious that his was not a strong creative faculty – by contrast with Proust – but a minor one; Gide's was essentially a critical intelligence, extremely sympathetic to ideas, sifting and trying everything, and there was always his style, translucently clear, limpid and pure. Proust remained as yet a closed book to me – the greatest experience in French literature in this century and, when all is said, my profoundest and most intimate admiration. Claudel – though I went to see *L'Annonce Faite à Marie* at the Odéon – I never responded to: in spite of his genius, he is all that Anglo-Saxons dislike in French literature, the endless rhetoric, the bombast and over-emphasis, the cult of *la gloire* and all that, the lack of sympathy, an intellectual bully, a sort of Belloc on a grander scale, a *Roi Soleil* of literature. He is like Bossuet, what we don't like in the French tradition, the declamatory and too self-confident; where what we like are the sympathetic and perceptive, the men of half-tones and subtler shades, Fénelon, Renan, above all Montaigne. François Poulenc once made to me a most revealing, if obvious contrast between Ravel, a Mediterranean type, with his cult of the boléro, his *Pavane pour une Infante défunte*, et cetera, and Debussy, the Nor-herner, with his *Les Nuages* and *La Mer*, the half-tones and imprecise contours.

Nor did Valéry, whom I came a little to know later, as yet loom on my horizon. I was engaged in catching up with Rimbaud, a fine edition of whose works I bought and read with avidity. These were years when André Maurois was in full spate (when has he not been?) and winning the English-speaking public with his books on Shelley and Byron and Disraeli. (He shortly after devoted a couple of kind pages to my little book *On History* in his *Aspects de la Biographie*, for which I was grateful and from then on we became friends.) These were years of the earlier, and best, novels of François Mauriac, *Thérèse Desqueyroux* and so on, all of which I read with

10

particular appreciation: as a provincial writer, with his rootedness in Bordeaux and the Garonne country, he specially spoke to me. But the writer whose attitude I most of all share, whose essential spirit is in large part mine, Henri de Montherlant, had not yet spoken for me: I was not moved by his early cult of athletics. In these post-war years Paul Morand had more popular *réclame* – one saw his books everywhere; there was the deplorable intellectual influence of Alain, very bad in its effects later on with the break-up of France, and the more respect-worthy rationalism of Julien Benda. I was naturally on the *qui vive* for the young men then beginning to make their name, Jean Prévost, Marcel Arland, Julian Green; but I never met any of them, for I knew no one.

A good result of the low rate at which the franc stood was that at last I was able to buy some music; I never had owned any and, in addition to learning to play the piano for myself, had had to make do for music with the leavings of my sister's low taste. Now at last I bought Paul Dukas's edition of the Beethoven Sonatas in two bulky volumes, Fauré's edition of Schumann's *Album à la Jeunesse*, Schubert's *Moments Musicaux* and *Impromptus*, some Chopin and Mozart – not, as yet, Bach. I don't think any of this would have been welcome in the old home at Tregonissey. Such music necessitated getting rid of the poor cottage-piano that had served our youth. In my rooms at Oxford I installed a Broadwood. In the summer vacation at home, going into the town I spied a fine Ibach and, somewhat breathlessly, plunged for it. It had a splendid ringing tone, built upon the foundation of a grand bass register, as with all Ibachs. Just the thing for Beethoven. So now I was in a position to tackle the Sonatas. In the confined space of a council-house it made plenty of noise.

As usual, it was not until I had returned from Paris that I savoured the experience to the full – in retrospect. I find that I had observed the menagerie at the pension pretty sharply. There was the good Bostonian lady, Miss Tufts, whom I used to tease by calling Mademoiselle Tüfts, a figure out of the lower tiers of Henry James, on her way to Rome. There were two women from the Middle West, a schoolteacher who used to engage me in conversation on highbrow subjects, neglecting her mother, a frail old lady with discouraged expression, whom her daughter never talked to on account of her deafness. There was Fritz, German-Swiss with a Jewish strain, an attractive young fellow with all the confidence of an advocate and

extraordinary temerity in his criticisms of the French. Madame Dessart, who kept the pension, I liked from the first, engaged in a struggle for existence to keep two inept sons going: one a coarse-looking ne'er-do-well, the other a languid and un-enterprising adolescent. Monsieur Girard, a notary of Angevin origin, was the purest French there: cold and egoistic, self-contained and indifferent to the point of impoliteness towards all foreigners. Next him there sat at table an impudent young student at the École des Chartes, who is working at a thesis on the Commune of Mantes: I hated his manners, those of an errand-boy, for ever showing off to amuse the other young men who egged him on in the salon. Monsieur and Madame Maertens, a pleasant couple: he a fat and agreeable Piedmontese who mounted the steep stairs with great difficulty in breathing, she speaking English incorrectly in a charming soft manner. I think I see them at table under the red shades of the *salle-à-manger*, or in the evenings in the salon where I sometimes used to play the piano to myself, rather than join the company. Charming, unique, only for that time, already irrecoverable.

What became of them all? I wonder.

I have often been urged to write a novel, or asked why I have not tried my hand at one. One or two novelists have urged that history plus poetry = the novel. But not so, and had I the faculty anyway? There is a fundamental psychological reason why I could never write a novel. I am not interested in the free flow of relations between people, indeed I am put off by them: the moment they get up to their tricks, the moment the tiresome old story begins, the man and the woman get interested in each other and the usual boring human pattern starts, my sympathy and interest vanish. My sympathy does not begin to operate until the pattern is complete and they are all dead: then I can feel sorry for them, appreciate perhaps the pathos of their lives. Not the equipment for a novelist, but perhaps the right outlook for an historian.

Two figures in the little pension came closer to me. There was Michel Popesco, a young Rumanian studying the mathematics of aviation to become an instructor in the army. He was rather handsome in his Rumanian way, full, sensitive lips, little curving moustache, large, dreamy, indolent eyes. My diminutive bedroom was inside his; we kept the door open and every night he would talk, half to himself, half to me. At the head of his bed was a picture of Christ, with a wreath of laurel-leaves, and this low dreamy voice sounded half in prayer. Michel was two years older than I, but to me he seemed a child: he would talk about 'mon avion' like a child with a toy, the aeroplane he was going to make was always running in his thoughts. He would count up the months still to go in Paris – he was frightfully homesick for 'mon pays' – and talk about his father and mother, his sister and sweetheart, and his dog that would run out to meet him as soon as he called. One day he would fly off in his aeroplane and see them all. It was an odd performance, I felt as if I were overhearing a child's confession. 'Vous gâtez vos yeux,' he would suddenly come to and call to me, my eyes glued to a book in bed. Now I wonder what happened to *him* in all the years since – Rumania trampled over first by the Nazis, then the Russians? It is hardly possible that he can have survived.

Then there was Jean Brière, who had been a student at the École des Beaux-Arts, when he had my room: now doing his army-service, a very dark, Italian type, with strong, well-knit body. He didn't seem to have much to do except escort Miss Tufts and me around Paris. Since he didn't speak English, I was very glad to have him to practise my French on, and naturally paid for our trips around the town, our teas together at a favourite café at the bottom of the Boulevard St-Michel. One day we went to Chartres, first of many visits for me to that cathedral which retains more of the mystery of the Middle Ages than any other: it is as if it is incarnate there, laid up for ever.

> Mais vous apparaissez, reine mystérieuse,
> Cette pointe là-bas dans le moutonnement

Des moissons et des bois et dans le flottement
De l'extrême horizon ce n'est point une yeuse,

Ni le profil connu d'un arbre interchangeable.
C'est déjà plus distante, et plus basse, et plus haute,
Ferme comme un espoir sur la dernière côte,
Sur le dernier coteau la flèche inimitable.

It was a gusty day, and the wind rushed round the mountain of stone – somehow large buildings always seem to have wind rushing round them. Jean and I went up the Clocher Neuf, he mounting higher and higher in the way such masculine types will,

till I felt quite dizzy when I looked out of the loopholes, on to the loose stones of the nave battlements that looked as if they might topple over, decayed and unsafe. They were oozing moisture down the sides in great streaks; two hundred feet below, the raindrops from the gutters dripped upon the pavement. Lower down the tower was a platform, more sheltered from the rain, but with the wind raging about the piers and through the openings in the wall. Looking out towards the west one saw the plain of the Beauce stretching away into the distance, the roads running silver ribbons through the grey spaces. We went down to wander through the grounds of the Bishop's Palace, the picture of desolation in its decayed splendour, paint peeling off woodwork, doors shaky on hinges, panes of glass wanting in the tall windows. Jean and I sat on a seat there in the derelict garden, the terrace looking out over miles of country to the east.

It reads like a parable of the Third Republic, decayed and seedy and rotting; this desolation was due to the Radical Combes's Laws that decreed the separation of Church and State. In later years I gather the palace has been renovated and become a museum – properly enough, for it is an exquisite Louis XV building, airy and elegant like a pavilion, with a series of tall-windowed rooms *en suite*, panelling and delicate fire-places, chapel with frivolous furbelows inlaid in the marble – one could see the wigged and soutaned ecclesiastics of the time floating round, courtiers and well-related, with not too severe an accent on piety. Robert Louis Stevenson stipulated that, if ever he were to join the Catholic Church, he be made Bishop of Noyon-sur-l'Oise; for myself, from that moment I chose Chartres.

I felt quite sentimental about Jean on leaving Paris. He promised to come and see me off at the station; but I knew he wouldn't, for the night before he had borrowed ten francs from me. One knew beforehand the ways of human beings, to which one would become inured.

*　　*　　*

Back in Oxford, I was at once immersed in all the arrangements for term. 'The hundred and one things to be done before settling in again soon put an end to my thoughts about Paris. The pull that Oxford has upon the mind is a hundred times stronger; in the course of the morning only I have slipped back into the groove.' In an access of loneliness in my new surroundings I had asked a friend from my old college, Robin Burn, to stay the week-end; and in the following week an earlier friend from school-days, Jimmy Crowther was coming to stay. Before the end of the last term I had been asked by my tutor to stand for the History donship that Christ Church was offering, and now I was asked to take on some pupil from the House – rather a mark of confidence, since the House made it a point of pride not to farm out its undergraduates outside the college. My mind and affections were still much more turned towards my old college, which had been so good to me, than the new.

Suddenly, in the second week of term when work was getting into its stride, the General Strike was upon us. There is no point in attempting its history here: that might give the episode a clarity which was wanting at the time and falsify the atmosphere. For the atmosphere was really one of confusion. The General Strike was a blunder, into which the other unions of the Trades Union Congress were reluctantly pulled, by a sense of obligation to the miners, who called on them to redeem their promises of support. The coal-miners were locked in struggle with the coal-owners, both sides mulish and obstinate, and stupidly led. A. J. Cook, the miners' leader, was a mere creature of emotions, a Left-Wing hot-head, not a grain of sense; the miners had turned down their chance of making Frank Hodges their leader, who had the brains – and in course of time he passed over to the other side. Serve them right: one cannot put up with stupidity indefinitely. The mine-owners were just, or almost, as stupid – but one is less intimately affected by the stupidity of one's opponents.

The coal-mining industry, which then had a considerable export trade, was the chief victim of the return to the gold standard at parity with the dollar: this made our exports too dear. The government had been paying a small subsidy of some £3 millions a month to keep the industry going and wages where they were. Of the various constructive recommendations made by the Samuel Commission – the acquisition by the state of the ownership of coal, for one – Baldwin's government chose only the easy but annihilating one, to discontinue the subsidy. This was bound to precipitate a show-down with the miners, and – to continue the clichés in which politicians talk – the government had already prepared its measures to meet the challenge.[1] The Trades Union Congress stumbled into a false situation, in attempting to fulfil its promises to support the miners. The confusion of mind may be glimpsed from the entries in my Diary. Naturally, all of us Labour men thought that our duty was to support the Trades Union Congress and the Labour Movement, not Mr Baldwin and his coal-owners' government.

Late Saturday night, 1 May 1926. News of a general strike ordered for Monday: what to think, or still more what to do? It is miserable to be here and doing nothing, when one ought to be up and doing ... What is impressive is the solidarity that exists in the trade union ranks; but the government seems equally determined: the preparations made for running essential services and for drafting soldiers into South Wales look ugly for us. What are the prospects of our taking over and running the mines? We could get the coal out; but could we organise

---

[1] 'The Government meanwhile had already taken steps to deal with a situation for which it had long been preparing.' *Annual Register*, 1926, 50.

the distributing agencies and rally sufficient technical ability to our side? ... I couldn't rest tonight in my rooms; I couldn't stand the talk in the Common Room. There was W., *petit bourgeois* that he is, pooh-poohing as usual, apeing the contemptuous attitude of the man of affairs, hoping that the general strike would crumble through dry-rot in the trade unions. I went to see Otis to get him to move the Labour Club and keep me informed of what the Committee will do in raising money, etc. Then I went down to Cole's house in Holywell, but hadn't the brazenness to persist in ringing at 11 p.m. Now I'd better write to my people and send them some money.

I was busy with my pupils, but in the interstices of work kept frequently in touch with Otis, who must have been then Chairman of the Labour Club.

5 May. The second day of the general strike: there is a curious silence over all the land and upon everybody, one can't say whether ominous or not. So far there doesn't seem to be any ugly temper in the people; but it is unthinkable what will happen if the general strike hangs on for a fortnight, and in places supplies begin to fail, while the government defeats the strikers bit by bit ... Last night the University Labour Club held a meeting to pledge members against black-legging, and the Master of Balliol [A. D. Lindsay] came to make a statement about the attitude of the authorities. Two lots of rowdies from the House and Hertford came and held up the meeting for a long time. At first there was an attempt to keep them out of the Hall [New Inn Hall]; but when they came in, led by an enormous hulking brute, who turned out to be full of good will and not entirely devoid of intelligence, they shouted Lindsay down and sang 'God Save the King'. After that things went well, except that Lindsay, tremendously on his dignity [he always was conscious of that] and white with indignation, made a very terse statement and left us to it. Otis made a plausible humanitarian appeal to the divided audience, which was responded to by the well-intentioned young men at the back. I took them at their word and, borrowing somebody's hat,

went back and collected money from them for a special fund
for women and children. It had a wonderful effect on the
House rowdies, who put their money into the hat and went
out like lambs!

Today I went to the Union to read the B.B.C. bulletins
which are all we have in the way of news. The Union lobby
thronged with people in gloomy silence; people discussing in
subdued voices and whispers in corners. Back to my rooms:
Aikin-Sneath came to be reassured about the Leaflet Committee we have formed, to whose pamphlets Frank Lee violently
objects – I reckon because he hasn't got the lead on such a job.
Then G. D. H. Cole came to tell me about his successful
negotiations with the ecclesiastics: he's moving them via
Lindsay, Sir Michael Sadler and Father Waggett to put pressure
on public opinion to support re-opening of negotiations.
[This had its effect with the Archbishop of Canterbury, who
called on the government to mediate a cessation of both the
lock-out and the strike. The Roman Archbishop of Westminster seized the chance to dissociate the Catholics from this
move and to line up with the government.] I am very well in
such excitement: I only wish I were in the real centre of things.
Now I must rush to Exeter College, where I am reading part
of my book on History to the Dialectical Society.

Late on Saturday, 8 May. Still no news, and the situation no
clearer. It is only now that people are settling in to the tug-
of-war with a certain grimness. But is the pressure of moderate
opinion, demanding immediate negotiations, likely to be
strong enough? If the Labour Movement as a whole has been
working solidly as we have here in Oxford, all would be well.
Our Leaflet Committee which was mainly the heir of my
invention is proceeding well, and this evening produced No. 8
of its leaflets on 'Sir John Simon and the Strike'. I wrote also
No. 2 on 'The Strikers and the Community': an argument on
the issue of sovereignty, not too explicit, for the idea is to side-
track the issue; and also No. 5 on 'The Daily Mail and the
Strike', which answers the argument about interference with

freedom of the press. I had a hand in others, and made suggestions for the rest of the series. Not a bad effort, what with meetings and the spiritual consolation which I offer free to the neurotics who resort to my rooms. Tomorrow night I have to hold forth to the waverers in T. B. L. Webster's rooms at Christ Church.

(He was a recruit of mine to the Labour Club – on his way to becoming a distinguished authority on Greek literature and art.)

Today a hurried morning, looking up the Trades Disputes Act in the Codrington, pondering Simon's wily speech to reply to it. Then lunch with the Master at Balliol: an extraordinary occasion, for the household seemed distraught. Lindsay himself fairly calm, though interrupted again and again by callers; Mrs Lindsay almost frantic, a state of nervous tension which made me fear tears; two silent children, both charming and rather grave.

Douglas Cole remembered one of these sessions with Mrs Lindsay twittering and jabbering to such an extent that Sandy took her by the shoulders and put her firmly outside the door. (When her husband was raised to the peerage, she no less firmly refused to be known by the title: *Mrs* Lindsay, she insisted, when actually she was Lady Lindsay.) A side-long glance registered,

What a vast Victorian barracks the Lodgings are, though no opportunity today to think of Jowett and his famous gatherings. Outside the dining-room bay-window, the chestnuts in full leaf and bloom. On the Master's door, a notice of a united religious service for tomorrow: it must be like war-days in Oxford.

On Wednesday, 12 May Trevelyan came over to give the Romanes Lecture in the Sheldonian. With so much excitement and anxiety growing at the time, I have no memory of the event. But the Diary records,

I am tired of people's obscurantism with regard to the obvious roots of party politics in economic interests; the fact that there was a certain cleavage inside the eighteenth-century governing class seems to have blinded people to the economic divisions upon which political parties rested – between the landed and the commercial interests (cf. Swift). They regard that governing class as homogeneous, and the divisions within it as of opinion and inclination, not interest. Perhaps my little book on that subject is on its way now.

Just after lunch there came through the news that the strike had ended. It is a great relief: I feel immensely glad, though a little tired; but we must wait to see what the terms of the settlement are before being rationally glad. The last two days have been a strain, with unpleasantness in the air, and I got tired of the ceaseless barrage of stupidities with which Holdsworth, Swinton & Co. have defended the rights of constitutional government. As if the precious heritage of Parliament was ever in danger from the leaders of the T.U.C.! It has nevertheless been a difficult job to make out a logical case for both Parliament and T.U.C.; in writing those pamphlets for the Labour Club, it exercised my wits to ward off such arguments as Simon's, without giving the case away for the Left. Moreover, I think the middle position, though uncomfortable as usual, is honest enough.

Simon, still a Liberal at the time, had come out with a declaration as a lawyer that the General Strike was illegal, and as such Trade Union funds might be open to confiscation by the government. This was honey to Baldwin's government, which made the utmost use of it in its propaganda during and after the strike. Simon's legal argument, construing the strike as unconstitutional, was dubious and not agreed to by many lawyers; but it was of the utmost political use to him – it obliterated his earlier Radicalism and made him acceptable to the Tories, when 1931, that fatal year, provided the chance for him to move over into association with them.

His ingenuous young colleague, writing pamphlets to counter Simon's all too effective campaign, was not so ingenuous in 'waiting to see what the terms of the settlement are before being rationally glad'. For in fact there was capitulation on the part of the Labour Movement; Baldwin won a victory without any conditions – no stipulations, no guarantees, for the miners or anyone else. The Tories were on velvet: they had successfully 'framed' the Labour Movement, which, by its own ineptitude, had let them do it, as they were to do again in 1931 and 1935. Of course the T.U.C. never had any intention of taking the place of the government or of usurping its authority; the Labour leaders declared throughout that it was a manifestation of sympathy with the miners – as it was – and had no political motive. But they had let the artful Baldwin catch them out in a false situation – as again in 1935, when Labour took a line far more sincerely in keeping with the interests and security of this country against Mussolini over Abyssinia.

The *Annual Register* comments impartially, 'the moderate tone of the speeches of the Labour leaders in the course of the week and the orderly way in which the strike was conducted led a considerable portion of the public to revise its opinion and to suspect the Government of having raised an unreal issue.'[1] Once the 'challenge to constituted authority', or 'the manifestation of sympathy with the miners' – whichever you will – was defeated, the miners were left to their fate. For months and months, until the end of the year the strike dragged on, accumulating misery and resentment on the part of the miners, and an immense economic loss to the country. The *Annual Register* describes it as 'by far the most disastrous industrial dispute which England ever experienced'. The loss to the country, direct and indirect, was vastly greater than the continuation of the subsidy would have cost. The cost in human misery, in social and political bitterness, was not to be estimated. When the turn of the miners came, with the social revolution after the second German war, they held the community up to ransom. Those of us who remember all that past can hardly blame them.

As for the Tories – Baldwin and Chamberlain and the rest of them – Oh, they had it all their own way all right in those decades, the 1920s and 1930s, when I was growing up and taking a young man's part. And see where they led the country in the end! – to the well-nigh irretrievable ruin of 1939.

*   *   *

[1] *Annual Register*, 1926, 52, 130.

The General Strike over, life lapsed back to the busy routine of Oxford term, for, in addition to my own reading and social life, I was teaching my St Edmund Hall pupils – I find a note from one of them asking to be excused for he was going down to do government work – as well as my pupils from the House. The day after the end of the strike was Ascension Day, and began with the charming ceremony of beating the bounds of St Mary's. As the parish boundary runs through All Souls, the clergy, wardens and choir, the boys in ruffs and cassocks, perambulate the large quadrangle with their wands, and then the boys scramble for pence on the grass; the whole winding up with a large breakfast for them in Hall. This was my first experience – always something new at All Souls!

Immediately the strike was over I started on my resolution to learn German – going for frequent lessons up a rickety pair of stairs in King Edward Street to an ancient German *Fräulein*, with no charm and the quasi-military ways of her tribe, enough to give anyone a complex against the language. Indeed, it never did have the appeal to me of French and the Romance languages, and I had difficulty in making myself learn it. Not until I went to live in Germany at the end of the year, and happened upon *modern* German poetry, with Rilke, Hofmannsthal, Stefan George, could I persuade myself to take it seriously or find anything congenial in it. All the same, what doors it opened in the end! – all the work of Rilke, so much of which I read, perhaps the greatest poet of our century, Hölderlin, Nietzsche, Goethe and Schiller (with less enthusiasm), Grimmelshausen's *Simplicissimus* (with much more), into the aborted, frustrating world of German history, into an intimate, if marginal, contact with the tragedy of Germany in our time, through my close friendship with Adam von Trott – all improbably opened before me by those uncongenial visits up the narrow stairs to the late German mistress of the Academy for Officers' Daughters at Bath.

All Souls was rather a lonely place for a Junior Fellow at that time – Roger was now away preparing for his Foreign Office examination, in Germany to learn the language, Richard Pares away in Liverpool on the *Liverpool Post*, Ernest Jacob at the House. Company in college was distinctly elderly – there was Sharp, but that was not much comfort to the emotions: the emotions had been left out of his composition. It was nice, when Chelmsford came down for a few days to hear Sharp address him reverently as 'Sir' – Sharp had been a member of his Legislative Council when Chelmsford was Viceroy of India. One occasionally listened to a fascinating conversation such as that between Chelmsford and Cruttwell on the events leading to the war, with Chelmsford 'letting us into a piece of secret history, the protest of the Government of India to the Mesopotamian Commission, which was never published nor its criticisms replied to'. Cruttwell was no less well-informed about the secret agreements entered into with Italy and Russia about Tripoli and Constantinople. One was at any rate learning all the time from the political conversation of one's elders – I was even beginning to doubt whether Russell, Brailsford and Co. had a monopoly of wisdom about the Germans and the origins of the war.

One evening in June 'Cruttwell dined alone with me on the last night before his operation. I gave him some good advice on his behaviour before and after – a nice reversal of our ordinary positions – then saw him out to the iron gate. As we said goodnight and I wished him luck, I saw him shudder as he turned away.' Alas, his operations did him no good: his comparatively early death was a loss to Oxford, to the study of history and to the country. For a young man there was something melancholy about the life of this lonely college.

Of course, it woke up when the grandees came down – Viceroys and Archbishops and such – and occasionally one or other of these put himself out to take a young Fellow under his wing. There was Simon, always filled with loyalty to All Souls (though nobody loved him), who took a party of us over to lunch at the Jacobean house he then had at Fritwell, up the charming Cherwell valley. I didn't take much of the house in, except a fine oak staircase brought from West Wales, grey Cotswold stone and cut yew hedges, I was so mesmerised by (the second) Lady Simon. She had the appearance of a female member of my family – and was a great authority on Slavery. My Catholic friend's sister had been her secretary, and said 'Talk about Slavery, it's nothing compared to being secretary to Lady Simon.'

Much more fun, indeed the greatest fun, on his rare visits to college was Henson, then Bishop of Durham, and a celebrated 'controversial' public figure. He took one look at me at our first meeting and said, 'Isn't it time the working classes had a little blood-letting?' I caught the twinkle, and from then on we always had a good understanding. Henson was a wonderful master of provocative phrase. His phrase, 'the Protestant under-world', did more than anything to lose the Revised Prayer-Book in the House of Commons. Once he returned from an unsatisfactory holiday at Sidmouth, where a barrel-organ had played outside his lodgings most of the time: 'It combined the *ennui* of eternity with the torments of the damned.' He was jealous of Lang, who, his junior in college, had long passed him in the egg-and-spoon race of ecclesiastical promotion. At Bishopthorpe one day Lang asked Henson what he thought of the new portrait of him by Orpen – 'People say that it makes me look proud, pompous and prelatical.' Henson saw his opportunity: 'And to which of these epithets does your Grace object?'

These amenities were somewhat elderly fare for a young man of twenty-two.

We had a French jurist staying in college, Le Bras, on his way up to eminence at the Sorbonne. He had the recommendation, for me, of being a Breton, but his subject wasn't mine. I made much more contact with André Siegfried, who came to stay for a term with us in successive years – he became a friend. I made friends with old Sir Robert Borden, the former Prime Minister of Canada, who came to give the Rhodes Lectures and stayed a couple of terms – charming old boy, very grave and deliberate of speech, with beautiful old-fashioned manners, spats and immensely crinkled, curly grey hair parted in the middle. When he went back to Canada he wrote to me now and again, and sent me the poems of Archibald Lampman, which I failed to appreciate.

Then there was Abraham Flexner, another old man, founder of and adviser on so many educational and philanthropic institutions in the United States. He came to study our universities, and All Souls in particular – and went back to blue-print the Institute for Advanced Study on its model. He told me something fascinating about Lloyd George. Flexner had been one of the first people into Germany after the war, and had been asked to give his impressions to Lord Balfour, then Foreign Secretary. Balfour took him by question and answer, and proper Scots intellectual method, through his story, and then said 'I think you should see the Prime Minister.' It took Flexner only half the time to give his report to Lloyd George – the Celt was intuitively *there* and had gathered the point before ever Flexner got to it.

One was learning all the time, but what food were these elderly gentlemen – all very kind to me – for one's emotional life?

There now turned up, through Kenneth Bell, a young American millionaire, of my own age and a fine specimen of American manhood – not precisely a Gene Tunney, but quite enough of it. I was much taken, and so it seemed was he; we spent a good deal of time together, around and about Oxford, walks around the Meadows and Parks, and up the river to Godstow, meals in All Souls. This was Louis J. Hill, grandson of the railway king, J. J. Hill, creator of the Great Northern and one of the great constructors of the later railway age. A Canadian by origin, he had come south of the border, where he was the opposite number to Lord Strathcona north of it. J.J., I gather, though not interested in money, left a fortune of $54 millions, nine children and no will. With the result that the next generation fought like cat and dog, providing the press with something of a saga by their epic quarrels. Now all the dust has settled, with Louis as the public-spirited head of the family, Hill Foundation and all, reigning benevolently over the dynasty of Minneapolis–St Paul.

It is nice to think that we have managed to keep contact, though so far apart, and over the years, though so many years. More through Louis's doing than mine, dogged by politics and illness and writing books; though at the time he made much more of an impression, with that magnificent head and taut muscular frame, on what I took to be my heart. My head, however, was not suspended: I observed that when the young millionaire went with me to a shop to buy a square of black silk for headdress for a ball he was going to as Pierrot, it occurred to him to have it cut across as a triangle: it would do as well, and be less expensive. Now that would not have occurred to me. At the end of term Louis came with his brother to say goodbye.

All day I have been getting rid of Louis J. in my mind; this evening I wrote in minute hand, so that it might not be read by strangers, 'L.J. gone: for ever.' And then, tonight he came back. I believe he had stolen a few minutes at the end of a busy day, on the excuse that he had left his camera in college, to come and see me once more alone. This time there was nothing to say. All the fine phrases which last night I might have said – but others were with us – vanished. Louis refused to say the words 'goodbye' even; I might at least have asked him not to forget, for a little while ... But it's no use moping; I have had the same experience with a dozen people for whom I cared: a kind of nostalgia for life itself, that comes down upon me in this companionless desert.

This defeatism about personal relations, which made me ready to abrogate beforehand, before there was any necessity, proved in this case not quite warranted. Actually, Louis remembered better than I did, sent me messages from Minneapolis, Chicago, Scandinavia, wherever in northern climes he happened to be. Many years after, when I was at the University of Wisconsin one winter, he invited me to stay with him on the family farm. The 'farm' turned out to be American democratic humbug for a beautiful estate of some four thousand acres, lakes and all. Life had moved on a long way for both of us, but we had no difficulty in resuming the old basis of easy understanding of when we were young, and life was before us. He took me to Carleton College, Minnesota, one of the Liberal Arts colleges in which the United States is so rich and which are the most attractive of its educational institutions. I hadn't been in the building five minutes before I found that the distinction of this college was the achievement, the life's work, of a fellow-Cornishman: Donald Cowling, brought over to the United States from Trevalga as a child.

New and old acquaintance mingled in my social life. Dear, vague, old Dr Lea, my former vicar at St Austell, came to lunch – I remembered how he had nearly had the church-bells rung, when

I won my scholarship to Christ Church. That evening I dined up at Elsfield with John Buchan – and was struck by the resemblance of type to our old church-organist, Brennand-Smith: curious how physical types produce the same characteristics – there was the same odd lisp, produced at the side of the lips through a gap in the teeth, the same ready smile playing about the features, with a quick change becoming a hearty laugh chuckling in the throat. I was in frequent company with David Cecil, now a Fellow of Wadham where he was the English Literature don, and beginning to turn his thoughts to his biography of Cowper.

Lady Ottoline was certainly determined to annex me to her salon: I suppose I was a 'discovery'. I was bidden out to lunch with her alone – I made it clear that I didn't care for parties – and then to meet Siegfried Sassoon, among the best of the war-poets. With my cult of the war-generation, he was rather a hero to me with lines like

> Everyone suddenly burst out singing,

and such verses as:

> I see them in foul dug-outs, gnawed by rats,
>   And in the ruined trenches, lashed with rain,
> Dreaming of things they did with balls and bats,
>   And mocked by hopeless longing to regain
> Bank-holidays, and picture shows, and spats,
>   And going to the office in the train.

Or such a summing-up of the ineptitude of the generalship in the first war as

> But he did for them all with his plan of attack.

Of that occasion I remember nothing but the poet's extraordinary beauty and inner quietude, as with de la Mare, for he said not a thing. On another occasion when I met Desmond McCarthy, I said far too much. He questioned one of my admirations, R. H. Tawney, and the value of the Marxist approach to history. That was enough to set me off: I remember haranguing McCarthy up and down those yew-hedged terraces, with the implication that he didn't know what he was talking about. Nor did he, when it came to Marxism and Tawney's *Religion and the Rise of Capitalism*. I remember a last occasion with Ottoline, when she walked down the slopes of Garsington alone with me, to set me on the road back to Oxford, and told me she was writing her Memoirs, all about the interesting people she had known. (Did they come to anything? Do they exist?)[1]

In July I was to stay at Garsington to meet Goldsworthy Dickinson, but instead was rushed to the Acland Home for an emergency operation. Ottoline sent me a basket of fruit, with a note in that elaborate handwriting written in the brown ink she affected. I was to go to Germany – the next phase – for the autumn and winter: she swore me to write to her from there. But I never did; when I returned to Oxford next year she had left Garsington for a house in Gower Street. She sent me messages through David Cecil, but I never went to see her. I think I felt that her exotic entourage was not for me; it was all I could do to get forward with my simple, fanatical life – I had found a vocation, almost received a call. Now I am sorry: she had been kind to me, even if I felt put off by the heartlessness, as it seemed, and the sophistication of her circle. I have never much liked the company of my fellow-intellectuals: I prefer cats, in their natural state.

* * *

This Whitsun of 1964 – nearly forty years later – I happened to be coming along that road at the foot of the slopes of Garsington, just before one enters now the vast and hideous industrial complex of Cowley. Suddenly I was at the corner of the turn where I had last seen Ottoline. There was hardly time for a glance up those luxuriant slopes, white with may, before the car had whisked by. But not before there came back upon an inner retina of the mind an image of that extraordinary figure – the spreading hat, the red hair underneath, the flowing draperies, the long Habsburg jaw, the astonishing way of talking English as if it were Italian, so exactly

[1] Since writing the above a first volume of her Memoirs to 1915 has been published.

caught in the cruel caricature of her which D. H. Lawrence perpetrated in *Women in Love*.

Hurrying back, the years closing in behind me, I turned to her *Early Memoirs*, published in the interval with a touching and most understanding portrait of her by Robert Gathorne-Hardy. I now see, with sorrow and regret, that this was the real Ottoline; for I, too, did her an injustice in my mind, or, rather, failed to appreciate her at her true value, fanatic and simpleton as I was – though I never caricatured her to myself or gave credence to the harsh things those clever sycophants said about her. The truth is that I was bent on my own path of development; instinct told me that her circle of conscious sophistication was not for me. But she had made it clear that she was willing to know me on my own terms, as a private friend, without all those intimidating people about. However, inhibited, possessed, recalcitrant, I was too much of a fanatic even for that.

And now that my own life is nearly over I am sorry; for, so like the unkindness of the young, I did not even appreciate that, under the sophistication that alarmed and put me off, under what I took to be exotic affectation (with her the exotic was natural), there was real warmth of heart, a genuine and passionate interest in human beings and an anxious desire to do what she could for them. I suppose I didn't want anyone, in any intimate sense, to do anything for me: I wanted to do it all for myself. It has meant going a long, and a hard, way round to achieve knowledge of life. (Lawrence, dying at forty-six: 'I have had a *hard* life.' He made it so, in large part.)

I write this about Ottoline as an act of reparation, though too late. I never responded to any of the messages she sent me from Gower Street; I never went – but then I never went to London, or hardly ever. So there was an enrichment, a complication of life, an alternation of course I missed, as the result of my determination to keep it simple. (I should have been engaged, if by nothing else, by the personality of the auburn-haired descendant of that famous Elizabethan red-head, Bess of Hardwick, to become so familiar to me summer after summer at Hardwick, and to appear in my later books. But all that was years ahead.) In the years to come

I met hardly any of the famous people of her circle, except marginally, on my own, in passing; and her not at all. What might have flowered if I had been willing to go out to meet life, instead of retreating within the fortress of myself, a fortress doubly entrenched by illness, cutting me off from life? Ottoline's epigraph for her own Memoirs gives me cause to think: 'Le hasard est le plus grand de tous les artistes.' But I never wished to expose myself to chance: I wished to have everything under my own control. That is not the way of love, though it may be of achievement. Obsessed at sixty with the idea of chances lost, opportunities deliberately not taken, the alternative lives that might have been mine (as Henry James was in those later stories), I feel now more open to experience, more willing, less recalcitrant. Then, as Picasso says: 'At sixty we are young; but it is too late.'

*   *   *

Ten days after the end of the General Strike I was summoned to Christ Church to be interviewed for their History lectureship. I had been asked to stand for this lectureship by my tutor; I was already tutoring undergraduates for Christ Church. It might have been supposed that the dons of my own college knew me well enough to dispense with the awkwardness of an interview; indeed it might have been supposed that, since they insisted on my going in for the job, they intended to appoint me to it. Trustful and confiding, and with a tremendous loyalty to Christ Church, which had been so good to me, I do not think I would have dared to say 'No' to my tutor's invitation, whatever my own inclinations were. With no one to back me, with no parents or people able to give me any advice, I assumed that my sponsors at my old college would know what was best for me.

What were my inclinations? I did not really wish to be a teaching don – too ambitious for that – though I knew I had it in me to become a good tutor, capable of interesting students and encouraging their interest. I did not really wish to leave All Souls, where I had but recently arrived; I was more proud to be a Fellow of All Souls than anything else – though when I was elected, Richard Pares told me, a doubt had been expressed whether I would stay. But I was a Christ Church man; I had not been a year at my new college, all my friends were House-men, all my loyalties turned in that direction. Moreover, here was security; All Souls Fellowships, very grand in honour, were very ill-paid – I was not in the least repining at that – but I had had quite enough struggle in my life and was tempted by the prospect of security and having to worry no more.

I went to the interview in the Senior Common Room of my old college, never having heard a word from anyone as to any other candidates, feeling self-conscious and nervous as always, faced with a barrage of people. But there were the familiar, friendly faces – the Dean with his pleasant smile of creased parchment, Dundas who, as Senior Censor, took the lead, Chaundy, Frank Taylor and a number of others. My tutors were conspicuously absent. In the ante-room waiting was the other candidate: a year my senior, though several years in maturity and bearing, for he was the son of a famous professor, a Public School man, Winchester and New College, a Greats man who had taken his First two years before and was now taking the Modern History School. An extremely nice man, with an engaging stammer, a much better scholar than I, he had all the right background for a Christ Church don. To all appearances a much better bet. After such a tribute to him, it would be an easy gambit to opt for bogus magnanimity and add – a better tutor. But that would not be true: a better pure scholar, really a professorial type – he would have done better to be a professor of his (somewhat specialist) subject; the joke is that I made a better common tutor with ordinary pupils.

And why a joke? – Because, at the interview, Dundas settled my hash with a tricky question. All was going not disagreeably for me when he asked, 'Would you be more interested in teaching clever pupils or stupid ones?' I answered honestly that I should be more interested in the clever ones – and immediately sensed from the reaction that he had gained his point; for, of course, Christ Church with its aristocratic clientèle in those days catered less for clever scholars than it did for very average, or even below, undergraduates. The irony was that, in fact, I turned out better with the latter; my successful rival, the pure scholar, with the specialists. Dundas had won – I never forgave him for it – but he was wrong.

I was thunderstruck that my own college, having made me stand and put me through this rigmarole, should have rejected me for an outsider. I was not only thunderstruck but, reacting actively as always, not passively, I was furious. No one could rationally object to the appointment of my rival: to all outward appearances he was the more suitable man. It was the superfluous humiliation of it that I resented – that having invited me, when left to myself I should never have thought of standing, they should then have turned me down. It appears that one of my tutors – so characteristic of him – changed horses in the middle of the proceedings: all he need have done was to have the courage to pass the word to me, 'Look, you don't really want this: withdraw your name'; he would have been on velvet with me. (Not so for a life-time afterwards.) The other tutor, a pretty cool customer so far as I was concerned, told me long after that he always thought that 'this was not the way to handle it.' This was when he was trying to persuade me to accept an invitation as 'the most distinguished of his academic pupils' to attend his Jubilee dinner in the House of Commons. The invitation was not accepted; no invitation from Christ Church has ever been accepted in all the years since.

For, of course, they chose quite the wrong man to humiliate. I reflected at the time – would they have behaved like that to David Cecil or Roger Makins? Certainly not. Then neither should they behave like that to me, with impunity. For I knew my own quality quite well: I am singularly little different at sixty from what I was at twenty-two. And I knew the quality of those people quite well, even then: who will remember who they were? The Diary has a quite rational estimate of it all as, in the long run, an advantage. The Christ Church dons in doing themselves a good turn (they may have acted wisely in choosing M. – after all his father was a don before him at the House, and I am still an unknown quantity) may have done me a good turn too. Not that I had the slightest intention, for my own part, of putting my name forward at Christ Church: it was for me the line of least resistance. Security after all is desirable, but not above all things.' I recognised that struggle towards real achievement would continue to be my lot, needs must, and I reminded myself of the work to be done, German and Italian to be learned, mastering Marx and Marxism, historical research and writing, some journalism (but not too much), poems, essays, books. 'It will keep me fully occupied; and, though not immediately remunerative – as Christ Church would have been – it will go towards a more enduring reputation than any drudgery as a tutor would achieve.'

After a few days of stunned resentment I was already registering

a rather more benevolent mood towards the House than has prevailed in my mind these last three days. As with all disappointments, the element of personal pique wears off quickly, and I am left merely regretful for prospective comfort. I know in my heart that the best course is not the easiest, and I have been providentially fortunate in my defeats ... I have been sitting near the open window, reading, and there's a fresh breeze from the west, whence I could hear the sighing chime of the quarters from the belfry at Christ Church, as I used to hear them at night from my room when I lived near by in Meadows. It made me unhappy to think I shall never go back there again.

But the fact was that I had received an emotional shock, for my affections were engaged; and this did not wear off so easily as I supposed. It reached to a much deeper level with me than with most ordinary, normal people. For it set up a kind of complex, a complex of rejection; I suppose with my inner insecurity about the family, and as good as having no parentage so far as any practical help or advice were concerned, I had transferred filial feelings, loyalties, affections to the House and the people who had been so kind to me there. The sudden revelation that they didn't care did untold damage psychologically, and the strange thing was that it set a pattern that recurred again and again all through my life: myself not wanting to be pushed into a position of asking something from my fellow-men, yet exposing myself – only to be denied and rejected. There is a very subtle psychological tie-up which I do not fully understand here. C. P. Snow has a searching phrase somewhere that our fate consists of the things that we really want to happen to us. Can I have wanted always to be denied and rejected by what I have loved most? I fear that this may be true.

On a more superficial level, perhaps I may say that I never had a word of apology, or was even given any explanation, by any of the people involved. That did not improve matters, and with regard to them I drew my own conclusions and took my own measures. They made no further contact, but kept silent; perhaps they thought that I could be ignored. Christ Church was a very stuck-up place in those days, insufferably complacent; since then it has, as a matter of fact, very much gone down in its rating among the colleges in the university. The next year there was an attempt to renew negotiations with me on the basis that I should come back as a don, teaching half English Literature, half History. I never gave it a moment's consideration: I took the opportunity to underline the fact that I had never wanted a teaching donship anyway by taking my name off the college books. I ceased to regard myself as a Christ Church man.

It would be untrue to say that this has not been a source of un-happiness to me, with my backward-looking temperament, with intense feelings of loyalty savaged by denial and rejection. It is obvious that I do not take things easily – one difference between myself and ordinary people. But, though I have made myself suffer much unhappiness in life this way – on the assumption that I can make myself stand anything – it has not been without its compen-sations. In fact, I could switch from this attitude tomorrow if I wished it (to my own and other people's comfort). Then why do I not even wish it now? There is the psychological problem I do not fully understand. Perhaps, because I have had so much of it from other people, it has become a fixation and I do not really wish to have to do with them; from that point of view, desperately busy and pushed for time as I am, it has certainly been a great convenience – it has freed me from obligations. And the prime compensation is that it has enabled me to preserve the experience of Christ Church as an undergraduate pure and unsoiled by subsequent layers of experience, to lay it up in my mind untouched, unchanged – like Joyce, the eternal exile from Dublin, who would never come back to it once he had left it. It would seem, then, that the underlying motive is an aesthetic one; and, if so, it would be true to my nature, in which aesthetic choices and experience are dominant.

Colleges often make mistakes. All Souls proceeded now to make a mistake in regard to T. S. Eliot, and since he has referred to the matter in print in his memorial address for Geoffrey Faber, there can be no objection to my mentioning it. Just at this time Faber proposed Eliot for a Research Fellowship. Faber, who was Estates Bursar, was then establishing the publishing firm which has made such a distinguished name, particularly for poetry, and Eliot, who was then in his first flight, was Faber's star of promise. (Faber once said to me, 'If I have achieved nothing else in life, I have accomplished something by saving Tom Eliot for literature.') Who more suitable, one would have thought, than Eliot for a Research Fellowship on the basis of the essays on the Elizabethan drama he submitted? Unfortunately, he had also written poetry, and, a Junior Fellow, I was the only person in college to possess a volume of his poems. I had no sense at all, or I would have hidden it or burned it. For someone asked to borrow it, and when the Scotch professors read some of the episodes of *The Waste Land* (the typist's tea-time hour, in Part III, for example), or 'Lune de Miel':

> Ils ont vu les Pays-Bas, ils rentrent à Terre Haute;
> Mais une nuit d'été, les voici à Ravenne,
> A l'aise entre deux draps, chez deux centaines de punaises;
> La sueur aestivale, et une forte odeur de chienne ...

they were horrified. How could they be expected to appreciate that this was in the best manner of Laforgue, Rimbaud, Tristan Corbière and all? The Diary has a complete account of the proceedings at the College meeting, which I am not at liberty to divulge – merely my own fatal part, for it was fatal of me to possess a copy of *Poems, 1909–1925*, and I have always felt myself responsible for his non-election. Eliot said in his Address, generously, that he was not really fitted for the part. On the contrary, no one would have fitted college life better, and think what All Souls lost by not electing him!

Colleges are sometimes great asses.

One way and another, I ended term in a stunned silence, working feverishly at my German, reading and reading, at last taking no exercise but 'cheating myself with nearly three hours' hard concentration on Beethoven by way of relaxation in the afternoons', as if waiting for something.

At last the blow fell – perforation of the ulcer and peritonitis. I remember well the ghastly immovable agony: where acute appendicitis was a clean flame of pain, with something pure about it, this was an ugly, impure pain, unendurable yet immovable, till the poison was running into one's system and one was passing out, into a coma. The young doctor who was sent was unable to diagnose what was wrong; so I passed all night and next day in my bed, under the arched beam, in that state. It took an intelligent young Fellow of All Souls, Reggie Harris, who had had some such experience himself, to diagnose the matter only just in time and off I was rushed to the Acland for an emergency operation.

Once more my people were sent for – simple as they were, I must have been a great worry to them. I knew nothing, except that they were arriving, and this gave a feeling of consolation; they must have had an awful journey, for railway disputes were still on, a sequel from the General Strike, and having got as far as Swindon, they had to come on by car in the night. I have an unconscious memory of the nastiness of a blood transfusion, and wondering in high fever why my arm was tethered to a pillow and what the gurgling noise was – and later the spots of blood spattered on the wall from my restlessness. People were very kind to my parents – especially Mary Coate, who had just been my first guest at an Encaenia Luncheon in the Codrington, Ernest Jacob's mother and good-hearted Marie Woodward. When I had turned the corner, with the inveterate vitality of youth, I was anxious that my people should see something of Oxford – and was amused to find that they were disappointed with the crumbling old stone buildings in the streets: they had expected colleges to be magnificent country houses all separate in their several estates. Natural enough, when one thinks of their country background, with the big house as the apex of society.

The doctors remained taciturn about my illness, hoping, I suppose, for the best. It was not long before I gathered, and learned from experience, that the source of the trouble, the ulcer, had still not been dealt with, could not be dealt with in such conditions of emergency. A good many years of worsening illness were to come before I got into the hands of a good doctor, and the fundamental trouble was grappled with.

Let me say no more about it, except what the Diary says when I was recovering: 'Is this really going to be the end of my troubles, and the beginning of new health which will enable me to do all that I want to do in my life? Or am I to be hampered at every turn by the ill-health which is the result of my efforts to make my way alone in the world?'

Index